Field Guide to the

MAMMALS

of the Kruger National Park

Heike Schütze

Struik Publishers (Pty) Ltd
(a division of New Holland Publishing
(South Africa) (Pty) Ltd)
Cornelis Struik House
80 McKenzie Street
Cape Town, 8001

New Holland Publishing is a member
of Johnnic Communications Ltd.
Visit us at **www.struik.co.za**
Log on to our photographic website
www.imagesofafrica.co.za for an African experience

First Published in 2002
10 9 8 7 6 5 4 3

Copyright © text: Heike Schütze 2002
Copyright © photographs: Heike Schütze 2002
and Individual photographers listed on page 219
Copyright © spoor drawings: Heike Schütze 2002
Copyright © maps: Heike Schütze 2002
Copyright © published edition: Struik Publishers (Pty)
Ltd 2002

Publishing manager: Pippa Parker
Managing editor: Helen de Villiers
Editors: Helena Reid, Katharina von Gerhardt
Designer: Bridgitte Chemaly
Cover design: Robin Cox
Picture researcher: Carmen Watts
Maps: Illana Fridkin

Reproduction by: Hirt & Carter Cape (Pty) Ltd.
Printed and bound by: Times Offset (M) Sdn Bhd
ISBN 1 86872 594 4

Acknowledgements

My thanks to the following, without whom this project would not have been possible:
To all the researchers, scientists, conservationists and wildlife enthusiasts who have collected and studied specimens and collated data over many hundreds of years: their valuable work has enabled this work to be collated.
To the many sources of help, support, encouragement, time and assistance: P. Schütze, A. Ruff, G. Smith, R. Driscoll, C. Winslow, J. Kingsley, H. Steynes, L. Patencia, A. Smith, A. Hutson, Dr G. Amori, N. Ratenbach, D. MacFadyen; G. Smit, R. Coetzee, C. van der Walt, G. Zambatis, H. Bryden.

Special thanks to:

Herbert Schütze, for tireless hours of help during the field work and for reviewing many drafts; the Kruger National Park for access, accommodation and use of facilities, and particularly Danie Pienaar, Kruger National Park Scientific Services Manager, for his generous time and assistance in providing data and information, and for reviewing the drafts; the African Hunting Co. for the kind permission to reproduce field signs listed in appendix 1; Jacana Education, for the kind permission to reproduce the Kruger National Park Ecozone Map; and Qantas, for their generous assistance with airfares.

Particular thanks to:

Billiton and Britz Africa, the corporate sponsors, for actively supporting and promoting education and environmental and wildlife conservation through their generous financial support, without which this project would still be an unfulfilled wish. I gratefully acknowledge their interest and support.

Preface

Having had the privilege of travelling extensively throughout southern Africa, I decided to compile this book for two reasons: first and foremost, to promote nature conservation through wildlife awareness. Although there are numerous wildlife protection bodies, their long-term success depends on sustained, honest management, as well as sound wildlife education aimed at the general public. Conservation is everyone's responsibility. Gaining an understanding of African wildlife leads to an interest in its welfare. At the same time, it underlines the importance of ways in which habitat and resource needs can be met, not only of growing human populations, but also of wildlife. How unfortunate it would be if future generations could not experience African wildlife in all its diversity. Thus, the second reason for writing this book – to compile a comprehensive, easy-to-use guide aimed at wildlife experts as well as novices, offering insight into mammalian behaviour, and how mammals interact with one another and their environment.

There is more to game-watching than simply keeping a checklist of sightings. If you stop to look and listen, immense rewards can be gained from observing animals in their natural environment. On one of my trips to the Kruger, I came across several tourists watching two impala rams sparring playfully. Suddenly, the rams' behaviour changed, and they seemed to start acting in a peculiar way: prancing with stiff legs, and jerking their heads while letting out loud snorts. While they were doing this, several of the tourist groups moved off to find 'the more glamorous species'. Yet if they had understood that they were witnessing impala signalling alarm, and had they waited a few more minutes, they would have had the opportunity to see a leopard not more than 30 metres away, stalking its prey!

This book covers all the mammalian species known to occur in the Kruger National Park, which accurately represents a large proportion of the mammals found in the southern African region. Data for the smaller species (bats, moles, shrews and rodents) is grouped according to families or subfamilies. Many of these species cannot be differentiated with the naked eye, and without the aid of dental and/or chromosomal analysis, so no attempt is made to discuss them separately. Instead, a general background is given to the different families/subfamilies, providing the reader with an overall understanding of these mammalian groups.

To aid the reader in identifying the different mammal species of the Kruger, field signs and tracking data are tabulated in Appendix 1, and predator/prey relationships are elucidated in tables and graphs in Appendix 2. For more in-depth information regarding the different species found in the region, 'Suggested Further Reading' on p 214 can be consulted.

DEDICATION

For my baby
Your life was taken before it could begin.
Spread your wings over the vast wonders of the world.

CONTENTS

Foreword

South African
NATIONAL PARKS

Since the Kruger National Park was founded more than 100 years ago, numerous books and articles have been written about its dazzling biotic diversity. To date, more than 2 000 plant species (including 336 tree species), 507 bird species, 147 mammals, 114 reptiles, 49 fish, 34 amphibians and many thousands of insects have been recorded, identified and described here. It is this spectacular variety, particularly among the larger mammals, that attracts the majority of the more than 1 million annual visitors to this best-known of all South African national parks.

Diversity is determined by the underlying geology, soils, water courses, altitude, slope and climate, which in combination create a mosaic of different habitat types. These different 'ecozones' detemine animal distribution. In order to assist visitors, this *Field Guide to the Mammals of the Kruger National Park* uses an excellent ecozone map to describe the areas favoured by the different mammalian species, providing the reader with the latest information on animal distribution in the Kruger Park, as well as across the African continent.

Ecosystems are not static, and climatic and rainfall cycles influence animal population numbers and distribution. The period from 1980 to 1997 were dry years with 1993 being the worst drought year in the recorded history of the Park. The buffalo population, for instance, crashed from 30 000 to below 15 000 and rare antelope species such as the roan antelope declined to worrying levels. The only herbivore species that did not decline during these droughts were elephant, white rhino and black rhino. Management strategies such as artificial water provision, or the burning policy, evolve as Park managers gain increasing knowledge on how ecosystems function. New initiatives such as the proposed extensive Transfrontier Park with Mozambique and Zimbabwe are being implemented. All these actions also influence game distribution and it is thus clear that guide-books have to be kept up to date.

This fine guide to the mammals of the Kruger National Park provides the reader with the latest information on distribution, habitat and behaviour of Kruger mammals, specifies activity peaks and includes some fascinating biological information unique to a species. Its informative text and pictures will enhance the experiences of visitors, be they experienced or amateur, in cars or on foot. I heartily recommend this book.

Danie J. Pienaar, Manager:
Scientific Services,
Kruger National Park

Sponsors' forewords

bhpbilliton
Development Trust
www.bhpbilliton.com

The Kruger National Park, founded by president Paul Kruger in 1898, is the oldest wildlife reserve in Africa. It is renowned for its excellence in wildlife management, its diversity of animal species, for which it is unparalleled in Africa, and its variety of vegetation zones. The Park covers nearly two million hectares, and is situated on the eastern boundary of South Africa, bounded by the Crocodile River in the south and the Limpopo River in the north. It stretches some 350 km from north to south, and is on average 60 km wide.

As natural resources the world over come under increasing threat from exponential population growth, the importance of the Kruger National Park takes on global significance. Never in the 100 years of the Park's existence has it faced as many challenges as it does today. The increasing numbers of tourists require additional facilities; development along the borders of the Park impacts on available resources, and the burgeoning populations outside the Park draw off more water from its vital rivers every year. As the population grows, the demands of local communities have to be balanced against the sustainability of wildlife reserves.

Education, particularly that of the people living close to the Park, is one way of dealing with these pressures. The Billiton Development Trust has focused on education by building schools, training teachers and administrators, and by supporting maths and science projects. Likewise, it is hoped that financial support for this informative book on the mammals of the Kruger National Park will enhance knowledge, understanding and thus respect for our natural environment, both among people living outside the Park, as well as those visiting the Park itself. It is our wish that, by making this gesture, we can help overcome the very real threats facing the Kruger National Park.

Sam Seepei, Senior Manager:
Billiton Development Trust

Britz
4 X 4 RENTALS
www.britz.co.za

More than 100 years of successful management has placed South Africa's Kruger National Park among the forerunners of the world's best conservation areas. Boasting a magnificent array of animal and plant life, its biological diversity is matched by none.

As human populations continue to grow, ever-increasing pressures are placed on resources currently set aside for wildlife. A sustainable balance between development and conservation depends directly on the people and their education.

Locally owned by Imperial Holdings, Maui and Britz 4 x 4 and Motorhome Rentals promote conservation through ecotourism. By supporting projects like this *Field Guide to the Mammals of the Kruger National Park*, it is hoped that people will gain knowledge and understanding of Africa's spectacular wildlife, and develop an interest in its welfare. We hope that both local residents and international visitors to the Park may see the real, long-term shared benefits of preserving natural heritage sites such as the Kruger.

Guy Stringer, Managing Director:
Britz 4 x 4 Rentals, Maui Rentals

Introduction to the Kruger National Park

The Kruger National Park is one of the largest national parks in the world, covering an area of 1 948 528 hectares (19 455 km²), lying between 22°25' to 25°32' latitude south and 30°50' to 32°2' longitude east. The Northern and Mpumalanga provinces of South Africa mark the western border, while the Lebombo Mountains form a barrier between the Park and Mozambique to the east. Two rivers, the Limpopo and Crocodile, form its northern and southern borders respectively. The road network in the Park covers nearly 2 000 km.

The history

This wildlife expanse owes its existence to the dedicated efforts of several men with the foresight and determination to conserve South African wildlife, the most important among them being Paul Kruger, James Stevenson-Hamilton and Piet Grobler. In 1884, the last president of the 'Zuid-Afrikaansche Republiek', Paul Kruger, proposed to the Volksraad (parliament of the South African Republic) that a

White rhino

tract of land be set aside where hunting would be prohibited, in order to conserve the country's natural heritage. This proposal initiated a debate that continued for the next five years. In 1889, he presented parliament with another proposal: that two specific areas be proclaimed as game reserves, one in the Pongola District on the Swaziland-Natal border, and one in the Zoutpansberg area (today's Shingwedzi area). Although the 1884 proposal was rejected, Kruger achieved considerable success when, on 13 June 1894, Africa's first game reserve, the Pongola Game Reserve, was proclaimed. For the next four years Kruger worked towards establishing a reserve in the eastern lowveld region, and on 26 March 1898, the 4 600 km² area between the Sabie and Crocodile rivers was proclaimed as the 'Gouvernement Wildtuin' (Government Game Reserve).

The newly established reserves faced an uncertain future with the onset of the Anglo-Boer War 18 months later. It was during this time that the Sabie Game Reserve was brought to the attention of British officials. Major Greenhill-Gardyne, an ardent conservationist, submitted a report on how to conserve the lowveld. Explorer, naturalist and writer, Abel Chapman, was so impressed during his visit in 1899 that he presented a report to the British Government in 1900, proposing that the entire

Wild dog and carcass

area, from the Limpopo River in the north to the Crocodile River in the south, from the Lebombo Mountains in the east to the Drakensberg Escarpment in the west, should be proclaimed a wildlife sanctuary. The International Convention for the Preservation of Wild Animals adopted his report, which was later presented to the British Government. Alfred Milner, then Governor of the Transvaal, was a committed conservationist. Armed with Chapman's report, and Greenhill-Gardyne's backing of Kruger's proposal, he proclaimed the Sabie Game Reserve.

After the Anglo-Boer War, Colonel James Stevenson-Hamilton was appointed head ranger of the Sabie Game Reserve. He stayed there for 44 years. He has been called the 'father of the Kruger National Park' due to his tireless efforts towards ensuring the proclamation and consolidation of the Park. During the first few years of his involvement, he managed to increase the total area of the Park to almost eight times the size of the original Sabie Reserve. He then embarked on an even more ambitious plan: to persuade the authorities to declare the Sabie and the Shingwedzi reserves (a piece of land in the Zoutpansberg District that was proclaimed a nature reserve in 1903) a united national park.

However, a major obstacle had to be overcome: the Sabie and Shingwedzi reserves were split by a wedge of land, about 32 km wide, between the Olifants and Letaba rivers. This area was owned by mining companies and private landowners. Stevenson-Hamilton negotiated tirelessly with the mining companies and landowners to gain protection rights over some of the land, and consequently to link the two reserves. In 1912, he approached government officials to consolidate the reserves into a national park.

At this stage, Piet Grobler, newly appointed Minister of Lands and grandnephew of Paul Kruger, played a key role in finally establishing the area as a national park. Being a supporter of Stevenson-Hamilton's conservation ideals, he succeeded in passing the National Parks Board Act in Parliament. The Act paved the way for the establishment of the Park, and on 31 May, 1926, the Kruger National Park was proclaimed.

Today, more than 1 000 000 tourists visit the Kruger National Park annually, drawn by the wide array of plant and animal species. 283 land mam-

Buffalo

Waterbuck calf

Cheetah

Porcupine

mammal species are known to occur in the southern African subregion, and more than half of these are found within the boundaries of the Kruger National Park. About 65% of the mammals occurring in the Park are classified as small mammals. Some of the rarer species, such as Commerson's leaf-nosed bat and Rufous hairy bat, are known to occur in South Africa only within the boundaries of the Park, and therefore particular attention is given to their conservation status.

The environment

The Kruger National Park falls within the southern African summer-rainfall zone, receiving rain from September to March in the form of short, severe thunderstorms or soft drizzles, lasting 2–3 days. The Park receives an overall average annual rainfall of 500 mm, with rainfall in the extreme northern regions averaging 400 mm, and in the southwestern Pretoriuskop area averaging 740 mm. Every 7–10 years, above or below normal rainfall patterns occur. These periods of prolonged drought or flood result in cyclical changes in grass height and therefore also cause fluctuations in the population densities and distribution patterns of many animals. In terms of climate, the Park straddles two transitional zones: the tropical/subtropical north and the temperate south; the moist and humid north and east, and the arid west. Summer temperatures may exceed 40˚C, while winter temperatures are moderate. Frost rarely occurs and is restricted to low-lying areas*.

Geologically the Park can be separated into two distinct zones: the undulating western parts, dominated by underlying granite formations, and the level plains to the east, characterized by basalt foundations. A narrow belt of sandstone stretches from the north to the south, dividing the western granites from the eastern basalt. The area north of Punda Maria is largely sandstone. Mountainous terrain occurs along the eastern border and in the southwestern corner of the Park between Pretoriuskop and Malelane; some rugged country occurs in the extreme north, in the Punda Maria area**. Overall, the vegetation is classified as sub-arid to arid wooded savanna. Park biologists recognize at least eight major vegetation zones and 36 landscape types***. Eight major rivers drain from west to east through the Park. Six of these are perennial, flowing during times of drought; the remaining two are seasonal.

The great number and variety of mammals occurring within the Kruger National Park can be attributed to the many different habitats in the Park, each supporting its own unique vegetation. The fact that the Park falls within more than one climatic zone, and the sheer size of the reserve, also contribute to a great abundance and variety of species. However, it is these same factors that restrict the population densities of some species with certain requirements. Samango monkeys and many bat species, for example, are found only in limited numbers in the Park since they are restricted to riparian vegetation that occurs in the Pafuri area.

The management plans of the Kruger National Park are complex and backed by comprehensive research programmes. The fine ecological balance within the Park can easily be disturbed by many factors: Natural disasters, such as drought and floods, and negative human influences, such as soil and water contamination from sites outside the Park, as well as poaching and introduced diseases. A team of dedicated scientists and management personnel are devoted to gaining more insight into the relationships between animal and plant life within the Park, and to finding ways of maintaining the delicate balance between them, thus ensuring that the magnificent natural heritage that is the Kruger National Park is conserved for future generations.

FOOTNOTE: For more data regarding the rainfall, geology and landscapes of the Kruger respectively, refer to: *Gertenbach, WPD 1980. *Rainfall Patterns in Kruger National Park.* Koedoe 23: 35–44; **Schutte, IC 1986. *The General Geology of the Kruger National Park.* Koedoe 29: 13–38; ***Gertenbach, WPD 1983. *Landscapes of the Kruger National Park.* Koedoe 26: 9–122.

The Great Limpopo Transfrontier Park

Today conservation has taken on an even broader scope. Political leaders have a vision – a vision of peace, where borders are being looked at as 'gates' to their neighbouring countries rather than 'walls' separating them. Throughout Africa, Transfrontier or Peace Parks are being proposed. Conservationists and political leaders have long recognized that country borders not only block ancient migration routes and cordon off ecosystems, but that they also split ethnic communities. The establishment of Transfrontier Parks hopes to achieve various results: Increased wildlife conservation by providing greater resources; sustained community development by introducing and maintaining a social ecology infrastructure with the new Parks; and the promotion of peace with neighbouring countries by working together on practical terms.

The largest proposed park is the Great Limpopo Transfrontier Park, which aims to join the Kruger National Park in South Africa, Coutada 16 in Mozambique, the Gonarezhou National Park in Zimbabwe, and some of their surrounding areas. The result will be a massive 155 440 km² super-park, where tourists and wildlife can freely cross from one Park into the other. Increased visitors will mean increased revenue to all Parks and will generate jobs, income and improved facilities for the surrounding communities.

The eastern border of the Kruger stretches nearly 400 km along the Mozambican border. The adjoining wilderness area is Coutada 16, which encompasses a huge portion of Mozambique's Gaza Province. Coutada 16's value lies in the fact that it has been virtually untouched by man; the area is virgin bush with streams and pans dotted throughout the Lebombo Mountains. On the southern section of Coutada 16 is Massingir Dam, with prime wildlife regions on its peninsulas. Coutada 16's eastern border is formed naturally by the Limpopo River. These areas are to become some of Coutada 16's most important tourism areas.

Although Mozambique's wildlife populations have been devastated by 20 years of civil war, it has something that the Kruger desperately needs: space. After increased pressures from animal rights groups, the Kruger's controversial management strategy of culling elephants has now ceased, resulting in an unsustainable increase in elephant populations. Opening borders and allowing free movement of animals into neighbouring protected areas will alleviate some of the overcrowding, without the disruptive and dangerous process of sedation and translocation.

After the initial relocation of approximately 1 000 elephants, which will be moved in family units, boundary fences will have to stay in place for 2 years to prevent the elephants from crossing back over into their old home ranges. Once the fences do come down, it is hoped that there will be a natural immigration process of other elephants, with antelope and predators following.

The Gonarezhou National Park in Zimbabwe lies 160 km north of the Kruger Park. However, Zimbabwe has recently experienced political upheaval, resulting in the cessation of bilateral aid and the collapse of tourism in Zimbabwe. The Save Conservancy, a large block adjacent to Gonarezhou, which was supposed to form part of the Transfrontier Park, has fallen victim to civil unrest and poaching.

Although the will to establish the Transfrontier Parks is present at the highest political levels, this is a stark reminder of how the success of the Transfrontier (Peace) Parks relies on political stability, still a delicate matter in Africa. Thus conservation is as concerned with people as it is with the environment. The long-term success of Transfrontier Parks lies in education and sustainable community development around them; safeguarding the environment must offer tangible benefits to those whose lives are affected directly – the local communities. Only through shared benefits will the future of game parks be secured.

Spotted hyaena cubs

How to use this book

To use this guide as a successful identification tool, the following procedure should be followed: first determine which group a particular animal belongs to (for example cat, dog or rodent); note characteristics, such as approximate size, colouring and any distinguishing features (spots, stripes, horns, or a prominently arched back, for example). Then note social and habitat settings – e.g. if the animal was alone or in a group; in open, grassy plains or on a rocky cliff. After narrowing down your choices to animals of similar appearance, use the diagnostic features in the text to determine the species.

Certain mammals are confined to specific habitats or geographical regions and this offers clues to their identity. Sixteen major eco- or vegetation zones can be distinguished within the Kruger National Park (see map on page 14), and habitat and distribution data are given for all species, not only for the Kruger National Park, but also for the rest of Africa. A regional map of the Kruger National Park is provided on page 15, indicating camp sites, entrance gates, major road networks and river systems.

The distribution maps are a quick and useful tool for establishing whether the animal occurs in a particular region. For example, if you are in the open eastern plains of the Kruger National Park, and you come across a small antelope, you can determine within seconds that it is not a red duiker by glancing at the distribution maps. Habitat also offers identification clues: impala, for example, are not likely to be found on steep, rocky cliffs; nor klipspringers on open, grassy plains. Likewise, distribution and habitat data can be used as identification pointers. When looking for serval, for example, first consult the habitat section for this animal in your field guide. Once you have established that serval generally occur in areas of rank vegetation, in tall grasses associated with water, and in reed beds, you will save yourself time and disappointment by not looking for them elsewhere. Also bear in mind that overall body colour is often linked to habitat, for purposes of camouflage. Animals with bold colouring or markings (nyala, kudu, bushbuck, or leopard, for example) are more likely to be encountered in bush or dense cover, whereas those with inconspicuous colouring

(impala, oribi and lions, for example) are usually encountered on open plains.

For the smaller mammals, which require dental and/or chromosomal analysis for differentiation and identification, this guide provides an overall description of the species within the subfamily or family, enabling readers to distinguish between a fruit bat and a horseshoe bat, for example, or to tell an acacia rat from a swamp rat.

It should be noted that certain animals might have more than one common name, especially if they occur in different regions. For example, the blue wildebeest is also known as the brindled wildebeest, blue gnu, and brindled gnu; and the common duiker as Grimms' duiker, bush duiker, and grey duiker. To avoid confusion, refer to scientific names, as these stay constant across regional and international borders.

Species descriptions

All species that are found within the park are grouped into their 13 orders and respective families, specified on the contents page (pages 4 and 5). Each species account contains a tinted box that summarizes key information such as mass, shoulder height, distinguishing features, life-span and main predators. A detailed table containing Kruger-specific predation rates is given in Appendix 2. Symbols in the key information box reflect whether the species is diurnal, nocturnal or both. The conservation status of endangered species is also provided. The written text contains detailed information regarding diagnostic physical features, distribution within the Park, behaviour (including calls, alarm signals and signs of aggression), reproduction, diet and habitat. The information goes beyond what is obvious to the casual observer, offering insight into particular behaviour, for example, why male elephants' faces are stained at certain times, why certain antelope thrash bushes and shrubs, or why male lions sometimes eat the cubs of their own kind. The more common species accounts are furthermore accompanied by a spoor drawing, which is of the frontfoot (F) for most species. Hindfeet (H) are occasionally depicted. All species accounts are accompanied by two distribution maps (Kruger and Africa).

Basic tips for mammal watching

When visiting a national park, always bear in mind that, although the animals are enclosed in a nature reserve, they are still untamed and wild. One cannot expect every encounter to be a picture-perfect opportunity. Hence, cameras should ideally be equipped with a good zoom lens; binoculars are useful for observing an animal and its behaviour from a distance without disturbing it.

The best time for mammal watching is early morning and late afternoon – periods when both nocturnal and diurnal species are active. To prevent water loss and overheating, many mammals lie up during the heat of the day, although more activity is likely to be encountered at this time on cooler overcast or rainy days. Watering holes are always good game-viewing sites, particularly in the afternoons.

Many animals find safety in numbers; therefore it is generally easier to approach large herds than individuals. Be mindful at all times of the effect you have on animals: try not to crowd

Wild dog pups

them (or to cut in front of other vehicles to get a better vantage point).

Finally, a point which I cannot stress enough: DO NOT FEED THE ANIMALS! It might be a novelty to see baboons, vervet monkeys or birds feed at arm's length, but in the long run, this causes havoc among wild populations: the wild animals may become dependent on humans, and more importantly, they may become pests and positively aggressive and dangerous, commonly resulting in the offenders having to be put down. One of South Africa's national parks does not allow its visitors to take citrus fruit in their vehicles on game-drives because certain animals, having developed such a fondness for citrus, have been known to attack vehicles to obtain the fruits. To drive this point home, signs in parks in Botswana read: 'You feed them, we shoot them.' Leave the animals as you found them, wild and free in their natural environment, so that future generations may also enjoy them.

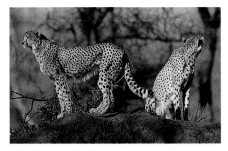

Cheetahs on the look-out

Major ecozones of Africa

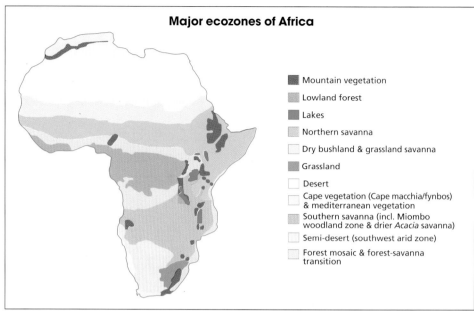

- Mountain vegetation
- Lowland forest
- Lakes
- Northern savanna
- Dry bushland & grassland savanna
- Grassland
- Desert
- Cape vegetation (Cape macchia/fynbos) & mediterranean vegetation
- Southern savanna (incl. Miombo woodland zone & drier *Acacia* savanna)
- Semi-desert (southwest arid zone)
- Forest mosaic & forest-savanna transition

Ecozones of the Kruger National Park

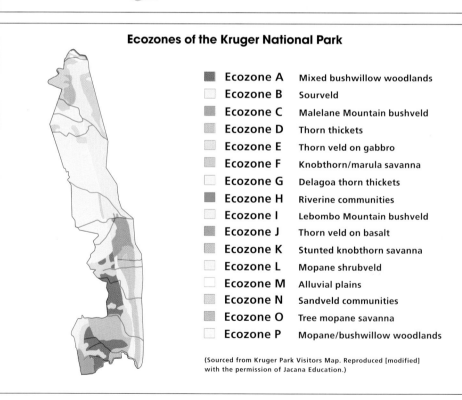

Ecozone A	Mixed bushwillow woodlands
Ecozone B	Sourveld
Ecozone C	Malelane Mountain bushveld
Ecozone D	Thorn thickets
Ecozone E	Thorn veld on gabbro
Ecozone F	Knobthorn/marula savanna
Ecozone G	Delagoa thorn thickets
Ecozone H	Riverine communities
Ecozone I	Lebombo Mountain bushveld
Ecozone J	Thorn veld on basalt
Ecozone K	Stunted knobthorn savanna
Ecozone L	Mopane shrubveld
Ecozone M	Alluvial plains
Ecozone N	Sandveld communities
Ecozone O	Tree mopane savanna
Ecozone P	Mopane/bushwillow woodlands

(Sourced from Kruger Park Visitors Map. Reproduced [modified] with the permission of Jacana Education.)

Regional map of the Kruger National Park

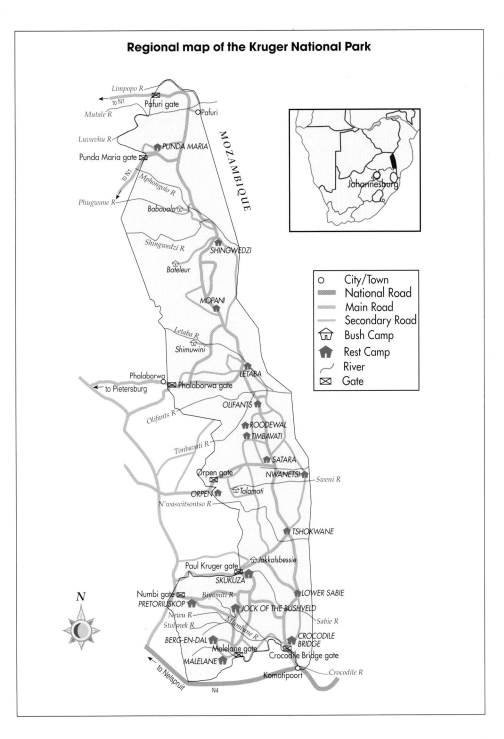

African Elephant

Loxodonta africana

Ger: Afrikanischer Elefant; **Fre:** Elephant d'Afrique; **Afr:** Olifant; **Nde:** indlovu ye-Afrika; **Xho, Zul,** **Swa:** indlovu; **Set, Sot:** tlou; **Xit:** ndlopfu; **Tsh:** ndou.

Status: IUCN: EN. CITES: App 1

Mass: ♂ 5 000–6 500 kg; ♀ 2 500–3 500 kg. **Shoulder height:** ♂ 3,0–4,0 m; ♀ 2,4–3,4 m. **Distinguishing features:** It is the largest land animal, recognized by its extremely long trunk (the only animal with a nose in this form), and its very large ears and tusks (both the largest found in any animal). **Life-span:** ± 60 yrs. Life cycle is similar to that of humans: puberty during teens, fertility cycle lasts ± 30 yrs. **Predators:** Main predator is man: the tusks are prized in the illegal ivory trade, and land resources are destroyed through human activity.

Front: 50 cm
Hind: 50 cm

DESCRIPTION

The skin is naked except for a few bristles. The overall body colour is dark grey or greyish brown, often taking on the colour of the local soil. Young calves are covered with sparse reddish-brown, brown or black hair. The African elephant can be distinguished from the Asiatic elephant by: (i) The absence of a depression behind the head. The forehead profile is rounded in bulls, angular in cows. (ii) A slightly hollow back that is not arched. (iii) A series of transverse ridges on the trunk. (iv) The tips of the upper and lower trunk have a finger-like projection, of the same size, which can be used as finger and thumb with much dexterity. (v) Enormous ears, up to 1,5 m wide and 2 m long. (vi) A loose skin fold that joins the hindquarters to the side of the body.

Age can be determined by studying the teeth. During a lifetime, an elephant will use 6 sets of teeth, each set comprising one molar tooth on either side of the upper and lower jaw (4 in total). As the molars get worn down, they are replaced by a set from the rear, with sets being replaced at about 1, 2, 6, 15, 28 and 47 years of age. The last set is worn down when the elephant is about 60 years old. After this, the animal slowly starves to death. Age can also be determined by size: elephants continue to grow throughout their lives.

Elephants walk at speeds of 5–10 km/h. During long journeys, the speed averages 10–15 km/h. They charge and stampede at about 40 km/h, but can only maintain this speed over short distances. Thick elastic pads under the feet enable the animal to move about without much sound. Feet expand when weight is applied and contract when weight is lifted. Superficial cracks in the horny covering of the soles show in the spoor.

Tusks: Elongated incisors, composed of prized ivory, project from the upper jaw and are used for fighting, digging and carrying objects. Tusk length is up to 2,8 m in bulls, smaller in cows. Average weight of tusks in bulls, 60 kg each; in cows, 18 kg each. (Tusk length of Kruger 'Magnificent 7' bulls: 2,5–3 m, weight 50–73 kg). Calves grow milk tusks up to 5 cm long that are replaced in young bulls at 2,5 years and in cows at 2 years.

Scent glands: Temporal gland (roughly halfway between eye and ear).

Senses: Poor sight, very good hearing (hear humans 1,5 km away), well-developed sense of smell (smell animals 3 km away).

DISTRIBUTION

Occur in all ecozones of the Kruger. Main density populations occur along the Letaba, Olifants, Tsende, Shingwedzi, Mphongolo and Shisha rivers, with smaller populations along the Timbavati, Sabie, Biyamiti and Crocodile rivers. A small population is found in the Stolsnek and Malelane Mountain regions.

Cow and calf

BEHAVIOUR

Diurnal and nocturnal. Bulls are solitary or can be found in bachelor herds of 2–12 individuals, occasionally more. Cows form nursery herds of 12 individuals on average, comprising a dominant cow known as the matriarch, and related cows and calves. Larger herds tend to split up into smaller groups that may stay within the same home range, keeping in constant contact with one another through rumblings and frequent visits. Cows stay within the natal herd while bulls leave at about 14 years of age. For both sexes, the size of the home range depends on habitat and distribution. It can be 15–52 km², as for example in the Manyara National Park in Tanzania, or up to 3 500 km² in arid regions. Kruger home ranges for both sexes are not smaller that 100 km². Home ranges contain well-worn paths.

The bonds between herd members are extremely strong, and maternal bonds may last a lifetime. Relations are maintained with much trunk caressing and touching. There have been reports of herd members attempting to raise fallen individuals. If the matriarch is injured or shot, the rest of the herd gather around in a state of panic, and very often become victims themselves.

Elephants greet one another by blowing into one another's mouths with their trunks, thereby stimulating a gland in the roof of the mouth. When curious about a sound, the ears are held out straight.

Elephants do not have sweat glands. They lower their body temperature by flapping their ears (which increases blood flow through a network of veins in the ears), by splashing themselves with water and by taking sand and mud baths. The trunk can hold up to 6 litres of water. Mud and sand also offer protection against sun and parasites.

Musth: A dark, oily, odorous secretion is discharged from the temporal gland once a year in bulls above 25 years of age, staining the face. This period of musth signifies elevated testosterone levels. Urine is also constantly dribbled, and a greenish fluid is secreted from the penis. Bulls in musth are more aggressive than other bulls, and oestrus cows are more likely to mate with bulls in musth than with those that are not.

Calls: Contact calls include rumbles, infrasonic sound, and trumpeting. Alarm calls include screams, bellows

The cow's forehead is angular (opposite, top); the bull's is more rounded (opposite, bottom)

and trumpeting, which can reach 110 decibels and can be heard over 5 km away. Calves squeak.

Alarm signals and aggression: When calves are present, adults form a circle around them. To signify aggression, adults trumpet and screech, hold their heads high or jerk them up and down, flap their ears and hold them out straight, kicking up dust with their forefeet. They may mock charge. If this fails, they charge the source of disturbance or stampede away from it. During a true charge, the ears are held back against the neck and the trunk is tucked under the chin. Within the herd structure, the matriarch usually charges.

REPRODUCTION

Breed all year. A single calf, weighing 100–165 kg, is born after a gestation period of 22 months, with an average interval of 4–9 years between births. During the birth process, cows surround and protect the cow giving birth. The calf stands within an hour of birth. Closely related females may cross-suckle calves. Calves are weaned at 2 years.

DIET

Browse on grass, roots, and the bark, branches, leaves and fruit of trees and shrubs. They enjoy sugar cane, bamboo and fruit, such as citrus, dates, plums, berries and coconuts. Elephants are particularly fond of fan palm and manketti tree and are often said to become intoxicated from marula fruits. Elephants visit salt licks and chew soil and rocks to supplement the mineral content of their diet. Approximately 150 kg of green fodder is required daily.

Elephants are water dependent. They can go without water for about 3 days, and will travel 80 km to the nearest water source. They will dig in dry riverbeds to reach the water below. Up to 200*l* of water are consumed daily.

HABITAT

Found in all habitats, provided there is sufficient water: forest, woodland and grassland savanna, river valleys and swamps. Occur in all the habitats of the Kruger.

This bull is in musth – note the temporal gland secretion

Black/Hook-lipped Rhinoceros

Diceros bicornis

Ger: Spitzmaulnashorn; **Fre:** Rhinocéros noir; **Afr:** Swartrenoster; **Xho:** umkhombe; **Nde:** umkhombo, ubhejane onzima, umkhombo onzima; **Zul:** ubhejane, isibhejane; **Set, Sot:** tshukudu; **Set:** bodile, tshukudu e ntsho; **Sot:** tshukudu e molomo wa haka; **Swa:** sibhejane; **Xit:** mhelembe, mhelemba; **Tsh:** thema, thema i re na milomo mitshena.

Status: IUCN: CR. CITES: App. I

☼ ☽

Mass: ♂ 800–1 400 kg; ♀ 800–1 100 kg. **Shoulder height:** ♂ 1,4–1,6 m; ♀ 1,4–1,5 m. **Distinguishing features:** Massive horns project from top of nose. Distinguished from white rhino by prehensile upper lip, which is pointed or hooked. Ears are fringed with brownish-black hair. Head is characteristically held high when the animal walks. **Lifespan:** ± 30 yrs. **Predators:** Main predator is man: horns are thought to have aphrodisiac and medicinal properties. Young fall prey to lion, spotted hyaena and wild dog.

Front: 22 cm
Hind: 20 cm

DESCRIPTION

The black rhino is smaller than its white relative. It has a huge, solid body with short stocky legs. Feet expand when weight is applied and contract when weight is lifted. The dark skin is greyish brown, often taking on the colour of the local soil. Regular mud and sand baths aid in lowering body temperature and offer protection against sun and parasites. Despite its size, it reaches speeds of up to 50 km/h.

Scent glands: None present.

Senses: Poor sight, very good hearing and sense of smell.

Horns: Anterior horn 0,5–1,3 m and posterior horn up to 0,5 m long. The cow's horns are longer and more slender than those of the bull. The smooth horns are composed of keratinised fibres. The strong anterior horn curves slightly backwards and has a round, thick base. It can be used for digging and easily uproots bushes and small trees. The posterior horn resembles an upside-down cone with flattened sides.

DISTRIBUTION

Occur in ecozones A, D, E, F, G and K of the Kruger. Populations are established in the Skukuza/Nwaswitshaka area, the Lubyelubye area near Lower Sabie, and along the N'waswitsonto and Sweni rivers between Tshokwane and Satara.

BEHAVIOUR

Diurnal and nocturnal, with activity peaks in the early morning and late afternoon; they tend to rest during the hotter hours of the day. Bulls and cows are solitary, but sometimes gather in groups at waterholes. The territorial behaviour of bulls varies according to habitat and population density. In high-density areas and in the Kruger, territories of 2,5–8 km² are loosely defended, although neighbours are tolerated, often sharing common paths. In the open Ngorongoro Crater, overlapping ranges of 2,6–44 km² are not defended, but in the Serengeti such ranges would be defended as territories. Territories/home ranges are marked with large, scattered communal dung middens, with well-worn paths, by spraying urine onto bushes, and with ground scuffing and vegetation horning, particularly on favourite posts, which become worn and smooth.

Cows are non-territorial. The size of the home range varies according to population density and habitat, and can range from 6–8 km² to 20 km² in poorer habitat conditions. Home ranges of neighbouring cows overlap and may cross several bull territories and are marked with communal dung middens and well-worn paths.

Note the distinct hook-shaped lips

Calls: Contact calls include puffs and puffing snorts. Alarm calls include snorts and shrieks. Calves squeal. They also respond to alarm calls of oxpeckers.

Alarm signals: When alarmed, trot a short distance with their tails curled onto their backs.

Aggression: May stare at the intruder. Approach with their heads held erect and the ears pinned back. A greater threat is signified when the head is lowered in a horn threat display, with ears cocked and tail raised. Other threat displays include dust raising, chasing, mock charges, vegetation horning, charging, grunting, snorting and shrieking.

REPRODUCTION

Breed all year with a peak in the summer rainy season. A single calf, weighing 40–50 kg, is born after a gestation period of 15 months, with an average interval of 3 years between births. The calf is born in heavy cover, and remains hidden for a week. It is able to walk within 3 hours, and can take solid food by one month. It is weaned after 1–1,5 years, but stays with the mother for about 3 years, or until the next calf is born. The calf always walks or runs behind or alongside its mother.

DIET

Selective browsers of leafy twigs and shrubs of a preferred height of 0,5–1,2 m, with a strong preference for *Acacia* spp and the Tamboti tree, with its poisonous milky latex. The pointed upper lip is used to grasp twigs and shoots, which are then snapped off or cut by the cheek teeth. They are water dependent, often drinking twice a day, but they can go without water for 4 days if the browse contains sufficient moisture. They are dependent on waterholes for mud wallows, and will dig for water in dry riverbeds.

HABITAT

Savanna woodland, scrub and forest with sufficient water, preferring areas on the edge of thickets and savanna which have dense vegetation cover in the form of numerous trees and shrubs. Seldom more than 25 km from water. In the Kruger Park, they are found in the mixed bushwillow woodlands, thorn thickets, thorn veld, delagoa thorn thickets as well as in knobthorn/marula savanna and stunted knobthorn savanna habitats.

White/Square-lipped Rhinoceros

Ceratotherium simum

Ger: Breitmaulnashorn; **Afr:** Witrenoster; **Fre:** Rhinocéros blanc; **Nde:** umkhombo omhlophe; **Zul, Xho, Swa:** umkhombe; **Zul:** ubhejane omhlophe; **Set, Sot:** tshukudu, mogohu; **Set:** kgetlaw, kôbaôba; **Sot:** tshukudu e molomo o sephara; **Xit:** mhelembe; **Tsh:** tshugula.

Mass: ♂ 1 800–2 400 kg; ♀ 1 400–1 850 kg. **Shoulder height:** ♂ 1,5–1,9 m; ♀ 1,5–1,75 m. **Distinguishing features:** Massive horns project from top of nose. Distinguished from black rhino by a 20 cm-wide, square lip and a pronounced neck hump. Head characteristically held low, just a few centimetres above the ground, even when not grazing. **Life-span:** ± 40 yrs. **Predators:** The main predator is man: the horns are thought to have aphrodisiac and medicinal properties. Young fall prey to lion, spotted hyaena and wild dog.

Front: 30 cm
Hind: 30 cm

DESCRIPTION

The white rhino is the second largest land mammal. It has a huge, solid body with short, stocky legs. Feet expand when weight is applied and contract when weight is lifted. A characteristic cleft at rear of foot distinguishes the spoor from black rhino spoor. The skin is dark greyish brown, often taking on the colour of the local soil. Regular mud and sand baths aid in lowering body temperature and offer protection against sun and parasites. Speeds of 45 km/h can be maintained over long distances.
Scent glands: Perineal.
Senses: Poor sight, very good hearing and sense of smell.
Horns: The anterior horn can grow up to 1,5 m long, average is 0,6 m. Cows' horns are longer and more slender than those of bulls. They are composed of keratinised fibres and are smooth in texture. The strong anterior horn curves slightly backwards and has a round, thick base. It is used for digging, easily uprooting bushes and small trees. The posterior horn resembles an upside-down cone with flattened sides.

DISTRIBUTION

Occur in ecozones A, B, C, D, E, F, G, K and P of the Kruger. Populations occur in the Tshokwane, Satara and Nwanetsi areas, in the Lower Sabie and Crocodile Bridge areas, with the most densely populated areas being between the Mbyamiti and the Mlambane rivers in the Pretoriuskop, Stolsnek and Malelane areas. Scattered populations also occur between the Tsende and Shingwedzi rivers.

BEHAVIOUR

Diurnal and nocturnal with activity peaks in the early morning and late afternoon; least active during the hotter hours of the day. The social structure consists of nursery herds, or herds comprised of a dominant bull, several cows and their calves. Average group size in the Kruger is 2–3.

Territories of neighbouring bulls do not overlap. Average territory size ranges from 6,5–13,2 km², with an average core range of 1,9–3,4 km². Outside of Kruger, bulls defend territories ranging from 1–10 km², but may tolerate up to four submissive bulls in their territory. Territory is marked with large, communal dung middens and with well-worn paths. The dominant bull marks the territory by spraying urine onto bushes, with ground scuffing and vegetation horning. Dominant bulls have favourite resting spots.

Cows are non-territorial and form nursery herds when not accompanied by a territorial bull. The size of the home range varies according to population density and

Note the distinct square-shaped lips

habitat, from 6–8 km² up to 20 km² in poorer habitat conditions outside of the Kruger. Home ranges of neighbouring cows overlap and may cross several bulls' territories. Home ranges are marked with large, communal dung middens and with well-worn paths. Home ranges in the Kruger average 11–34,7 km², with an average core range of 2,6–6,8 km². During the dry winter season, home ranges are reduced to 11,5 km².

Calls: Contact calls include grunts and bellows. Alarm calls include snorts, roars and shrieks. Calves squeal. They also respond to alarm calls of oxpeckers.

Alarm signals: Herd members stand rump against rump, facing outwards, while snarling, grunting, and snorting; when alarmed, trot a short distance, with their tails curled onto their backs.

Aggression: May simply stare at the intruder. Approach the threat with their heads held high and ears pinned back. A greater threat is signified when the head is lowered in a horn threat display, with ears cocked and tail raised. Other threat displays include dust raising, chasing, charging and mock charging, vegetation horning, grunting, snorting and shrieking.

REPRODUCTION

Breed all year with a peak in the summer rainy season. A single calf, weighing 50–65 kg, is born after a gestation period of 16 months, with an average interval of 3 years between births. The calf is born in heavy cover, and remains hidden for 3 days. It takes solid food at 2 months. It is weaned after one year, but remains with the mother for about 2 years. The calf always walks or runs in front of or alongside its mother.

DIET

Selective grazers of short, new grasses, favouring perennials. Water dependent, often drinking twice a day but can go without water for 4 days. Dependent on waterholes for mud wallows.

HABITAT

Open woodland in close proximity of open grassland, thickets, mud wallows and water. In the Kruger, found in the mixed bushwillow woodlands, Malelane Mountain bushveld, thorn thickets, delagoa thorn thickets, thorn veld, knobthorn/marula savanna, stunted knobthorn savanna and sourveld habitats. Found marginally in the north-central parts of the mopane/bushwillow woodlands habitat where it borders thorn veld. Moderately undulating granitoid plains with *Combretum zeyheri* woodland is the favoured landscape in the southern parts of the Kruger.

Burchell's/Plains Zebra

Equus burchelli

Ger: Burchell's/Steppenzebra; **Fre:** Zèbre de burchell/steppe; **Afr:** Bontsebra, Bontkwagga; **Nde:** idube, iduba, iduba elimibalabala, idube elibhondo; **Xho:** iqwarhashe; **Zul:** indube; **Set, Sot:** pitse ya naga; **Sot:** pitsi ya naha; **Swa:** lidvubu, lidvuba; **Xit:** mangwa, mbizi, duva; **Tsh:** mbidi.

Status: not endangered ☼ ☽

Mass: ♂ 290–340 kg; ♀ 260–320 kg. **Shoulder height:** ♂ 1,3–1,4 m; ♀ 1,3–1,4 m. **Distinguishing features:** Black and white striped patterning is unique for each individual. An erect black and white mane extends from the head to the shoulders. **Life-span:** ± 25 yrs. **Predators:** Main predators include lion and spotted hyaena; others include leopard and crocodile. Young also fall prey to wild dog and cheetah.

Front: 11 cm
Hind: 10 cm

DESCRIPTION
The coat is short and sleek, with broad black stripes on a white-buff background. The patterning varies between subspecies and individuals, and ranges from solid stripes only, to solid stripes with paler buff-brownish shadow stripes. The stripes may extend to the undersides and hooves in some individuals, in others the legs and belly are not striped. The muzzle and chin are black. Zebra can reach speeds of up to 65 km/h.
Scent glands: None present.
Senses: Very good sight, hearing and sense of smell.

DISTRIBUTION
Occur widely and commonly in suitable habitat in all ecozones of the Kruger. Densest concentrations are found on the open plains of the central regions and in the eastern parts of the Park.

BEHAVIOUR
Diurnal and nocturnal. Form harem herds, comprising a dominant stallion, 2–6 mares and their foals, but herds numbering several hundred are not uncommon. Average group size within the Kruger is 2–5, but groups of over 50 individuals are sometimes seen north of the Letaba River. Home range size is determined by habitat and distribution, and can be as small as 30 km² and up to 600 km² for migratory herds. Home ranges of neighbouring herds overlap. Home ranges in the Kruger are 49–566 km² (depending on distribution), with an overall average of 165 km². Zebras utilize well-used paths within the home range. Mares remain with the stallion that sired their offspring. Young stallions leave the natal herd at 2–3 years of age, residing on the fringes of harem herds, and remain at the rear of the herd, behind the dominant stallion.
   Zebra condition their coats by rolling on the ground, dust bathing, rubbing themselves against trees and rocks (which often become smooth from continued use), and by grooming other herd members' coats. Mutual grooming plays an important role in maintaining relations between herd members.
   Zebra herds are often seen in association with herds of other species, such as wildebeest, giraffe and impala. Zebra always stay in groups as a protective measure. It is thought that the mass of stripes may confuse predators, as they are unable to distinguish individual herd members. At dawn and night, the striping also distorts distance, making it difficult for predators to judge the distance for attack.
Calls: Contact calls include a distinctive loud, high-pitched `qua-ha' bark. Short whinnying calls serve as an initial warning; snorts signal alarm.

The striped pattern is unique for each individual

Alarm signals: When approached by a predator, herd members form a semi-circle around the intruder, ready to kick with the hind hooves and to bite if the attack continues. When fleeing danger, stallions always run at the rear of the herd, kicking and biting in defence. Zebra deliver a powerful kick with their hind hooves.

Aggression: To signal aggression, the head is held high, the ears are turned inward and pinned back, the teeth are bared and the tail is whipped from side to side. Lowering the head with an open-mouthed gape indicates a greater threat. Other signs of aggression include stamping, ground pawing, kicking and biting.

REPRODUCTION

Breed all year with a peak in the summer rainy season. A single foal, weighing 30–36 kg, is born after a gestation period of 12 months, with an average interval of 2 years between births. Foals are able to stand within 15 minutes of birth. They are kept away from the herd for 2–3 days until maternal imprinting has been established. It takes solid food at 1 month, but is suckled for up to a year. It is weaned at 11 months.

DIET

Graze over 50 grass species, preferring short grasses and new grasses that sprout after fires. Occasionally browse on herbs, bark, fruit and leaves, especially mopane and kiaat leaves. Zebra are water dependent, drinking daily.

HABITAT

Open woodland and grassland savanna; shrubveld. Seldom more than 12 km from water. Occur in all the habitats of the Kruger but are absent from areas with dense shrub, tree thickets and dense riparian vegetation.

Hippopotamus

Hippopotamus amphibius

Ger: Nilpferd, Flußpferd; **Fre:** Hippopotame; **Afr:** Seekoei; **Nde, Xho, Zul, Swa:** imvubu; **Set, Sot:** kubu; **Xit:** mpfubu, mpfuvu; **Tsh:** mvuvhu.

Status: CITES: App.II

Mass: ♂ 1 600–3 200 kg; ♀ 650–2 400 kg. **Shoulder height:** ♂ 1,4–1,7 m; ♀ 1,3–1,6 m. **Distinguishing features:** The third largest land mammal. Large, barrel-shaped body, with short legs and tail. Huge head with a 50 cm-wide muzzle, which opens to 90–120 cm (150°), exposing long, pointed incisors and curved canines. **Life-span:** ± 30 yrs. **Predators:** Main predator is man: farmers shoot hippo because they trample their crops; hippo meat and hide are used in soups; and the canines are a source of ivory. Young fall prey to lion, spotted hyaena, wild dog, crocodile and leopard.

Front: 25 cm
Hind: 25 cm

DESCRIPTION

The naked skin is greyish brown with a purplish tinge. Areas around the eyes, ears, throat and lips, in the neck fold and on the underparts are tinged pink. The eyes are small and protrude from the side of the head. Adults have long, pointed incisors and tusk-like canines. The upper canines can grow 60 cm long, weighing up to 3 kg. Lower canines average 22 cm for bulls, 14 cm for cows. Hippo can remain submerged for 6 minutes, and the ears and nose can be closed down when underwater. On land, they reach speeds of 30 km/h. Despite their huge size, they can climb steep banks and turn around in a very small area, but they cannot jump, and move around obstacles rather than stepping over them.

Glands: Subdermal glands produce a reddish-pink secretion (also referred to as 'blood sweat'), which protects the skin against the sun and dehydration, and enables the hippo to stay in water for long periods.

Senses: Fairly good sight, good hearing and sense of smell.

DISTRIBUTION

Occur in ecozone H of the Kruger, in perennial rivers and in permanent and semi-permanent pools formed in seasonal rivers. Also found in large dams throughout the Park. The highest densities are found in the Olifants River.

BEHAVIOUR

Days are spent mainly in the water to protect their delicate skin against the sun; nights are spent grazing on land. Found in mixed herds averaging 5–30 individuals, although larger aggregations occur at higher population densities. A typical herd consists of a dominant bull, cows and calves. Mature bulls hold mating territories, which range over 50–100 m of river and 250–500 m of shores and shallows. Bulls mark the territory by flicking their dung with their tail into the water, onto bushes and rocks, and particularly in communal dung heaps on paths leaving the water. Cows remain in the natal herd. Young bulls reside in bachelor herds on the periphery of the dominant bull's territory.

Herds have fixed paths leading to their grazing grounds. These paths are worn into two parallel ruts, and are marked with communal dung middens. Hippo graze about 5 hours every night, travelling 3–5 km while feeding. When they are in the water, they walk along the bed of the river or other water body, often forming trails that can be seen through clear water. Paths are also cleared through reed beds and deltas. Hippo

The yawning gape is a sign of aggression

are often seen basking in the sun on sandbanks. They mate in water.

Calls: Contact calls include wheeze-honks and grunts. Alarm calls include wheeze-honks, exhaling extremely loudly above or below the water, and loud staccato grunts that are followed by bellows as loud as 120 decibels.

Alarm signals: When threatened on land, hippo run to the water. When threatened in the water, they dive and swim away.

Aggression: Wide, open-mouthed gapes and wide yawning gapes displaying the tusks and canines, signify aggression. Other threat displays include water scooping, head shaking, chasing, mock or real charges, exhaling loudly above or below water, and grunting.

REPRODUCTION

Breed all year with a peak in the summer rainy season. A single calf, weighing 25–50 kg, is born after a gestation period of 8 months, with an average interval of 2–3 years between births. Cows leave the herd to give birth in isolation. Calves are born in shallow water, on land in reed beds or in dense cover. They are kept from the herd for 2–3 weeks until maternal imprinting has been established. Calves can swim almost immediately and suckle underwater. In deep water they climb onto their mothers' back. Calves take solid food at 4–6 months and are weaned at 8–12 months.

DIET

Selective grazers, favouring short, new green grasses. They can consume up to about 60 kg of grass in one day. They also browse on leaves, fruit and vegetables; fond of sugar cane and corn. Hippos obtain enough moisture and water from their food and dew. However, they are dependent on water for the protection of their sensitive skin pigmentation, and must have water that is 1,5 m deep into which they can submerge themselves.

HABITAT

Lakes, streams, rivers, swamps and deltas, and near marshes and grassland for grazing. Prefer quiet waters, deep enough to submerge in by standing or kneeling on the bottom of the waterbed. Found in riverine communities habitats throughout the Kruger.

Southern Giraffe

Giraffa camelopardalis giraffa

Ger, Fre: Giraffe; **Afr:** Kameelperd; **Nde, Xho, Zul:** indlulamithi; **Nde:** intudla; **Xho:** icowa, umcheya; **Set, Sot:** thuhlo; **Set:** thutlwa, thitlwa; **Swa:** indlulamitsi, lihudla; **Xit:** nhutlwa, nthutlwa; **Tsh:** thuda, thudwa.

Mass: ♂ 1 000–1 900 kg, ♀ 700–1 200 kg; **Shoulder height:** ♂ 4,5–5,5 m; ♀ 3,9–4,5 m. **Total height:** ♂ 2–3,5 m; ♀ 1–2,5 m. **Distinguishing features:** The tallest animal in the world, its long neck rendering it unmistakable. Patchwork patterning of the coat is unique for each individual. Body slopes downwards towards the rear, with the forequarters appearing longer than the hindquarters, but they are the same length. **Life-span:** ± 20 yrs. **Predators:** Main predators include lion and leopard. Young fall prey to cheetah, spotted hyaena and crocodile.

Front: 22 cm
Hind: 18 cm

DESCRIPTION

The coat is tawny, covered with large chestnut-brown patches separated by tawny or white bands. The patches darken with age. A stiff mane extends from the back of the head to the shoulders. The tail tassel is black. The long neck contains 7 vertebrae, like that of most mammals. Each vertebra is about 30 cm long. Elasticized blood vessels in the neck prevent a surge of blood to the head when the head is lowered or swung. When giraffe walk or run, they move both legs on the same side of their body forward simultaneously. At a full gallop, speeds of over 55 km/h can be reached. Bulls exude a pungent smell.

Scent glands: Possibly on the lips and eyes.

Senses: Very good sight, recognize herd members 1,5 km away. Good hearing and sense of smell.

Horns: The knob-like protrusions on the head are not true horns. They are straight, up to 13,5 cm long, and covered with hair. Cows have tufts of hair on the tips of their 'horns', the tips of bulls' 'horns' are bald. Bulls may have a large, central 'horn' arising from the forehead, between the eyes.

DISTRIBUTION

Occur in all the ecozones of the Kruger, except L, with the highest density concentrations occurring between the Sabie and the Olifants rivers. They are also common south of the Olifants River, and north of the Olifants River around the Olifants Camp area. Further to the north they are rare, being almost absent north of Punda Maria.

BEHAVIOUR

Diurnal and nocturnal, with nocturnal activity being confined mostly to rumination. They are solitary or may occur in loosely associated same-sex and mixed herds. Dominant bulls stand with their heads held high; subordinates show submission by bowing their heads and dropping their ears. Young bulls tend to form bachelor herds. Nursery herds are comprised of cows and their calves, consisting of 4–30 (average 12) individuals. Average group size in the Kruger is 2–3, but groups of up to 10 individuals can be encountered in the central areas where the highest densities occur. Giraffe move over core home ranges of up to 80 km², through a yearly home range that is up to 650 km². The home ranges of neighbouring individuals and herds overlap. The average home range in the central parts of the Kruger is 282 km². Giraffe are often seen in association with herds of zebra, wildebeest and impala.

The 'horns' of a giraffe bull (above) are bald, whereas the female's 'horns' are covered with tufts of hair

Calls: Although the vocal cords are rudimentary, giraffe can emit a number of sounds. Contact calls include bellows, coughs, grunts and moans. Calves mew. Alarm calls include grunts and snorts. They bleat when distressed.

Alarm signals: Head fully raised in alert posture. Flee with their tails curled onto their backs.

Aggression: Dominance displays include horn threats and sparring, which involves striking the opponent with the head against the neck, rump and flanks. Predators are kicked during attack, and a well-aimed blow can kill a lion.

REPRODUCTION

Breed all year. A single calf (rarely two), weighing 70–100 kg, is born after a gestation period of 14–14,5 months, with an average interval of 1,5–2 years between births. The calf is born in isolation, and can stand within an hour of birth; it joins the herd after 2–3 weeks. It takes solid food at 3 weeks but is suckled up to 9–10 months. For the first 4–5 months calves form nursery crèches. The calf is weaned after 1 year but stays with its mother until it is 1,5–2 years old.

DIET

Browse more than 100 species of plants, preferring *Acacia, Combretum* and *Terminalia* spp, browsed at 2–5,5 m. During the rainy season their diet consists mainly of broad-leaved deciduous plants; these are replaced by evergreens in the dry season. A study undertaken in 1990 showed that 42 different woody species were browsed in the central parts of the Kruger. Leaves are grasped with the 45 cm-long tongue, and thorns are chewed with the long, muscular upper lip. Fruit, such as monkey oranges and sausage tree fruit, is also taken. Salt licks are visited and bones and soil are chewed to supplement the mineral content of their diet. Bulls tend to eat at full stretch, with their heads tilted upwards. Cows eat from lower branches, or nibble from the tops of bushes, with their heads tilted downwards and their necks angled. Giraffe prune trees into a distinctive hourglass shape when browsing. They can browse for over 15 hours a day, consuming up to 80 kg. They very occasionally graze on new sprouting grasses. They are water dependent and drink regularly when water is available, but can go without water for up to a month, obtaining enough moisture from their food.

HABITAT

Savanna and open woodland, particularly *Acacia, Commiphora* and *Terminalia* dominated woodland. Occur in all the habitats of the Kruger, except mopane shrubveld.

African/Cape Buffalo

Syncerus caffer

Ger: Büffel; Fre: Buffle, Afr: Buffel; Nde, Xho, Zul: inyathi; Set, Sot: nare; Set, Tsh: nari; Swa: inyatsi; Xit: nyarhi.

Status: not endangered

Mass: ♂ 450–870 kg; ♀ 550 kg. **Shoulder height:** ♂ 1,4–1,65 m; ♀ 1,0–1,4 m. **Distinguishing features:** Massive, heavy build. Distinctive W-shaped horns grow from heavy bosses on the forehead. Large ears, fringed with hair, droop below the horns. **Life-span:** ± 15–20 yrs. **Predators:** Main predators include lion and man. Young also fall prey to spotted hyaena, crocodile and wild dog.

Front: 13 cm
Hind: 12 cm

DESCRIPTION

The coat is short, thin and scanty. Bulls are brownish black, cows reddish brown. The underside of the chin is often paler or cream coloured. Calves are reddish brown, covered with a dense coat of hair. The broad, splayed feet enable Cape buffalo to utilize marshy habitats and to wallow in water and mud. They can run at speeds of up to 55 km/h.

Scent glands: None present.

Senses: Poor sight and hearing, good sense of smell.

Horns: Horns grow from heavily ridged bosses on the forehead. They curve downward, outward and then upward. When viewed together, the two horns form a shallow W-shape. Bulls' horns and bosses are heavier than those of cows, and in old bulls the bosses join across the head. The horns are heavily rugose for one third of their length, then smooth to the tips. ♂ width: 0,5–1,0 m; length along curve: 1,15–1,50 m. ♀ width: 0,5–1,0 m; length along curve:1,0–1,35 m.

DISTRIBUTION

Found in suitable habitat in all ecozones of the Kruger, with the highest numbers occurring in the northern districts.

BEHAVIOUR

Diurnal and nocturnal, grazing mostly at night, but may become nocturnal in disturbed areas. Herds usually consist of several hundred individuals, but may number up to 3 000 in East Africa. In the Kruger, average herd size is 250, although herds of over 800 individuals are also encountered. Herds consist of small clans, comprised of one to several dominant bulls, cows and calves. Clans share home ranges of 10–300 km², the range being determined by the size of the herd. Individual clans within the herd do not necessarily come together. 3–6 km are covered daily whilst grazing; up to 25 km per day in the dry season. Individuals known as 'pathfinders' always take the lead when the herd moves. When they are 3 years old, young bulls join bachelor herds of about 3–6 individuals. Their home ranges can be as small as a few square kilometres. Older bulls tend to be solitary.

Calls: Contact calls include grunts, honks and croaks. Alarm calls include snorts and bellows.

Alarm signals: Alert posture with arched tail. May advance to investigate the source of the disturbance, circling the predator whilst tossing the head. Flee in stampeding flight, or mob-attack (*see* below).

Aggression: Stiff-legged gait, head level or raised, horn threats, head tossing and grunting. Herds will defend any member that is attacked, and adults encircle

Note the typical W-shape of the horns

vulnerable members. During an attack, herd members defend themselves by lowering and tossing their heads, while presenting their horns. They may mob-attack intruders.

REPRODUCTION
Breed all year, with a peak in the summer rainy season. A single calf, weighing 30–50 kg, is born after a gestation period of 11 months, with an average interval of 2 years between births. The calf joins the herd within hours of birth. It is suckled for 1 year, but stays with its mother for 2 years. Calves always stay in the centre of the herd.

Horns and bosses are heavier in bulls than in cows

DIET
Grazers, preferring long, coarse grasses, 5–80 cm long. The long prehensile tongue bundles the grass, which is then snapped off by the incisors. Eat up to 17 kg daily. Water dependent, drinking once or twice a day (early mornings and late afternoons).

HABITAT
Open woodland savanna with mosaics of dense cover (thickets, reeds or patches of forest), associated with rivers, lakes and swamps. Not found in regions with an annual rainfall of less than 250 mm. Found in all the habitats of the Kruger.

Eland

Taurotragus oryx

Ger: Elenantilope; **Fre, Afr:** Eland; **Fre:** Élan du Cap; **Nde, Xho, Zul, Swa:** impofu; **Nde:** ipofu; **Swa:** impophi, imphofu; **Set, Sot, Tsh:** phofu; **Sot, Set:** phohu; **Xit:** mhofu.

Status: not endangered	

Mass: ♂ 700–940 kg; ♀ 450–600 kg. **Shoulder height:** ♂ 1,4–1,8 m; ♀ 1,3–1,6 m. **Distinguishing features:** The largest of the antelopes. Both sexes have a dorsal crest and a tufted dewlap on the throat, the latter very prominent in bulls. Bulls also have a thick tuft of long hair on the forehead. When moving, adult bulls produce a distinctive clicking sound with their front hooves. **Life-span:** ± 15–20 yrs. **Predators:** Main predators include lion and spotted hyaena. Young also fall prey to leopard, cheetah and wild dog.

Front: 11 cm
Hind: 10 cm

DESCRIPTION

The coat is pale buff, fawn or tawny, with 10–16 transverse white stripes down the sides that may be very faint or absent in southern populations. In bulls, the hair on the neck and shoulders turns blue-grey with age. The back of the forelegs, above the knees, is covered with dark patches. The sides of the muzzle, the lips and lower legs have whitish patches. The tail tuft is black. Although the slowest of all the antelope (max. speed 40 km/h), eland can maintain a trotting speed of 20 km/h indefinitely. They are very good jumpers: adults clear heights of 2 m, the young clearing 3 m.
Scent glands: Hoof.
Senses: Very good sight, hearing and sense of smell.
Horns: Both sexes carry horns. They are smooth and straight with shallow spirals (1–2 twists). Bulls have a thicker and more pronounced spiral than cows. Length: ♂ 0,4–0,67 m; ♀ 0,5–0,7 m.

DISTRIBUTION

Found in ecozones B, L, M, N, O and P of the Kruger, occurring widely to the north of the Olifants River. Major concentrations are found in woodland savanna in the western parts of this range, in the eastern open plains north of the Shingwedzi River, and in the sandveld and floodplain areas between the Luvuvhu and Limpopo rivers. Very occasionally they are found in the Pretoriuskop area.

BEHAVIOUR

Diurnal and nocturnal. They tend to graze at night when the vegetation has a higher water content. The herd structure is open and fluid, with loosely associated same-sex and mixed herds occurring. Outside of the Kruger, herds usually consist of up to 60 individuals, but aggregations of as many as 2 000 or more have been recorded, particularly during the dry season. Herd sizes in the Kruger average 2–5, but a few herds of 20–50 individuals occur in the north-western sections of the Park, north of the Letaba River. Nursery herds consisting of young calves form the nucleus of large aggregations, with mothers and other herd members staying on the periphery. Young cows are more nomadic than bulls; the latter tending to be more static, occurring singly or in loosely associated bachelor or mixed herds. Home ranges of neighbouring herds overlap. The size of the home range is determined by habitat as well as the social structure of the herd, and can cover up to 1 400 km². Eland herds often associate with herds of other species, such as zebra and giraffe.
Calls: The alarm call is a loud bark.

Cow

Alarm signals: Alert posture, stamping. Freeze; or flee, often with high, leaping bounds. Calves lie flat and motionless, with ears pinned back.

Aggression: Horn threats, head tossing, head nodding (symbolic butting), vegetation horning, ground horning, mock and real charges, rushing, chasing and kicking. The herd may mob-attack intruders. Even solitary individuals fight lions.

REPRODUCTION

Breed all year with a peak in the summer rainy season. A single calf, weighing 25–35 kg, is born after a gestation period of 8,5–9 months, with an average interval of 1 year between births. The calf remains hidden for 2 weeks or joins a nursery crèche a few days after birth. It is weaned at 6–8 months.

DIET

Browse leaves, fruit, berries, seeds and herbs, and also dig for roots and bulbs. Graze short grasses, favouring new growth sprouting after fires. Grazing increases during the dry winter season. Water independent, obtaining enough moisture from food, but will drink when water is available.

Bull (left) – note the pronounced dewlap. Cow (right)

HABITAT

Found in a variety of habitats: open arid plains covered with scrub, grassland and woodland savanna, forest fringes and bush country. Avoid forest, desert, swamps and extensive open grassy plains. In the Kruger, found predominantly in the mopane shrubveld, tree mopane savanna, mopane/bushwillow woodland, alluvial plains and sandveld communities habitats; they very occasionally occur in sourveld habitat.

Nyala

Tragelaphus angasii

Ger: Tieflandnyala; **Ger, Fre, Set, Xit, Tsh:** Nyala; **Afr:** Njala; **Xit:** imbala-intendi; **Nde, Xho, Zul, Swa:** inyala; **Zul:** inxala; **Swa:** litagayezi.

Status: not endangered

Mass: ♂ 100–140 kg; ♀ 55–90 kg. **Shoulder height:** ♂ 1,0–1,2 m; ♀ 0,8–1,1 m. **Distinguishing features:** Bulls have a long, erect dorsal crest (grey-brown up to the shoulders, then white-tipped) extending from head to tail base. A fringe of long, grey-black hair extends from the throat to between the hindlegs. Ewes have a very short, brown-black dorsal crest, extending from head to tail base. **Life-span:** ± 15 yrs. **Predators:** Main predators include lion, leopard, wild dog and spotted hyaena.

Front: 6 cm
Hind: 5 cm

DESCRIPTION

Bulls have a long, shaggy coat, greyish-brown in colour with 8–14 transverse white stripes down the sides, which may be absent in some individuals. The dorsal crest is dark on the neck, white-tipped on the back. A fringe of dark hair extends from the belly. The lower legs are yellow-brown. There are white spots on the haunches.

Ewes have a short coat, yellow-brown to chestnut in colour, with up to 18 white stripes down the flanks. The lower legs are paler than the body, and the haunches may or may not have white spots. The dorsal crest is short and dark.

Both sexes have white facial markings on the upper lip and chin, a white spot below the eyes and white bars between the eyes that almost meet at the muzzle (the latter is much more pronounced in bulls). The dark, bushy tail is white underneath. Calves resemble cows.

Scent glands: Hoof.

Senses: Very good sight, hearing and sense of smell.

Horns: Only bulls carry horns. They are straight, smooth and white-tipped, with a shallow spiral (1–2 twists). Length: 0,6–0,8 m.

DISTRIBUTION

Found in suitable habitat in ecozones H, M, N and O of the Kruger, and marginally along waterways into ecozones I and L. Common along the Limpopo, Luvuvhu and Shingwedzi rivers, in mountainous terrain north of Punda Maria and in Nyandu sandveld south of Pafuri. Smaller population densities occur along the Sabie River and in the Tshokwane/Orpen Dam area.

BEHAVIOUR

Diurnal and nocturnal. Feed mainly at night, and are least active during the hotter hours of the day. Herds of 1–2 ewes and their lambs are common, although temporary nursery and mixed herds of up to 30–100 individuals may aggregate in grazing pastures, at waterholes or near fruiting trees. In the Kruger, solitary individuals, pairs or pairs with their young are common, although groups of 5–10 individuals have been recorded. Bulls join mixed herds or associate briefly (usually for less than 2 hours) in bachelor herds. At 6 years of age, bulls mature and tend to become solitary. Home ranges of same-sex and mixed herds cover 0,8–3,6 km², and may overlap those of neighbouring herds.

Calls: The alarm call is a bark; they bleat when distressed. Nyala also respond to the alarm calls of other species, such as baboon, impala and kudu.

Nyala have white spots on the haunches. Rams have distinct yellow-brown lower legs (ewe, above; bull, below)

Alarm signals: Alert posture, stamping. Freeze motionless to avoid detection. Flee. Lambs lie flat and motionless, with ears pinned back.

Aggression: Threat displays include horn threats, head tossing, head nodding (symbolic butting), vegetation horning, ground horning, ground pawing, mock and real charges, rushing and chasing. Displays of dominance and/or aggression among bulls are impressive: when they raise their fringe and their dorsal crest, their apparent body size is increased by 40 %.

REPRODUCTION

Breed all year, with a peak in the summer rainy season. A single lamb, weighing 4,5–5,5 kg, is born after a gestation period of 7–7,5 months. The lamb is born in thickets and remains hidden for up to 2–3 weeks. It is weaned at 6 months. Young bulls attain adult coloration by 1 year.

DIET

Browse leaves, twigs, flowers, fruit, and occasionally bark. Graze grasses and herbs. Water independent, obtaining enough moisture from food, but will drink when water is available.

HABITAT

Nyala are generally found in dry savanna woodland, dry forest and riverine woodland, usually within a few hundred metres of thickets and with access to grassland. In the Kruger Park, nyala are found mainly in the tree mopane savanna, the alluvial plains and riverine and sandveld communities habitats, and marginally in the mopane shrubveld and Lebombo Mountain bushveld habitats along waterways.

Greater Kudu

Tragelaphus strepsiceros

Ger: Kudu; **Fre:** Grand koudou; **Afr:** Koedoe; **Nde:** ibhalabhala; **Xho:** iqudu; **Zul:** umgankla, igogo, igoqo imbodwane; **Set, Sot:** thôlô; **Swa:** lishongololo; **Xit:** nhongo; **Tsh:** tholo, tholo-lurango.

Mass: ♂ 190–315 kg; ♀ 130–215 kg. **Shoulder height:** ♂ 1,3–1,5 m; ♀ 1,0–1,4 m. **Distinguishing features:** Sides marked with a distinctive series of 6–10 white vertical stripes. Tail bushy and black-tipped with white underside. Ears very large and rounded. Long, majestic spiral horns of mature bulls are unique. **Life-span:** ± 15 yrs. **Predators:** Main predators include lion, leopard, wild dog and spotted hyaena. Young also fall prey to cheetah, serval, caracal and large snakes.

Front: 10 cm
Hind: 9 cm

DESCRIPTION

The coat is reddish brown to dark bluish grey, with 6–10 white stripes down the sides of the body, and a whitish dorsal crest. Facial markings consist of a white bar between the eyes, extending across the muzzle and broken in the middle; white patches under the eyes; white lips and a white chin. The black-tipped tail is white underneath and the legs have a characteristic dark brown band above the hooves. Bulls have a dark beard, throat and belly fringe, and darken in colour with age. Kudu are very good jumpers, easily clearing heights of 2,5 m.
Scent glands: Hoof.
Senses: Very good sight, hearing and sense of smell.
Horns: Only bulls carry horns. They are long, smooth and distinctively spiralled, with two and one quarter turns to the horn spiral of a mature bull. Length: average 1,3 m, record 1,8 m.

DISTRIBUTION

Found in suitable habitat in all the ecozones of the Kruger, but only in small numbers in ecozone L.

BEHAVIOUR

Diurnal and nocturnal, but may become nocturnal in disturbed areas; least active during the hotter hours of the day. Nursery herds are comprised of 1–3 cows and their calves. Kruger herds generally consist of 3–5 individuals, but herds of 5–15 individuals also occur and temporary aggregations of up to 30 individuals may be seen when two herds merge. Home ranges within the Kruger are generally smaller than those outside of the Park, averaging 3,5–5,5 km², and up to 22 km² in the central parts.

Bulls are either solitary or form bachelor herds of 2–10 individuals when they reach the age of two. Their home range (10–50 km² in size) may overlap with those of several nursery herds, but do not overlap those of other bulls.
Calls: The alarm call is a loud bark; they bleat when distressed.
Alarm signals: Alert posture; stamping. Freeze motionless to avoid detection, skulking away if not detected. Flee in bounding flight, with the tail raised to expose the white underside. May stop after a while to check if they are still being pursued. Bulls flee with their heads held back and their horns resting on the shoulders to prevent them from becoming entangled in vegetation. Calves lie flat and motionless, with ears pinned back.

Bulls have long (around 1,3 m), distinctively spiralled horns

Aggression: Bristle the hair on the dorsal crest and tail. Other threat displays include horn threats, head tossing, head nodding (symbolic butting), vegetation horning, ground horning, mock and real charges, rushing and chasing.

REPRODUCTION

Breed in the summer rainy season. A single calf, weighing 15 kg, is born after a gestation period of 9 months. Cows leave the herd to give birth in dense cover, and the calf remains hidden for 2–4 weeks. It is weaned at 6 months, but remains with the mother for 2 years.

DIET

Browse leaves, shoots, succulents, vines, tubers, seedpods, flowers and fruit. Feed on 148 plant species in the Kruger, favouring *Acacia* and *Combretum* spp. Forbs are preferred over woody plants, and constitute up to 65 % of their diet in the Kruger. However, during the pre-rain period, when trees sprout new leaves, forbs constitute only 20 % of their food intake. Occasionally graze on green grasses and herbs. Water independent, obtaining enough moisture from food, but will drink when water is available.

Cow and calf

HABITAT

Lowlands, hills and mountains in savanna woodland; mixed scrub woodland and dense bush and thickets. During the dry season, found along waterways and at the bottom of hills where the vegetation is lush. Absent from desert, forest and open grassland. Found in all habitats of the Kruger, but only in small numbers in the mopane shrubveld.

Bushbuck   *Tragelaphus scriptus*

Ger: Schirrantilope, Buschbock; **Fre:** Antilope harnaché, Guib; **Afr:** Bosbok; **Nde, Xho, Zul, Swa:** imbabala; **Xho:** unkonka, ungece; **Zul:** unkonka omdaka; **Swa:** inkonka; **Set:** serôlôbotlhôkô, serolobotlhoko; **Sot:** pabala, tshoso; **Xit, Tsh:** mbavhala; **Xit:** xoxwe, hodzolume; **Tsh:** tshishosho, luvhengammbwa.

Status: not endangered   B

Mass: ♂ 40–80 kg; ♀ 25–60 kg. **Shoulder height:** ♂ 0,7–1 m; ♀ 0,65–0,95 m. **Distinguishing features:** Characteristic white patch on throat, a horizontal band at the base of the neck, white spots below the eyes and near the base of the ears, white lips and a white chin. **Life-span:** ± 12 yrs. **Predators:** Main predators are lion, leopard, hyaena, wild dog and crocodile. Young also fall prey to baboon, civet, caracal and pythons.

Front: 4 cm
Hind: 4 cm

DESCRIPTION

Colour varies according to distribution. In the east and south, bushbuck are yellowish brown to dark brown with a few whitish spots and stripes; in the north and west they are chestnut with numerous whitish spots and stripes. The lower limbs are paler than the upperparts, becoming whitish above the hooves. The inner parts of the upper forelegs are white, with a central, dark brown band. The throat, facial markings, and underside of the tail are white. Rams have a yellowish-white dorsal crest, and ewes tend to be paler than rams. Bushbuck are very good swimmers, easily covering distances of 3 km.

Scent glands: Inguinal.

Senses: Very good sight, hearing and sense of smell.

Horns: Only rams carry horns. They are smooth with a slight spiral (1 twist). Length: 0,3–0,5 m.

DISTRIBUTION

Patchily distributed over all the ecozones of the Kruger. Highest population densities are found in the riverine forests on the Sabie, Luvuvhu and Limpopo rivers, and in well-wooded areas near Punda Maria and Pretoriuskop.

BEHAVIOUR

Nocturnal, but can be diurnal in undisturbed areas. They are usually solitary, but sometimes form small nursery herds. In the Kruger they are generally solitary, but are also seen in pairs or pairs with their young. Home ranges vary between 0,05–0,6 km² in size, and may overlap with those of neighbours. Both sexes mark the home range by rubbing their head and neck against trees and bushes. Rams also mark vegetation with their horns.

Bushbuck often associate with baboons and monkeys, feeding on leaves and fruit dropped by the latter. They may remain under certain flowering trees for many hours.

Calls: The alarm call is a loud bark, similar to the sawing grunt of a leopard.

Alarm signals: Alert posture; stamping. Freeze motionless to avoid detection, skulking away if not detected. Readily take to water if threatened.

Aggression: Bristle the hair on the dorsal crest and tail. Other threat displays include horn threats, head tossing, head nodding (symbolic butting), vegetation horning, ground horning, mock and real charges, rushing and chasing.

Ewe (top). Bushbuck have a characteristic white band at the base of the neck

REPRODUCTION

Breed all year, with a peak in the summer rainy season in the southern parts of their range. A single lamb, weighing 3,5–4,5 kg, is born after a gestation period of 6 months. It remains hidden for up to 4 months, and is weaned at 6–8 months.

DIET

Bushbuck are selective browsers of leaves, buds, shoots, twigs, flowers and fruit. They are especially fond of *Acacia*, *Combretum*, *Kigela*, *Ximenia* and *Ziziphus* spp, also grazing on green grasses and herbs. Bushbuck are water dependent and drink water daily.

HABITAT

Bushbuck occur in a wide range of forest and bush habitats with dense underbrush and near water. They are found in all the habitats of the Kruger, but are restricted to the riparian vegetation along waterways and other dense vegetation.

Ram (juvenile)

Sable Antelope

Hippotragus niger

Ger: Rappenantilope; **Fre:** Hippotrague noir; **Afr:** Swartwitpens; **Nde:** umtjwayeli, ingwalathi, ngwaladi, umtshwayeli; **Xho:** iliza; **Zul:** impalampala; **Set:** kwalata, potokwane; **Sot:** phalafala, kgama; **Swa:** impapampala, imphalamphala; **Xit:** mhalamhala; **Tsh:** phalaphala, phalafhala.

Status: not endangered	

Mass: ♂ 200–270 kg; ♀ 190–230 kg. **Shoulder height:** ♂ 1,2–1,6 m; ♀ 1–1,4 m. **Distinguishing features:** Black and white facial mask, a dark brownish-black face, with a white patch over the muzzle, mouth, chin and lower jaw; and a white patch extending from the base of the horns through the eyes, down the cheeks and on to the mouth. Ears fringed with white. **Life-span:** ± 15 yrs. **Predators:** Adults have no major predators. Young fall prey to lion, leopard, wild dog, spotted hyaena and crocodile.

Front: 11 cm
Hind: 10 cm

DESCRIPTION

Bulls have a rich brownish-black coat, with white underparts and a white rump patch. Cows have a reddish-brown to dark brown coat that becomes black in southern populations. The underparts and rump patch are paler than the upperparts. The black and white facial mask is present in both sexes. An erect, black mane stretches from the top of the neck to just beyond the shoulders; the tail has a black tassel. Calves' coats are pale reddish brown. Sable can reach speeds of 57 km/h.

Scent glands: Preorbital and hoof.

Senses: Very good sight, hearing and sense of smell.

Horns: Both sexes carry horns, sweeping backwards with a pronounced curve. They are heavily ridged but smooth at the tips. Bulls' horns are more robust than those of cows. Length: ♂ 0,8–1,65 m; ♀ 0,6–1,0 m.

DISTRIBUTION

Found in suitable habitat in ecozones A, B, C, D, F, J, K, L, N, O and P of the Kruger. The highest population densities are found in the Pretoriuskop area, on Hlangelene Road near Manzimhlope (around 15 km southwest of Tshokwane), and near Phalaborwa Gate.

BEHAVIOUR

Diurnal and nocturnal, with activity peaks in the morning and afternoon. They form herds averaging 30–100 individuals, consisting of cows and calves grouped into clans of 15–25 members. Clans rarely associate with one another, but temporary aggregations of up to 200 individuals are sometimes encountered, particularly at the end of the dry season. In the Kruger, average group size is 2–4, but groups of up to 10 individuals are occasionally seen in the Pretoriuskop/Malelane area and northwest of Tshokwane. Clans share home ranges of 10–25 km², which may cross up to 5 dominant bull territories of 4–9 km². Territories are marked with ground pawing (depositing digital gland secretions), with vegetation horning, and with dung and urine.

A strict hierarchy is maintained within the herd: there is one dominant bull and one or more dominant cows; the rest of the herd is ranked according to age, with young bulls ranking after young cows. The dominant cow determines the herd movement, with the other dominant cows acting as sentinels on the periphery of the herd. The dominant bull follows at the rear of the herd. Young bulls join bache-

The white patch over the eyes extends to the mouth

lor herds of about 10 individuals at 3–4 years of age, or may remain solitary. Older bulls may be solitary, regardless of whether they have territories or not.

Calls: The alarm call is a loud snort.

Alarm signals: Alert posture, stamping, style trotting, and flight with herd members scattering in all directions. Calves lie flat and motionless, with ears pinned back.

Aggression: Threat displays include horn threats, head tossing, head nodding (symbolic butting), horn clashing (often from a kneeling position), vegetation horning, ground horning, ground pawing, rushing, chasing, mock and real charges, and slashing out sideways or stabbing with the horns.

REPRODUCTION

Breed in the summer rainy season. A single calf, weighing 13–18 kg, is born after a gestation period of 8–9 months. Cows leave the herd and give birth in isolation. The calf is born in dense cover and remains hidden for 2–3 weeks before joining a nursery crèche. It is weaned at 6–8 months.

DIET

Graze medium-tall grasses. Browse sparingly in the dry season, losing condition as grasses become scarce. Visit salt licks, and chew bones and soil to obtain minerals. Water dependent, drinking daily.

HABITAT

Occur in open savanna woodland near medium-high grassland, with water, favouring areas with well-drained, sandy soils. Seldom more than 2–4 km from water. In the Kruger, found in the mixed bush-willow woodland, mopane/bushwillow woodland, Malelane Mountain bushveld, Lebombo Mountain bushveld, tree mopane savanna, mopane shrub-veld, knobthorn/marula savanna, stunted knobthorn savanna, thorn thickets, delagoa thorn thickets, rugged veld and sourveld habitats.

Roan Antelope

Hippotragus equinus

Ger: Pferdeantilope, Roan; **Fre:** Antilope cheval, Hippotrague rouanne; **Afr:** Bastergemsbok; **Nde, Zul:** inoni; **Nde:** ithaka; **Xho:** iliza; **Set:** kunkuri, kwalata e tshehla; **Sot:** hlaba-ka-lele, kgama; **Swa:** litagayezi, inyamatane, linoni; **Xit:** ndakadzi, xidya-na-mani; **Tsh:** thavha-nda-lila, thavhandalila, ndi-la-na-nnyi.

Status: CITES: App. II   ☼ ☽

Mass: ♂ 260–300 kg; ♀ 220–280 kg. **Shoulder height:** ♂ 1,4–1,5 m; ♀ 1,3–1,4 m. **Distinguishing features:** Distinctive black and white facial mask: brown-black face, with a white patch over the muzzle, mouth and chin, and a white patch extending from the base of the horns through the eyes onto the cheeks. The ears are long and narrow (measuring 30 cm) with dark brown tassels at the tips. **Life-span:** ± 15 yrs. **Predators:** Main predator is lion. Other predators include leopard, wild dog, spotted hyaena and crocodile. Roan are extremely susceptible to anthrax.

Front: 11 cm
Hind: 10 cm

DESCRIPTION

Coat is greyish brown, often with a strawberry tinge, particularly in northern and West African populations; underparts are paler. The legs are darker than the upperparts. Distinct black and white facial mask. Black erectile mane extending from the top of the neck to just beyond the shoulders. Tail has a black tassel. Calves are light to dark reddish brown.

Scent glands: Preorbital and hoof.

Senses: Very good sight, hearing and sense of smell.

Horns: Both sexes carry horns, sweeping backwards with a pronounced curve. They are heavily ridged, with smooth tips. Bulls' horns are more robust than those of cows. Length: ♂ 0,7–1,0 m; ♀ 0,6–0,8 m.

DISTRIBUTION

Found in ecozones L and P of the Kruger, with the major concentration occurring in the basalt plains adjoining the Lebombo Mountains in the eastern parts of the Park.

BEHAVIOUR

Diurnal and nocturnal, with activity peaks in the afternoon. They form herds of 5–20 individuals, comprising a dominant bull, cows and calves; temporary aggregations of up to 80 individuals may be seen outside of the Kruger. In the Kruger, average group size is 2–5, but groups of over 10 individuals are occasionally seen in the northern districts. The core home range is as small as a few square kilometres, with overall ranges reaching up to 60–100 km² in poorer habitat conditions. Although home ranges of neighbouring herds overlap outside of the Kruger, there is little overlap within the Park. Herds remain faithful to their range. Home ranges are marked with ground pawing (depositing digital gland secretions), with vegetation horning, and with dung and urine. The dominant bull does not defend the whole home range, but rather a 300–500 m area around the cows.

A strict hierarchy is maintained within the herd: there is one dominant bull and one or more dominant cows; the rest of the herd is ranked according to age, with young bulls ranking after young cows. The dominant cow determines herd movement, with the other dominant cows acting as sentinels on the periphery of the herd. The dominant bull follows at the rear of the herd. Young bulls join bachelor herds of about 8 individuals at 2 years of age. Older bulls that do not hold territories remain solitary.

Calls: The alarm call is a loud snort.

Alarm signals: Alert posture, stamping, style trotting, flight with herd members scattering in all directions. Calves lie flat and motionless, with ears pinned back.

Aggression: Horn threats, head tossing, head nodding (symbolic butting), horn clashing (often from a kneeling position), vegetation horning, ground horning, ground pawing, rushing, chasing, mock and real charges, lashing out sideways and stabbing with the horns.

REPRODUCTION

Breed all year with a peak in spring. A single calf, weighing 16–18 kg, is born after a gestation period of 9 months, with an average interval of 1 year between births. Cows withdraw from the herd to give birth in isolation. The calf is born in dense cover and remains hidden for 4–6 weeks. It attains adult coloration at 4 months, and is weaned at 6 months.

DIET

Graze medium to high grasses, usually selecting the top parts (80 mm and more from the ground). In the Kruger, show a strong preference for *Heteropogon contortus* and *Themeda triandra*, with these two species constituting more than 70 % of the diet. Will browse if the grass is poor, preferring leaf to stem. Visit salt licks and chew bones and soil to obtain minerals. Water dependent, drinking at least every second day, often 1–3 times a day.

HABITAT

Lightly wooded or open woodland savanna with vast areas of medium-tall grasses, near water. They are seldom more than 2–4 km from water. In the Kruger, found predominantly in the mopane shrubveld and mopane/bushwillow woodland habitats.

The white patch over the eyes does not extend over the cheeks

Blue Wildebeest/Brindled Gnu   *Connochaetes taurinus*

Ger: Streifengnu, Blaues Gnu; **Fre:** Gnou bleu; **Afr:** Blouwildebees; **Nde, Xho, Zul:** inkonkoni; **Nde:** imbudumo, imbuduma ehlaza; **Zul:** inkonkoni enombala oluhlaza; **Set, Sot:** kgokong; **Sot:** kgaranyane; **Swa:** ingongoni, ngongoni; **Xit:** hongonyi; **Tsh:** khongoni, khongoini.

Status: not endangered	

Mass: ♂ 170–290 kg; ♀ 140–260 kg. **Shoulder height:** ♂ 1,3–1,5 m; ♀ 1,2–1,4 m. **Distinguishing features:** Head long and broad with a blunt muzzle and a black beard. Shoulders higher than the hindquarters. Neck arched with an erect, black bristling mane running down the back of the neck, and black hair extending along the throat. Head bowed while moving about. **Life-span:** ± 15 yrs. **Predators:** Main predators include lion, spotted hyaena and crocodile. Young also fall prey to leopard, cheetah and wild dog.

Front: 10 cm
Hind: 9 cm

DESCRIPTION
Coat is dark grey to brownish with a silver-bluish tinge. Vertical, dark stripes (brindling) run down the sides of the body, from the neck to just before the hindquarters. The mane, beard, muzzle, throat fringe and horse-like tail are black. Cows tend to be browner than bulls, and calves are fawn-brown with dark faces. Wildebeest can maintain high speeds over long distances.
Scent glands: Preorbital and hoof.
Senses: Very good sight, hearing and sense of smell.
Horns: Both sexes carry robust horns that grow from bosses on the forehead. They are smooth and curve downward, outward and then upward. When viewed together from end-to-end, they form a shallow 'W'. Bulls' horns are more robust than those of cows, growing from heavier bosses and usually extending past the ears. In old adults, the horns cover and protect the head. Length: ♂ 55–80 cm; ♀ 45–65 cm.

DISTRIBUTION
Found in suitable habitat in ecozones A, B, D, E, F, G, I, J, K, L, N, O and P of the Kruger. Scattered herds are found north of the Olifants River. South of the river, three major areas of concentration are found: in the Mavumbye/Gudzani/Bangu region northeast of Satara; between the Sweni River and Mlondozi Dam (about 10 km north of Lower Sabie), and on the open plains between Lower Sabie and Crocodile Bridge. Smaller populations occur at Orpen Gate and in the Pretoriuskop area.

BEHAVIOUR
Diurnal and nocturnal. In non-migratory populations (which constitute the majority of populations found in the Kruger), cows and calves form nursery herds of 2–30 individuals. Average group size in the Kruger is 3–6, but groups of over 20 individuals can be encountered in the northern parts of the Park. Herd structure is open and fluid. Cow home ranges overlap with the territories of several bulls. Bulls mark their territories with preorbital gland secretions (that smell like tar), with ground pawing (depositing digital gland secretions), and with dung and urine middens. Cows sometimes mate with more than one bull. At the age of one, young bulls join bachelor groups, remaining on the periphery of the herd.
In migratory populations, herds come together to form one unit, losing their separate identities. Territorial bulls join bachelor herds, which mix with nursery

Both sexes carry horns

herds. Some bulls remain territorial but because of the high population density, the size of their territory may be as small as 15 m. Wildebeest herds are often seen in association with giraffe, zebra and impala.

Calls: Contact calls include deep grunts and a high-pitched 'ge-nu' snort, from which the common name is derived. The alarm call is a snort.

Alarm signals: Alert posture, stamping, and style trotting. May flee in leaping bounds.

Aggression: Horn threats, horn clashing (often from a kneeling position), head tossing, ground horning, rubbing preorbital gland secretions into the ground, frantic leaping, cavorting, mock or real charges.

REPRODUCTION

Breed in the summer rainy season, with 90 % of the calves born during a 3-week calving peak. Cows do not leave the herd to give birth. A single calf, weighing 15–20 kg, is born after a gestation period of 8–8,5 months. It is born early in the morning, and is able to stand within minutes of birth. It takes solid

food at 2 weeks, and is weaned by 8 months. The calf joins a nursery crèche at 2–3 months, and attains adult coloration after 2–4 months. Horns grow straight up until 8 months, and then start growing sideways.

DIET

Non-selective grazers of short green grasses. Drink daily when water is available, usually in the afternoons, but can go without water for a few days.

HABITAT

Prefer short open grassland, scrub and woodland savanna, but can be found in dense bush with short grasses. Usually occur within 20 km of water. In the Kruger, found in the mixed bushwillow woodland, rugged veld, mopane/bushwillow woodland, mopane shrubveld, thorn veld, Lebombo Mountain bushveld, knobthorn/marula savanna, tree mopane savanna, stunted knobthorn savanna, thorn thickets, delagoa thorn thickets, sandveld communities, and sourveld habitats.

Lichtenstein's Hartebeest

Sigmoceros lichtensteinii

Ger: Lichtensteins Kuhantilope, Lichtensteins Hartebeest; **Fre:** Bubale de Lichtenstein; **Afr:** Lichtensteinse hartebees.

Status: not endangered

Mass: ♂ 135–200 kg; ♀ 100–185 kg. **Shoulder height:** ♂ 1,2–1,4 m; ♀ 1,2–1,3 m. **Distinguishing features:** Head long and narrow, shoulders higher than hindquarters. Have distinct habit of rubbing their flanks with their face, particularly after ground horning. This leaves streaks of black preorbital gland secretion mixed with soil and dust on the flanks. **Life-span:** ± 12-15 yrs. **Predators:** Main predators include lion, leopard, spotted hyaena and wild dog. Young also fall prey to cheetah, serval, caracal, jackals and pythons.

Front: 8 cm
Hind: 8 cm

DESCRIPTION

The coat is tawny yellow, with a darker saddle extending from the shoulders over the rump, and ending at the base of the tail. The underparts are paler than the upperparts. The rump, upper hindlegs, front of the lower legs, tail base, tail tuft, and chin are whitish. They are capable of reaching 60–70 km/h at top speed.

Scent glands: Preorbital and hoof.

Senses: Very good sight, hearing, and sense of smell.

Horns: Both sexes carry horns. They are 60 cm long, are strongly ringed, and have a 'Z'-shaped curvature. They are located in the centre of the head, and are flattened at the partially ridged base.

DISTRIBUTION

Although once widely distributed in Africa, Lichtenstein's hartebeest is now very rare in southern Africa. In 1985, populations were translocated from Malawi and were reintroduced into the Kruger. They have bred successfully ever since their reintroduction. These antelope are found in ecozone B, in the grasslands adjoining savanna woodland in the Pretoriuskop area, and in ecozone L, 25 km south of Punda Maria .

BEHAVIOUR

Predominantly diurnal. They form herds of 10–20 individuals, comprising a territorial bull, cows and calves. Both sexes defend the territory, ranging in size from 0,3–3 km². Territories include elevated areas, such as termite mounds, which are used as lookout points. These vantage points are also used by bulls as territorial markers. Territories are marked with preorbital gland secretions, ground pawing (depositing digital gland secretions), vegetation horning, ground horning, and with dung heaps. At 10–12 months of age, young bulls either remain solitary or join bachelor herds of 2–4 individuals that remain on the fringes of the bull territories.

Calls: The alarm call is a sneeze-snort. Bulls often bellow loudly during territorial disputes.

Alarm signals: Alert posture, foot stamping, style trotting, and stotting. Flee in zigzags with stiff-legged gait, with females taking the lead. Calves that cannot keep up with the herd lie flat and motionless, with ears pinned back.

Aggression: Horn threats, horn clashing (often from a kneeling position), head tossing, ground horning, mock or real charges.

A dark saddle extends from the shoulders to the base of the tail

REPRODUCTION

Breed annually, peaking in September-October. A single calf, weighing 13–15 kg, is born after a gestation period of 8 months. It is born in thick cover, and remains hidden for 2 weeks. The calf is weaned at 4 months.

DIET

Graze on medium to tall grasses, favouring perennial grasses. Also fond of new sprouting grasses after fires. Tend to graze during the cooler hours of the day (early morning and late afternoon), when the moisture content of the grass is higher. Water dependent, drinking regularly when water is available, but can go without water for several weeks.

HABITAT

Grassland floodplains and open savanna grassland adjacent to open savanna woodland and bushland. In the Kruger, found in the mopane shrubveld habitats, and in the sourveld bordering mixed bushwillow woodland.

Tsessebe
Damaliscus lunatus

Ger: Leierantilope, Halbmondantilope; **Fre:** Sassaby; **Afr:** Tsessebe; **Nde:** inkolome, inkomozane; **Set:** tshêbêbe; **Sot:** tshentshebe, kgama ya lebasetere; **Swa:** mzanxi, inyamatane; **Xit:** ndzandzi, nondo.

Mass: ♂ 130–160 kg; ♀ 100–130 kg. **Shoulder height:** ♂ 1,0–1,3 m; ♀ 1,0–1,2 m. **Distinguishing features:** Head long and narrow; shoulders higher than hindquarters. **Life-span:** ± 12–15 yrs. **Predators:** Main predators include lion, leopard, spotted hyaena and wild dog. Young also fall prey to cheetah, serval, caracal, jackals and pythons.

Front: 9 cm
Hind: 8 cm

DESCRIPTION
The coat is glossy, reddish brown with a purplish tinge; the underparts are paler. A blackish blaze marks the upper legs, shoulders and head. The lower legs are fawn coloured, with a dark brown stripe down the front of the forelegs. There is a black tassel on the tail. Calves are tawny coloured.

Scent glands: Preorbital and hoof.

Senses: Very good sight, hearing, and sense of smell.

Horns: Both sexes carry horns. They initially curve backwards, and then forwards and upwards. They are heavily ridged, with smooth tips. Length: ♂ 30–60 cm; ♀ 30–50 cm.

DISTRIBUTION
Found in ecozones L, N, O and P of the Kruger, north of the Letaba River. The highest concentration is found in the eastern parts of this range. South of the Letaba River, they are found in small, scattered herds in ecozones A and E, and in ecozones F and I in the Mlondozi Dam area, situated around 10 km north of Lower Sabie. They are also found in ecozone B, where they have been reintroduced into the Pretoriuskop area.

BEHAVIOUR
Diurnal and nocturnal. They form herds comprising a dominant bull and 2–10 cows and their calves. In the Kruger, average group size is 2–4 individuals (sometimes up to 10), but herds of hundreds are also found. A dominance hierarchy is maintained among cows, with the alpha female leading the herd. Both sexes defend the territory, ranging in size from 0,7–4 km². Territories include elevated areas, for example termite mounds, which are used as lookout points. These vantage points are also used by bulls as territorial markers. Territories are marked with preorbital gland secretions, ground pawing (depositing digital gland secretions), vegetation horning, ground horning, and with dung heaps. At 1 year of age, young bulls join bachelor herds of up to 30 individuals (average 10), which remain on the fringes of bull territories. Tsessebe are the fastest of all the antelopes.

Calls: The alarm call is a snort.

Alarm signals: Alert posture, foot stamping, style trotting, and stotting. Freeze when predators approach, then dart away or remain frozen, often becoming victims of hunters.

Aggression: Horn threats, head tossing and pronounced head nodding, horn clashing (often from a kneeling position), pushing, chasing, cavorting, ground horning, ground pawing, and mock or real charges.

A blackish blaze extends over the legs, shoulders and head

REPRODUCTION

Breed in the summer rainy season. A single calf, weighing 10–12 kg, is born after a gestation period of 8 months. Calves are either 'followers' (keeping up with the herd) or 'hiders' (remaining hidden for a few months after birth). Calves are weaned at 6 months but remain with the mother for about a year. Calves often gather in nursery crèches, which may be surrounded by protective mothers.

DIET

Graze on medium-high grasses and herbs; and fond of new sprouting grasses after fires. Obtain enough moisture from their food when the grass is saturated with moisture, otherwise will drink every 1–2 days.

HABITAT

Restricted to open savanna woodland with medium-high grasses, grassland and floodplains. Avoid heavily utilized areas or areas with dense trees and shrubs. In the Kruger, found in the sourveld, mopane shrubveld, mopane/bushwillow woodlands, tree mopane savanna and sandveld communities habitats, and occur marginally in the mixed bushwillow woodlands, thornveld, knobthorn/marula savanna and Lebombo Mountain bushveld habitats. Optimum habitat is best represented by the mopane shrubveld of the northeastern Lebombo flats north of the Letaba River. Here *Colophospermum mopane* is the dominant shrub species, and *Panicum coloratum*, *Themeda triandra* and *Cenchrus ciliaris* the dominant grass species.

Common Waterbuck

Kobus ellipsiprymnus

Ger: Wasserbock; **Fre:** Cobe à croissant; **Afr:** Waterbok; **Nde:** isidumuka; **Zul, Swa:** isiphiva; **Zul:** iphiva; **Swa:** liphiva; **Swa, Xit:** phiva; **Xit:** mhitlwa; **Sot:** pitlhwa; **Sot, Set:** lepitlhwa; **Tsh:** phidwa, ngwele-ngwele.

Status: not endangered

Mass: ♂ 160–260 kg; ♀ 150–200 kg. **Shoulder height:** ♂ 1,1–1,3 m; ♀ 1,0–1,25 m. **Distinguishing features:** Very distinctive white ring encircles the rump. Bulls have a characteristic, pungent musty odour, which is secreted by the sebaceous glands. **Life-span:** ± 12-15 yrs. **Predators:** Main predators include lion, spotted hyaena and crocodile. Young also fall prey to leopard and wild dog.

Front: 8 cm
Hind: 8 cm

DESCRIPTION

The coat is coarse and shaggy; grey to reddish brown in colour. The lower legs are brown-black with white bands above the hooves. The underside and the ring encircling the rump are white. Waterbuck have distinctive facial markings: white eye patches, white around the muzzle, white lips and chin, and a white band running from the base of each ear to the throat. Ears are rimmed black with black tips. The overall body colour of bulls darkens with age. Calves resemble cows, but overall body colour is lighter.

Scent glands: None present.

Senses: Very good sight, hearing and sense of smell.

Horns: Only bulls carry horns. They are heavily ridged with smooth tips, sweeping backwards and curving forwards at the tips. Length: 70–99 cm.

DISTRIBUTION

Although their distribution is patchy, waterbuck occur in suitable habitat in all the ecozones of the Kruger near permanent water. During the dry winter season, they are very common along the banks of the Letaba and Olifants rivers.

BEHAVIOUR

Diurnal and nocturnal, becoming more nocturnal in disturbed areas. Various social structures are found among waterbuck. Cows and calves form loosely associated herds of about 5–10 individuals, but larger aggregations of up to 30 individuals may be seen, particularly in summer. Their home ranges vary between 0,6–2 km², and overlap with those of neighbouring herds. The territories may cross several bull territories. Average group size in the Kruger is 2–6, but groups of 10–20 or even larger groups of 30 are also occasionally seen north of the Letaba River.

Bulls remain faithful to their territories, which range in size from 0,6–2,8 km². At 8–12 months of age, young bulls join bachelor herds of 5–10 individuals, remaining on the fringes of dominant bulls' territories.

Calls: The alarm call is a snort.

Alarm signals: Alert posture, stamping. They freeze motionless to avoid detection, skulking away if not detected. Style trotting and stotting. Waterbuck readily take refuge in water.

Aggression: Threat displays include horn threats, head tossing, head nodding (symbolic butting), ground horning, mock and real charges, rushing, butting and chasing.

Bull

REPRODUCTION

Waterbuck breed all year, with a peak in the summer rainy season. A single calf, weighing 13 kg, is born after a gestation period of 8–8,5 months. It is born in a thicket, and remains hidden for 2–4 weeks. It is able to walk within 30 minutes of birth, and is weaned at 6–8 months. At 8–9 months, horns begin to develop in males.

DIET

Mainly grazers, feeding on a variety of short and medium grasses, including reeds and rushes. Show a strong preference for *Cynodon dactylon* in the Kruger, as well as in other areas. When the quality of the grass is poor, they browse leaves, herbs and fruit. Require water daily.

HABITAT

Open grassland and woodland savanna, forest mosaics, reed beds and thickets, close to cover and

Ewes

near permanent water. Found in all the habitats of the Kruger, but restricted to areas near permanent water, occurring particularly in rocky areas along streams and rivers.

Southern Reedbuck

Redunca arundinum

Ger: Großer Riedbock; **Fre:** Redunca grande; **Afr:** Rietbok; **Nde, Zul:** umziki; **Nde:** umzigi; **Zul:** inxala, inhlangu, umsagogo, isagogo; **Xho:** intlangu; **Set:** sebugatla, motsosa, motlobo; **Sot:** lekwena, motlapasi; **Swa:** inhlangu; **Xit:** nhlangu; **Tsh:** davhu.

Status: not endangered

Mass: ♂ 60–95 kg; ♀ 50–85 kg. **Shoulder height:** ♂ 0,80–1,05 m; ♀ 0,65–0,95 m. **Distinguishing features:** Distinctive dark line runs down front of forelegs; a less prominent one runs down the lower hindlegs. A dark, glandular patch is present under the ears. Underside of the short, bushy tail is white. When stotting, inguinal glands open with a distinctive popping sound. **Life-span:** ± 10 yrs. **Predators:** Main predators include lion, leopard, wild dog, spotted hyaena and cheetah. Other predators include crocodile and large snakes. Young also fall prey to serval, jackals and eagles.

Front: 6 cm
Hind: 6 cm

DESCRIPTION

Colour of coat is variable: from buff, buffy grey, grey to greyish brown. Neck and chest are paler, often tinged grey. Underparts, lips and chin are white. A dark band runs down the front of the forelegs and down the lower hindlegs.
Scent glands: Beneath the ears and inguinal.
Senses: Very good sight, hearing and sense of smell.
Horns: Only rams carry horns. They curve forward, are partly ridged for two thirds of their length, and have smooth tips. At the base of the horns there is a distinct band of pale, rubbery tissue. Length: 30–45 cm.

DISTRIBUTION

Found in suitable habitat in ecozones B and C of the Kruger, and marginally into ecozone L. Common in the tall grassed areas between the Pretoriuskop and Malelane areas, and in the Nxawu Valley north of Letaba, and also in the vlei areas on the northern plains.

BEHAVIOUR

Diurnal and nocturnal. Move independently, but monogamous pairs share a territory (ranging in size from 0,3–0,6 km²) that is defended by the territorial ram. Regularly used paths are followed within the territory. Larger groups usually consist of a pair with their young, and in the Kruger small nursery herds are also encountered. Although the ram is dominant, the ewe initiates the movements of the family party.
Calls: Alarm calls are loud, shrill nasal whistles and snorts.
Alarm signals: Alert posture, stamping. Freeze motionless to avoid detection, skulking away if not detected. Style trotting and stotting, causing the inguinal glands to open with a popping sound. Flee with 'rocking-horse' canter and a series of leaps, with the bushy tail raised, exposing the white underside.
Aggression: Threat displays include horn threats, head tossing, head nodding (symbolic butting), ground horning, mock and real charges, rushing, butting, and chasing.

REPRODUCTION

Breed all year with a peak in the summer rainy season. A single lamb, weighing 5 kg, is born after a gestation period of 7,5–8 months. It is born in dense cover, and remains hidden for 2 months.

Ewe

DIET

Mainly grazers, feeding on grasses and herbs, and showing a preference for green grasses and newly sprouted grasses after fires. The main components of the diet are 'unpalatable' grasses, which are avoided by other antelope. In the Kruger, the most important grass species are *Hyparrhenia dissolute, Heteropogon contortus, Trachypogon spicatus,* and *Panicum maximum.* During the dry winter season, the latter two species become the staple diet, and grassy plants and herbaceous vegetation, which are largely ignored by other species, supplement the diet.

Southern reedbuck are water dependent, requiring water every few days during the rainy season, and daily or several times a day during the latter part of the dry season.

HABITAT

Areas with tall grass cover near water, preferably with some scrub or reed beds. Occur in the sourveld and Malelane Mountain bushveld habitats of the Kruger, and marginally in vlei areas in the mopane shrubveld.

Ram

Mountain Reedbuck

Redunca fulvorufula

Ger: Bergriedbock; **Fre:** Redunca de montagne; **Afr:** Rooirietbok; **Xho, Zul:** inxala; **Zul:** ingxala, inhlangu; **Set:** lehele, mohele, lefala; **Sot:** letlabo, lebele; **Swa:** lincala; **Xit:** nhlangu, nhlangu ya ntshava; **Tsh:** davhu.

Mass: ♂ 25–38 kg; ♀ 19–35 kg. **Shoulder height:** ♂ 0,6–0,8 m; ♀ 0,6–0,75 m. **Distinguishing features:** Dark, glandular patch under ears. Underside of short, bushy tail is white. When stotting, the inguinal glands open with a distinctive popping sound. **Life-span:** ± 10 yrs **Predators:** Main predators include lion, leopard, caracal, wild dog, spotted hyaena and cheetah. Other predators include crocodile and large snakes. Young also fall prey to serval, jackals and eagles.

Front: 5 cm
Hind: 5 cm

DESCRIPTION

The coat is soft and woolly. The upperparts are grey-fawn and the underparts whitish. The head and neck usually have a reddish, yellowish tinge. The tail is bushy and white underneath.

Scent glands: Beneath the ears, and inguinal.

Senses: Very good sight, hearing and sense of smell.

Horns: Only rams carry horns. They are straight but curve forward at the tips, and are heavily ridged with smooth tips. Length: 15–38 cm.

DISTRIBUTION

Found in suitable habitat in ecozone C of the Kruger. The main population occurs in suitable habitat in the Berg-en-dal and Stolsnek areas.

BEHAVIOUR

Diurnal and nocturnal, but least active during the daylight hours. Cows and calves form nursery herds of 2–6 individuals, but larger aggregations of 15 or more may be seen, particularly in summer. Average group size in the Kruger is 2–3, but solitary individuals are also common. Average home range is 0,3–0,75 km², and overlaps with the territories of several rams. Ram territories are 0,3 km² in size. At 9–12 months of age, young rams join bachelor herds, remaining on the fringes of dominant rams' territories.

Calls: The alarm call is a loud, shrill nasal whistle.

Alarm signals: Alert posture and stamping. They freeze to avoid detection, skulking away if not detected. Style trotting and stotting, causing the inguinal glands to open with a popping sound. Flee to higher ground with a 'rocking-horse' canter and intermittent leaps, raising the bushy tail to expose the white underside. May stop after 300–400 m to check if they are still being pursued.

Aggression: Threat displays include horn threats and head tossing, as well as head nodding (symbolic butting), ground horning, mock and real charges, butting and chasing.

REPRODUCTION

Breed in the summer rainy season. A single lamb, weighing 3 kg, is born after a gestation period of 7,5–8 months. It is born in dense cover, and remains hidden for 2–3 months.

Ram

DIET
Graze on grasses and herbs, favouring short green grasses and newly sprouted grasses after fires. Very occasionally browse on leaves. Water dependent. They can go without water for a few days when the grass contains sufficient moisture, but require water regularly in the dry season.

HABITAT
Mountain reedbuck are found on the dry, grass-covered, stony slopes of mountains and hills, where there is sufficient cover available in the form of bushes and trees, and within the proximity of water. Found in the Malelane Mountain bushveld habitat of the Kruger.

Grey Rhebok

Pelea capreolus

Ger: Rehantilope, Rehböckchen; **Fre:** Rhebok gris, Pelea; **Afr:** Vaalribbok; **Xho, Zul:** iza, iliza; **Set:** pelea, lehele; **Sot:** letsa; **Swa:** liza.

Mass: ♂ 18–30 kg; ♀ 16–27 kg. **Shoulder height:** ♂ 0,7–0,8 m; ♀ 0,6–0,72 m. **Distinguishing features:** Very long, narrow ears; swollen nose. Distinctive white ring around eyes. **Life-span:** ± 10 yrs. **Predators:** Main predators include caracal, wild dog and large snakes. Other predators include leopard. Young also fall prey to serval, jackals, eagles and baboons.

Front: 5 cm
Hind: 4 cm

DESCRIPTION

The thick coat is soft and woolly. The upperparts are greyish brown. The underparts, ring around the eyes and patches on the muzzle and chin are white. A dark, narrow stripe runs down the front of the legs. The tail has a white tip and underside. The ears are long and narrow. Grey rhebok are swift runners, reaching speeds of up to 60 km/h.

Scent glands: Hoof. Rams also have preputial glands.

Senses: Very good sight, hearing and sense of smell.

Horns: Only rams carry horns. They are straight, long, thin and pointed. The horns are partially ridged at the base, with smooth tips. Length: 15–29 cm.

DISTRIBUTION

In the Kruger, found in suitable habitat in ecozone C, on the high mountain plateaus in the Malelane area.

BEHAVIOUR

Predominantly diurnal, with activity peaks in the afternoon; least active during the hotter hours of the day. They form herds of up to 12 individuals, comprising a dominant ram, and several ewes and their lambs. Temporary aggregations of up to 30 individuals are also encountered. The average size of a territory is 0,3 km² in summer, and up to 0,75 km² in winter. The territories are marked with dung and urine. Rams mix their urine with strong-smelling, black preputial gland secretions, and may spend up to several hours daily marking their territory boundaries.

Young rams without territories remain on the periphery of the dominant ram's territory. At 1,5–2 years of age, these young rams leave in order to claim their own territories, but they have to wait patiently for females to immigrate into their area, as abductions from another ram's territory are rarely successful. Females tend to move between territories during the winter months when rams are less territorial.

Calls: The alarm call is a snort.

Alarm signals: Close bunching of herd members; stotting and fleeing with 'rocking horse' canter, displaying the white underside of the tail; fleeing to hilly terrain with straight and/or swerving flight. Lambs run to their mothers, and follow them very closely.

Aggression: Threat displays include horn threats, stabbing with the horns, stamping, and chasing.

Rams carry straight, thin and pointed horns

REPRODUCTION

Breed in the summer rainy season. A single lamb (rarely two), weighing 3 kg, is born after a gestation period of 8,5 months. Ewes give birth in isolation, rejoining the herd after 1–2 weeks. The lamb is born in dense cover, and remains hidden for 6 weeks. It is weaned at 6–8 months.

DIET

Browse broad-leaved plants, forbs, roots, seeds and flowers, and graze sourveld grasses. The level of browsing increases during the dry season, whereas grazing increases in the wet season. Grey rhebok are water independent, obtaining enough moisture from their food. They will, however, drink when water is available.

HABITAT

Rocky hills, hill plateaus, rocky mountain slopes, as well as valleys and scrub savanna, all with good sourveld grass cover. Avoid tall grasslands. In the Kruger, found in the Malelane Mountain bushveld habitat.

Impala

Aepyceros melampus

Ger: Schwarzfersenantilope; **Ger, Fre, Nde, Xho, Zul, Swa:** Impala; **Fre:** Phallah; **Afr:** Rooibok; **Nde, Xho, Zul, Swa:** impala; **Nde:** ipala; **Set, Sot, Tsh:** phala; **Swa:** mpala, imphala; **Xit:** mhala.

Status: not endangered	

Mass: ♂ 45–80 kg; ♀ 40–60 kg. **Shoulder height:** ♂ 0,80–0,95 m; ♀ 0,75–0,90 m. **Distinguishing features:** Distinctive tufts of black hair on the lower hindlegs cover the glands situated above the hooves. Vertical black stripe down each buttock and down the center of the tail. **Life-span:** ± 12–15 yrs. **Predators:** Main predators include lion, leopard, cheetah, wild dog, spotted hyaena and crocodile. Other predators include python. Young also fall prey to jackals and eagles.

Front: 6 cm
Hind: 5 cm

DESCRIPTION

One of Africa's most graceful antelopes. Rich and glossy coat; tan torso with reddish-brown saddle. Underparts, throat, lips, chin, and patches around the eyes are white. Black-tipped ears. Very good jumpers, easily leaping 3 m high, covering 9 m. Reach speeds of up to 80 km/h.

Scent glands: Above the hooves on the hindlegs. Rams also have forehead glands.
Senses: Very good sight, hearing, and sense of smell.
Horns: Only rams carry horns. The horns are heavily ridged with smooth tips. Length: 50–90 cm.

DISTRIBUTION

Found in all the ecozones of the Kruger in suitable habitat, but are almost absent from ecozone L. They are particularly numerous along rivers and other permanent water supplies. Only low population densities are found in the tall grassed areas of the Pretoriuskop area, and they are almost absent from the rank, tall grasses of the plains north of the Letaba River.

BEHAVIOUR

Predominantly diurnal, with a late-night grazing bout. Social structure varies according to the different phases of the breeding cycle. Herds generally comprise ewes and lambs residing in clans of 30–120 individuals (average 10–60). Average group size in the Kruger is 10, but groups of 50 individuals are also encountered. Home ranges of neighbouring herds overlap. The core home range is 0,8–1,8 km², and the overall home range size expands during the dry season. The average home range in the central districts of the Kruger is 5,8 km². Rams form bachelor herds at about 8 months of age, sharing the natal range. As young rams mature, they move up to 4 km away from the natal herd and join other clans. During the rut (an intensely active mating season from April to June) older rams become territorial, holding short tenures (average 3–13 days) over harem herds. Rams mark territories with urine, dung, and by pasting secretions from the glands above the hind hooves and forehead onto bushes and grass stalks, by constantly 'herding' the ewes, strutting and 'roaring' with their tails raised, heads lifted and chins pointed. Because so much energy is spent keeping ewes within the territory and keeping other rams out, little time is left for eating, causing rams to lose form quickly.

Impala are very wary of danger. At least one herd member acts as a sentinel. Herds are often found in association with baboons, wildebeest, giraffe and zebra.

Ewes

Calls: The alarm call is a loud snort.

Alarm signals: Head jerking whilst flicking the tail; kicking back and up with the hindfeet, thereby releasing scent from the glands above the hindfeet. They also flee into dense vegetation by running in zigzags with sudden changes in direction and high, long leaps, with individual herd members scattering in all directions.

Aggression: Threat displays include horn threats, head tossing, head bobbing as well as vegetation horning, mock or real charges, chasing and stabbing with the horns. Ewes dip their heads and butt with their hooves.

REPRODUCTION

Breed all year, with most births occurring in a lambing peak of a few weeks in spring and autumn. A single lamb, weighing 4,5–5,5 kg, is born after a gestation period of 6,5 months. The ewe gives birth in isolation, and the lamb remains hidden for 1–3 days before joining a nursery crèche. It is weaned at 4–6 months.

DIET

Mixed feeders. Graze a variety of grasses, favouring green grasses. Browse mainly during the dry season, taking leaves, bark, herbs, seedpods, succulents, fruit, and flowers, particularly those of the sausage tree. Generally live near water, drinking once, but usually twice a day, in the early morning and

Ram with oxpecker on head

evening. However, impala are water independent, and can obtain enough moisture from succulents.

HABITAT

Found in open savanna woodland, and on the peripheries of grassland in open woodland, particularly *Acacia* woodland. Avoid tall grasslands. Found in all the habitats of the Kruger, but are almost absent from the mopane shrubveld.

Klipspringer

Oreotragus oreotragus

Ger: Klippspringer; **Fre:** Oréotrague; **Afr:** Klipspringer; **Nde, Zul:** igogo; **Set:** kololo, mokabaowane; **Sot:** kome, sekome; **Swa:** ligoga, ligoka, inyamatane; **Xit:** ngululu, xemi.

Mass: ♂ 9–12 kg; ♀ 10–15 kg. **Shoulder height:** ♂ 0,5–0,6 m; ♀ 0,5–0,6 m. **Distinguishing features:** Large, black preorbital glands are prominent. The hindquarters are massive relative to body size. Walk on the tips of their hooves, which are almost circular. The rounded spoor is unique. **Life-span:** ± 10–12 yrs. **Predators:** Main predators include leopard, caracal, serval, spotted hyaena and jackal. Other predators include large snakes. Young also fall prey to baboon, eagle, monitor and ratel.

Front: 2 cm
Hind: 2 cm

DESCRIPTION

Grizzled coat with brittle, hollow hair. Colour varies according to distribution: northern populations are yellowish, speckled with brown, with a greyish tinge on the legs; other populations are yellowish to yellow-olive, with or without brown or grey speckling. The underparts, chin and lips are white; the ears are white inside, with a black border. The two digits of the hooves are tightly connected so that they do not splay, allowing for great agility on rocky terrain.

Scent glands: Preorbital. Rams also have preputial glands.

Senses: Very good sight, hearing and sense of smell.

Horns: Only rams carry horns. They are wide set, straight, partly ridged at the base and smooth towards the tips. Length: 10–15 cm.

DISTRIBUTION

Found in suitable habitat in all the ecozones of the Kruger. Particularly common in the Lebombo Mountain region north of the Letaba River, and in the extreme northern hilly areas north of the Punda Maria and Pafuri roads.

BEHAVIOUR

Predominantly diurnal with activity peaks in the late afternoon; may be active all day in cool weather. Monogamous pairs share a territory of 0,08 km² (up to 0,5 km² in sub-desert). Both sexes defend the territory from intruders. Territories are marked with dung middens and black preorbital gland secretions that are pasted onto grass and bushes. Rams also mark their territory with vegetation horning.

Single klipspringers are usually unmated rams. When larger groups are encountered, they are either a pair with their young, or temporary aggregations of 2–3 pairs. Groups are more common during the dry season, and separate into individual pairs again when food becomes more available. Relations between pairs are maintained through mutual grooming.

Calls: Alarm calls are loud, shrill nasal whistles that are given in duet, the male calling first. Klipspringers also respond to the alarm calls of other species.

Alarm signals: Freeze, call in duet, and then flee for cover or higher ground, halting on high vantage points to see if they are still being pursued. Klipspringers can outrun any land predator over rocky terrain. Lambs lie flat and motionless, with ears pinned back.

Aggression: Threat displays include horn threats, vegetation horning, ground pawing, mock attacks, chasing, and stabbing intruders with the horns. Both sexes bite.

Ewe (above). The spoor is unique

REPRODUCTION
Breed all year. A single lamb, weighing 1 kg, is born after a gestation period of 7 months in rocky recesses or in thick vegetation in rocky habitats. It remains hidden for 2–3 weeks, and is weaned at 4–5 months.

DIET
Browsers, favouring evergreen shrubs, succulents and herbs. Also take fruit, berries, seedpods, flowers, lichen and new grass shoots. Bones and soil are chewed for their mineral content. Water independent, obtaining enough moisture from food, but will drink when water is available.

HABITAT
Steep, rocky terrain (rocky outcrops, mountainsides and river gorges) with brush cover. In the Kruger, found in rocky terrain in all habitats, and common in the northern parts of the Lebombo Mountain bushveld and in hilly and mountainous terrain of the extreme northern portions of the alluvial plains and sandveld habitats.

Rams carry straight, thin and pointed horns

Steenbok

Raphicerus campestris

Ger: Steinböckchen; **Fre, Afr:** Steenbok; **Nde, Zul:** iqhina; **Nde:** ingina, iqina; **Xho:** itshabanqa; **Set:** phuduhudu; **Sot:** thiane; **Swa:** lingcina; **Xit:** xipene; **Tsh:** phuluvhulu.

Mass: ♂ 10–15 kg; ♀ 10–15 kg. **Shoulder height:** ♂ 0,45–0,55 m; ♀ 0,45–0,55 m. **Distinguishing features:** Distinctive, black Y-shaped marking on the snout, prominent preorbital glands, and large ears with white lining. **Life-span:** ± 8–10 yrs. **Predators:** Main predators include lion, leopard, cheetah, caracal, wild dog and spotted hyaena. Young also fall prey to baboon, jackal, eagle, monitor, ratel and python.

Front: 3 cm
Hind: 3 cm

DESCRIPTION

The coat is smooth and glossy. The upperparts are reddish fawn or reddish brown, while the underparts, the throat and the inner legs are white. The tail is short and has a white underside.

Scent glands: Preorbital, between the halves of the lower jaw, and hoof.
Senses: Very good sight, hearing and sense of smell.
Horns: Only rams carry horns. They are short, straight and curve forward slightly. The horns are smooth and lightly ridged at the base. Length: 13–19 cm.

DISTRIBUTION

Found in all the ecozones of the Kruger, with high-density populations occurring in the open plains of the eastern districts. Lower population densities occur in the western parts of the Park.

BEHAVIOUR

Diurnal and nocturnal, becoming predominantly nocturnal in disturbed areas. Activity peaks are in the early morning and late afternoon, but they may be active all day in cool weather.

They are usually solitary, although it is thought that monogamous pairs may share territories of 0,5–1 km². The territory is marked with dung and urine middens that are deposited in scrapes. Scrapes are mixed with soil and then covered with soil (thereby depositing digital gland secretions). Rams also mark territories with preorbital gland secretions.

Calls: The alarm call is a nasal snort.
Alarm signals: Freeze when a predator approaches, then flee in zigzags with intermittent leaps, stopping to see if they are still being pursued. Often dart down abandoned burrows or lie flat on the ground. Lambs lie flat and motionless, with ears pinned back.
Aggression: Threat displays include horn threats, vegetation horning, ground pawing as well as mock attacks, chasing. When threatened, they will readily stab intruders with their horns.

REPRODUCTION

Breed all year round, with a peak in the summer rainy season. A single lamb, weighing 1 kg, is born after a gestation period of 5,5 months. The lamb is born in dense cover, where it remains hidden for up to a month. It is fully weaned at 3 months.

Steenbok are solitary creatures

DIET

Selective browsers of tree and shrub leaves, forbs and shoots. During the wet season, forbs are the dominant browse; in the dry season, when forbs are scarce, woody plants are taken. In the Kruger, *Flueggea virosa* is a favourite during the dry season. They also take bulbs, tubers, roots, berries and fruit. Graze occasionally on newly sprouted grasses in the early rainy season and after fires. Water independent, obtaining enough moisture from food, but will drink when water is available.

HABITAT

Dry, open plains or lightly wooded habitats with stands of tall grass or brush cover. Absent from forest, thick woodland, rocky habitats and desert. Found in all the habitats of the Kruger, showing a very strong preference for *Acacia tortilis* savanna throughout the year.

Ram (top), ewe (bottom)

Sharpe's Grysbok

Raphicerus sharpei

Ger: Sharpes Greisbock; **Fre:** Grysbok de Sharpe; **Afr:** Sharpese grysbok; **Nde:** isanempa; **Swa:** mawumbane; **Xit:** pitsipitsi, xipitsipitsi, zipitipiti.

Mass: ♂ 8–13 kg; ♀ 8–13 kg. **Shoulder height:** ♂ 0,45–0,55 m; ♀ 0,45–0,55 m. **Distinguishing features:** Large, rounded ears; grey on the outside with black borders. Short, inconspicuous tail. **Life-span:** ± 10 yrs. **Predators:** Main predators include leopard, cheetah, caracal, wild dog, spotted hyaena and python. Young also fall prey to baboon, jackal, eagle, monitor and ratel.

Front: 3 cm
Hind: 3 cm

DESCRIPTION

The coat is reddish brown to reddish fawn, generously speckled with white hair, resulting in an almost grizzled appearance. The face is paler than the body, with white rings around the eyes and a dark band on the muzzle. Whitish lips, throat, inner legs and underparts.

Scent glands: Preorbital and hoof. Rams also have preputial glands.

Senses: Very good sight, hearing and sense of smell.

Horns: Only rams carry horns. They are short and straight; smooth and lightly ridged at the base. Length: 4–5 cm.

DISTRIBUTION

Patchily distributed in the Kruger, occurring in ecozones A, E, F, I, J, L, M, N, O and P. Major population densities are found in the Lebombo Mountain area south of the Olifants River, and in the extreme northern hilly areas north of the Punda Maria and Pafuri roads.

BEHAVIOUR

Predominantly nocturnal. Although sightings are usually of solitary individuals, it is thought that pairs may share a territory range, which is defended by the ram. Territories are marked with preorbital gland secretions, as well as with dung and urine middens.

Calls: The alarm call is a snort.

Alarm signals: Lie low in dense cover; flee in a straight line, with the head and body held low. May dart down abandoned aardvark burrows, or other similar holes in the ground.

Aggression: Threat displays include horn threats, vegetation horning, ground pawing, mock attacks, chasing, and stabbing intruders with their horns.

REPRODUCTION

Breed all year. A single lamb, weighing 1 kg, is born after a gestation period of 5,5–6 months. The lamb is born in dense cover, where it remains hidden for up to a month. It is weaned at 3 months.

DIET

Browse broad-leaved shrubs including *Acacia*, *Grewia*, *Ziziphus* and *Diospyrus* spp; fruit and berries. Occasionally graze on grasses and herbs. Water independent, obtaining enough moisture from food, but will drink when water is available.

Ewe (above) – the large round ears are a distinguishing feature of this species

HABITAT

Favour low scrub and brush with medium grasses, open woodland savanna and thickets. These habitats often contain rocky outcrops and adjacent grasslands. Avoid thick, tall grassland. In the Kruger Park, these grysbok are found in the mixed bushwillow woodlands, mopane/bushwillow woodlands, tree mopane savanna as well as knobthorn/marula savanna, mopane shrubveld, thorn veld, rugged veld and the Lebombo Mountain bushveld. Also found in the alluvial plains and the sandveld communities habitats.

Oribi

Ourebia ourebi

Ger: Bleichböckchen, Oribi; **Fre:** Ourébie; **Afr:** Oorbietjie; **Nde:** insinza; **Xho, Zul, Swa:** iwula; **Swa:** liwula; **Set:** phuduhudu kgamane, tlhwaele; **Sot:** hlwaele; **Xit:** mhala.

Mass: ♂ 12–22 kg; ♀ 12–22 kg. **Shoulder height:** ♂ 0,5–0,67 m; ♀ 0,50–0,67 m. **Distinguishing features:** A small, round naked skin patch under the large, oval ears; a relatively long neck and a short black-tipped tail. **Life-span:** ± 12 yrs. **Predators:** Main predators include leopard, cheetah, caracal, wild dog and spotted hyaena. Young also fall prey to baboon, jackal, eagle, monitor, ratel and python.

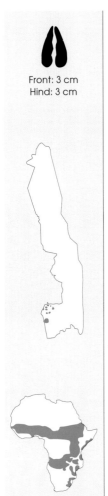

Front: 3 cm
Hind: 3 cm

DESCRIPTION

The largest of the pygmy antelope. Similar to steenbok but larger. The overall body colour varies geographically, ranging from yellowish brown to reddish. The long, woolly coat tends to curl. There is a white patch on the upper throat, and there are white patches on the eyes, lips and chin. The white of the underparts extends one third up the flanks. The short tail is black, with a white underside. Lambs are much darker than adults.

Scent glands: Preorbital, below the ears, inguinal and hoof.

Senses: Very good sight, hearing and sense of smell.

Horns: Only rams carry horns. The horns are straight and curve forward slightly. The upper two thirds are smooth while the base is heavily ridged. Length: 8–19 cm.

DISTRIBUTION

Although no sightings have been recorded in the Kruger over the past few years, oribi are known to occur in suitable habitat in ecozone B, in the higher altitudes areas of the Pretoriuskop area.

BEHAVIOUR

Predominantly diurnal, becoming nocturnal in disturbed areas. Social structure is determined by habitat. In areas with sufficient grass cover, monogamous pairs or small family herds (a dominant ram, 1–2 ewes and lambs) share a territory of 0,3–1 km². Grazing pastures and salt licks are shared with other family groups, with temporary associations of up to 12 individuals being formed, particularly after fires. Territories are defended against same-sex intruders and are marked with urine and communal dung middens. Only rams mark territories with preorbital gland secretions, pasting them onto grass stems and twigs, which may be bitten off to shoulder height.

Calls: The alarm call is a sharp, snorting whistle. They bleat when distressed.

Alarm signals: Alarm signals include distinctive stotting action, displaying the black tail, and stopping every few paces to see if they are still being pursued. Lambs lie flat and motionless, with ears pinned back. Where temporary aggregations occur, separate groupings scatter in different directions.

Aggression: Threat displays include horn threats with the head lowered, chin pushed forward, ears cocked and tail raised; vegetation horning; ground pawing; mock attacks; chasing; and stabbing intruders with their horns. An upward jerk of the head precedes a horn attack.

Ram (above). Oribi have white underparts and a short, black-tipped tail

REPRODUCTION

Breed all year, with a peak in the summer rainy season. A single lamb, weighing 1,6–2,5 kg, is born after a gestation period of 6,5 months. It is born in dense cover where it remains hidden for 2–3 months. It attains adult coloration at 2–5 weeks, and is weaned at 4–5 months.

DIET

Graze short, green grasses and herbs, showing a preference for newly sprouted grasses after fires. Water independent, obtaining enough moisture from food. Drink rarely, even when water is available.

HABITAT

Open, short grassland and floodplains (with patches of tall grasses and bushes or solitary trees), and hilly and mountainous terrain. Absent from desert, forest or areas with dense, tall grass. In the Kruger, found in the sourveld habitat.

Ewe

Suni/Livingstone's Antelope

Neotragus moschatus

Ger: Moschusböckchen; **Fre:** Suni, Antilope musquée; **Afr:** Soenie; **Zul, Swa:** inhlengane; **Xit:** nhlengane.

Mass: ♂ 4,5–5,0 kg; ♀ 5,0–6,0 kg. **Shoulder height:** ♂ 33–38 cm; ♀ 33–38 cm. **Distinguishing features:** Pink-lined ears appear translucent. The tail is flicked constantly. The prominent preorbital glands emit a strong, musky odour. **Life-span:** ± 8 yrs. **Predators:** Main predators include leopard, cheetah, caracal, wild dog, spotted hyaena, crocodile and python. Young also fall prey to baboon, jackal, eagle, monitor and ratel.

Front: 2 cm
Hind: 2 cm

DESCRIPTION

The reddish-brown upperparts are flecked with buff-white hairs, while the underparts are whitish. White patches are above the eyes and on the chin and throat; there is a dark marking on the snout. The tail is edged in white and has a white underside. The tail is characteristically flicked from side to side.
Scent glands: Preorbital and hoof.
Senses: Very good sight, hearing and sense of smell.
Horns: Only rams carry horns. They are straight and backward pointing, and heavily ridged. Length: 7–13 cm.

DISTRIBUTION

Very rare in the Kruger, occurring marginally in suitable habitat in the extreme northeastern parts of ecozones M and N, and marginally into the extreme northwestern parts of ecozone N, west of Punda Maria.

BEHAVIOUR

Diurnal and nocturnal, with activity peaks in the early morning, late afternoon, and between 10 pm and 4 am; least active during the hotter hours of the day. Most active after rain or dense mist. Found in pairs or herds comprising a dominant ram, and up to 4 ewes with their young.

Territories of 0,01–0,1 km² are marked with communal dung middens, digital gland secretions, and with preorbital gland secretions that are pasted onto bushes and grass stalks. The territory includes regularly used paths and favourite resting sites. Relations between pairs and herd members are maintained through mutual grooming.
Calls: Alarm calls include a high-pitched squeal, a sharp, whistling snort (if the threat is close), and a bark (if the threat is distant).
Alarm signals: When approached by predators, they initially freeze, then flee for cover.
Aggression: Threat displays include horn threats, mock attacks, chasing, and stabbing intruders with the horns.

REPRODUCTION

Breed all year, with a peak in the summer rainy season. A single lamb, weighing 0,65–1,0 kg, is born after a gestation period of 6 months, with an average interval of 7 months between births. The lamb is born in dense cover and remains hidden for a week. It takes solid food at 1 week, and is weaned at 2–3 months.

Ewe (top). Suni constantly flick their tails

DIET

Browse leaves (including *Crotalaria*, *Commelina*, *Acacia* and *Grewia* spp), flowers, fruit, shoots, herbs, and mushrooms and other fungi. Commonly found following monkeys, feeding on the fallen leaves and shoots that are dropped during their activities. Water independent, obtaining enough moisture from food, but will drink when water is available.

HABITAT

Woodlands and forests with thickets and dense underbrush; scrub and bush along rivers. In the Kruger, found in dense thickets of the alluvial plains and sandveld community habitats.

Ram

Common/Grimm's/Grey/Bush Duiker *Sylvicapra grimmia*

Ger: Buschducker, Kronenducker; **Fre:** Cephalophe commun, Cephalophe de Grimm; **Afr:** Gewone duiker; **Nde, Xho, Zul:** impunzi; **Nde:** ipunzi ejayelekileko; **Swa:** imphunzi; **Set:** phutï, photi; **Sot:** phuthi; **Xit:** mhunti; **Tsh:** nfsa, ntsa.

Status: not endangered   ☼ ☽

Mass: ♂ 15–21 kg; ♀ 17–25 kg. **Shoulder height:** ♂ 0,5–0,6 m; ♀ 0,45–0,6 m. **Distinguishing features:** A dark, tufted crest on the head; prominent, slit-like preorbital glands. Dark facial blaze: a dark, vertical band extending from the muzzle to the lower forehead. **Life-span:** ± 10 yrs. **Predators:** Main predators include lion, leopard, cheetah, wild dog, spotted hyaena and crocodile. Other predators include pythons. Young also fall prey to large owls, jackals and eagles.

Front: 4 cm
Hind: 4 cm

DESCRIPTION
Grey-buff to reddish-yellow upperparts; white underparts, occasionally tinged with red, grey or off-white; a dark facial blaze. The front of the forelegs are dark brown to dark brown-black. The tail is black with a white edge, and is white underneath.
Scent glands: Preorbital, hoof and inguinal.
Senses: Very good sight, hearing and sense of smell.
Horns: Only rams carry horns. They are straight, heavily ridged at the base, with smooth tips. Length: 10–18 cm.

DISTRIBUTION
Found in suitable habitat in all the ecozones of the Kruger.

BEHAVIOUR
Diurnal and nocturnal, with activity peaks at night and during the cooler hours of the day (morning and late afternoon); active all day in cool or over-cast weather. Predominantly nocturnal in disturbed areas. They are solitary, defending territories of 0,2 km². The territories of neighbouring same-sex and opposite-sex individuals do not overlap. Territories are marked with preorbital gland secretions that are rubbed onto bushes and grass stalks, and with digital gland secretions.
Calls: Contact and alarm calls include snorts; bleat when distressed.
Alarm signals: Sneak off into cover, if undetected. When predators approach, freeze, duck or lie low, fleeing at the last moment in distinctive zigzag fashion interspersed with leaps, and diving for the nearest cover. Lambs lie flat and motionless, with ears pinned back.
Aggression: Threat displays include horn threats with head held low, vegetation horning, ground pawing, rushing towards the intruder, mock or real charges, chasing, stabbing the intruder with the horns; both sexes kick with the sharp back hooves.

REPRODUCTION
Breed all year. A single lamb, weighing 1,4–1,9 kg, is born after a gestation period of 7 months. It is born in dense cover, where it remains hidden for 2–3 months. It is able to run within a day, and is weaned at 5 months.

Ewe (above), ram (below) – note the dark tufted crest on the head

DIET

Browse leaves from a variety of broad-leaved trees and bushes. Also take twigs, fruit, melons, seeds, roots as well as bark, bulbs, tubers, flowers and fungi. Occasionally feed on birds. Water independent, obtaining enough moisture from their food, and drink rarely even when water is available.

HABITAT

Found in a variety of habitat types, favouring woodland savanna, scrub and bush. Absent from short open grassland, rain-forest, and true desert, but penetrate desert along drainage lines if cover is available. In the Kruger, found in all habitats, and occur commonly in riparian vegetation along rivers and watercourses.

Red Duiker

Cephalophus natalensis

Ger: Rotducker; **Fre:** Cephalophe de Natal; **Afr:** Rooiduiker; **Nde:** ipunzi ebovu; **Xho:** impunzu; **Zul, Swa:** umsumpe; **Zul:** umkhumbi; **Swa:** umsumbi, imphunzi; **Set:** photi; **Sot:** phuthi e kgubedu; **Xit:** mhunti; **Tsh:** phithi, tshipiti.

Mass: ♂ 11–13 kg; ♀ 11–16 kg. **Shoulder height:** ♂ 0,4–0,5 m; ♀ 0,4–0,5 m. **Distinguishing features:** A dark, tufted crest on the head; prominent, slit-like preorbital glands; and a distinctive black-and-white-tipped tail. **Life-span:** ± 8 yrs. **Predators:** Main predators include lion, leopard, cheetah, wild dog, spotted hyaena, serval, civet and crocodile. Other predators include pythons. Young also fall prey to jackals, large owls and eagles.

Front: 3 cm
Hind: 3 cm

DESCRIPTION

Deep chestnut to reddish-brown upperparts; paler lower flanks and underparts. White throat turns grey with age; the tail has a black-and-white tip. Lambs are darker than adults.

Scent glands: Preorbital and hoof.

Senses: Very good sight, hearing and sense of smell.

Horns: Both sexes carry horns, but ewes may not have horns in some populations. The horns are straight and backward pointing. They are heavily ridged at the base, the middle portion is grooved lengthwise, and the tips are smooth. Length: 7–10 cm.

DISTRIBUTION

Found in suitable habitat in ecozones B and D of the Kruger, in the Pretoriuskop and Skukuza areas, and east of Skukuza along the Sabie River.

BEHAVIOUR

Predominantly diurnal, with activity peaks at dawn and dusk. They may be solitary, or are found in monogamous pairs or family parties (a pair with their offspring). Home ranges (0,02–0,1 km²) may overlap with those of neighbouring individuals or family parties. They are marked with preorbital gland secretions that are rubbed onto bushes and grass stalks, with digital gland secretions, and with communal urine and dung middens. Home ranges include favourite resting sites.

Social relations between individuals are maintained by pressing their preorbital glands together, and with mutual grooming.

Calls: Contact calls include a 'tchie-tchie' call. Alarm calls include snorts and whistles; they bleat when distressed.

Alarm signals: Sneak off into cover, if undetected. When predators approach, freeze, duck or lie low, fleeing at the last moment, and diving for the nearest cover.

Aggression: Threat displays include horn threats with the head held low, vegetation horning, ground pawing, rushing towards the intruder, mock or real charges, chasing, stabbing the intruder with the horns, and kicking with the sharp back hooves; snorting.

REPRODUCTION

Breed all year. A single lamb, weighing 1 kg, is born after a gestation period of 7 months, with an average interval of 9 months between births. The lamb is born in dense cover, and remains hidden for 2–3 months. It is fully weaned by 5 months.

Ewe (above). The black-and-white-tipped tail is a distinguishing feature of this species

DIET

Browse on leaves, buds, shoots, berries and fruits. Also take termites, ants, snails and eggs. Occasionally graze on grasses and herbs. Commonly found following monkeys, feeding on the fallen leaves and shoots that are dropped during their activities. Water independent, obtaining enough moisture from food, but will drink when water is available.

HABITAT

Forest, thickets, dense woodland, thick bush, and scrub forest with thick underbrush. A requirement of these habitats is the availability of a range of trees which flower and bear fruit throughout most of the year. Occur predominantly in the sourveld habitats of the Kruger, and marginally into the thorn thickets habitat.

Warthog

Phacochoerus aethiopicus

Ger: Warzenschwein; **Fre:** Phacochère; **Afr:** Vlakvark; **Nde, Swa:** indayikazane; **Nde:** ingulube yesiganga, isavukazana sommango, ifarigi yommango; **Swa:** budzayikatana; **Xho:** ingulube; **Zul:** indlovudawana, indlovudalana, intibane; **Set:** kolobê; **Sot:** kolobe, kolobe-moru, mokhesi, mokgesi; **Xit:** ngulube, nguluve, ndaekedzane; **Tsh:** phangwa.

Mass: ♂ 60–150 kg; ♀ 45–75 kg. **Shoulder height:** ♂ 60–80 cm; ♀ 50–70 cm. **Distinguishing features:** Boars have two pairs of facial warts that can reach up to 13 cm: one situated next to the eyes, the other above the tusks. The facial warts of sows are much smaller and are situated next to the eyes. When warthog run, their long, tasseled tails are characteristically held straight up like antennae. **Life-span:** ± 10–15 yrs. **Predators:** Main predators include lion and wild dog. Other predators include leopard, cheetah and spotted hyaena. Young also fall prey to eagles and jackals.

Front: 5 cm
Hind: 5 cm

DESCRIPTION

The skin is grey (often taking on the colour of the local soil) and almost naked, except for a few sparse bristles. A black, brown or yellowish bristly mane runs down the back, and is longest over the neck and shoulders and shorter on the back. There are whitish whiskers on the jaw line. Warthog are fond of mud and sand baths, which aid in lowering body temperature and offer protection against sun and parasites. Hooves are narrower than those of the bushpig; the difference is visible in the spoor.

Scent glands: Underlying the warts of the face; lips and chin. Boars also have preputial glands.

Senses: Poor sight, very good hearing and sense of smell.

Tusks: In boars, upper tusks can reach up to 60 cm; in sows, 30 cm. The lower tusks reach up to 10 cm. Upper tusks curve upward and inward, those protruding from the lower jaw are straight and pointed.

DISTRIBUTION

Occur in suitable habitat in all the ecozones of the Kruger. High-density populations are found in the areas between Lower Sabie and Crocodile Bridge; in the Orpen, Tshokwane, Nwanetsi and Phalaborwa areas; and between the Luvuvhu and Limpopo rivers.

BEHAVIOUR

Diurnal; least active in the hotter hours of the day. Sows form nursery sounders, comprising 1–2 sows and their piglets. Average group size in the Kruger is 2–5. Mature boars tend to be solitary, while young boars form bachelor sounders with siblings remaining within the natal home range. Warthog mark the home range (0,65–4,2 km²) by wiping their mouths against vegetation and other objects, and with secretions from the glands enclosing the warts. Home ranges of neighbouring individuals and sounders overlap, and only the core area around the burrow is defended. Home ranges include several burrows that are used communally by different sounders at different times on a 'first in, first served' basis. Relations between group members are maintained through mutual grooming. During the course of a day's foraging, warthog can travel up to 7 km over their home range. Warthog shelter mainly in abandoned aardvark burrows, which they modify and

Due to the near-naked skin, warthogs have a low tolerance to cold temperatures

line with grass. Occasionally they shelter in caves, under riverbank overhangs, and in holes in erosion gulleys. Adults enter and exit the burrows head-first.

Because their skin is almost naked, and they contain virtually no fat reserves, warthog have a very low tolerance to cold temperatures. To conserve heat, they insulate their burrows, bask in the sun and huddle together.

Calls: Contact calls include grunts and snorts. Piglets squeak. The alarm call is a single, loud grunt, and they squeal when distressed. Warthog also respond to the alarm calls of oxpeckers.

Alarm signals: Flee with ears flattened and tail held upright like an antenna.

Aggression: Aggression is shown by raising the mane, stiff-legged gaits, ground pawing, rushing, charging, snarling, snorting, and grunting. During fights, they drop to their knees and head-butt their opponents. The warts protect the face against blows.

REPRODUCTION

Breed in the summer rainy season in southern and East Africa; all year in higher-rainfall equatorial regions. 1–8 (average 2–3) piglets, weighing 450–900 g each, are born after a gestation period of 160–170 days. Sows leave the sounder to give birth. Piglets are born in grass-lined burrows, but are moved to raised recesses within the burrow to protect them against drowning during heavy rains. Each piglet is allocated its own teat and is not allowed to suckle from another. Piglets remain in the burrow for 6–7 weeks, but start leaving it for short periods by 1–3 weeks of age, to feed on grass. They are weaned at 6 months, but remain with the mother for up to a year. Piglets follow behind their mother in fixed order. Sows sometimes adopt orphaned piglets.

DIET

Selective grazers, favouring short grasses and newly sprouted grasses after fires. Also browse on tubers, bulbs and roots, which are dug out with the snout, and on fruits, berries, carrion, birds, rodents, reptiles, and snakes. Feed by kneeling on the front knees, which have protective calluses on them. Chew bones, soil and rocks to supplement the mineral content of their diet. Water independent, obtaining enough moisture from food, but will drink regularly when water is available.

HABITAT

Grassland and open woodland savanna, sparse forest and floodplains, favouring areas with alluvial soil and abundant aardvark burrows. Absent from desert and rain-forest. Found in all the habitats of the Kruger.

Bushpig

Potamochoerus larvatus

Ger: Buschschwein; **Fre:** Potamochère; **Afr:** Bosvark; **Nde:** ingulungun-du, ifarigi yommango, isavukazana sommango; **Xho, Zul, Swa:** ingu-lube; **Zul:** ingulube yasahlathini; **Swa:** ingulube ye siganga, inhontji; **Set:** kolobê, kolobe ya naga; **Sot:** kolobe, kolobe ya thaba, moru, kolobe-sodi, kolobe-moru; **Xit:** khumba, nguluve m'hlati; **Tsh:** ngulu-vhe, nguluvhe ya daka.

Status: not endangered   ☽ B

Mass: ♂ 45–115 kg; ♀ 45–90 kg. **Shoulder height:** ♂ 55–80 cm; ♀ 55–80 cm. **Distinguishing features:** A mane of long, bristly hair extends from neck to tail base. Horn-like, bony processes protrude from either side of the upper jaw. Unlike the warthog, the tail is held down when the animal runs. **Life-span:** ± 15 yrs. **Predators:** Main predators include lion, leopard and spotted hyaena. Young also fall prey to eagles and rock python.

Front: 5 cm
Hind: 5 cm

DESCRIPTION

The coat is coarse and shaggy. Overall colour varies according to habitat and distri-bution: from tawny to reddish brown to brownish black, turning grey with age. Yellowish dorsal mane, and yellowish-white tufts on the ear tips. Piglets are brown with faint stripes that fade at 4 months. Mud and sand baths aid in lowering body temper-ature and offer protection against sun and parasites. Bushpigs are strong swimmers. They raise their tails when they dive in water. Hooves are broader than those of the warthog; the difference is visible in the spoor.

Scent glands: Hoof, neck, lip and chin. Boars also have preputial glands.

Senses: Poor sight, good hearing, very good sense of smell.

Tusks: Upper tusks reach up to 16 cm. They curve upward and sometimes protrude from the upper jaw.

DISTRIBUTION

In the Kruger, found in ecozone M, the extreme northern parts of ecozone N, and parts of ecozone H. Highest-density populations are found north of the Luvuvhu River, and in riverine forests of the Limpopo Mountains. Small populations occur along the Olifants River, and sightings have been reported along the Sabie and Crocodile rivers.

BEHAVIOUR

Predominantly nocturnal, but sometimes forage during the early morning and late afternoon in undisturbed areas. Diurnal activity may increase during the cold winter months. They are found in mixed sounders, comprising a dominant boar and sow, and subordinate sows and their piglets, averaging 6–8 individuals, although larger aggregations may be encountered at times. The home range (0,2–10 km²) is marked with digital and neck gland secretions, with dung middens and urine, and with well-worn rubbing posts and regularly used paths. The dominant boar also gouges trees to mark his territory. Mature boars tend to be solitary, while young boars form bachelor sounders. During the course of a night's foraging, bushpigs can travel up to 6 km.

Calls: Contact calls include grunts and snorts. Piglets squeak. Alarm calls include grunts; they squeal in distress.

Alarm signals: Freeze, then flee for cover with sounder members scattering in all directions. The tail is held down when fleeing.

Note the coarse and shaggy coat

Aggression: Raising the mane whilst holding their heads high and cocking their ears, and by ground pawing, throwing up dust and clumps of earth, snapping and gashing with their canines, mock or real charges, grunting, growling, squealing and snorting. Sounder members may mob-attack.

REPRODUCTION

Breed in the summer rainy season. 3–10 (average 3–4) piglets, weighing 700–900 g each, are born after a gestation period of 4 months. Piglets are born in grass 'nests' (up to 3 m wide and 1 m high), and are weaned at 3–6 months. They are cared for by the dominant boar.

DIET

Omnivorous, favouring roots, tubers, bulbs, corms and fruit. Also take larvae, worms, eggs, carrion, snakes and rodents. Water independent, obtaining enough moisture from food, but will drink when water is available.

HABITAT

Well-watered areas with dense cover, including forests, thickets, swamps, marshes as well as reed beds and tall grasslands. In the Kruger, found in the alluvial plains habitat, and also in some parts of the northern sandveld and riverine communities habitats.

Rock Dassie/Cape Hyrax

Procavia capensis

Ger: Klippschliefer; **Fre:** Daman de rocher; **Afr:** Klipdassie; **Nde, Xho, Zul, Swa:** imbila; **Set, Sot:** pela; **Xit, Tsh:** mbila.

Mass: ♂ 3,5–5,5 kg; ♀ 3,5–4,5 kg. **Head-and-body length:** ♂ 36–60 cm; ♀ 36–58 cm. **Distinguishing features:** A patch of long, blackish or whitish hair around the dorsal gland in the centre of the back. **Life-span:** ± 10 yrs. **Predators:** Main predators include leopard, cheetah, jackal, caracal, serval and civet. Other predators include black eagle, rock python, mongooses and large snakes.

H

Front: 5 cm
Hind: 7 cm

DESCRIPTION

The coat is coarse with long, black tactile hairs scattered amongst the shorter hair. Overall body colour varies according to habitat: grizzled greyish brown in moister areas, buff in arid regions. The underparts are paler. The dorsal crest is blackish in *P.c. capensis*, and whitish cream in *P.c. welwitchii*. The soles of the feet are naked with soft, elastic pads that are moistened with sweat gland secretions. The moist soles function as suction pads, enabling the hyrax to climb trees and steep, smooth rock surfaces.

Scent glands: Dorsal.

Senses: Very good sight and hearing, good sense of smell.

DISTRIBUTION

Found in suitable habitat in ecozones E, J, L and P of the Kruger, between the Olifants and Bububu rivers, and in the northern parts of ecozone I, in the Lebombo Mountain bushveld north of the Olifants River.

BEHAVIOUR

Predominantly diurnal, but may be active on moonlit evenings during the warm summer months; least active during the hotter hours of the day. They form harem clans of up to 25 individuals, comprising a dominant male, and several (usually related) females and their young. Several clans may share the same area, but core areas are defended as territories. Subordinate males remain on the periphery of the dominant male's territory. The home range covers 4–6 km², and is marked with communal dung and urine middens. The dung is distinctly bright white, and the urine leaves whitish stains on rock surfaces, caused by crystallized calcium carbonate.

They shelter in rock crevices and cavities, or in the burrows of other animals, including suricates and aardvarks. Cape hyraxes may shelter and forage with or alongside yellow-spotted hyraxes. Hyraxes have a very low tolerance of cold temperatures, and therefore conserve energy by basking in the sun or huddling together.

Calls: Contact calls include twitters, whistles, chirrups, growls, grunts, yips and screams. Alarm calls include squeaks, shrieks and sharp barks.

Alarm signals: When alarmed, the hair surrounding the dorsal gland is raised and dorsal gland secretions are released. To escape danger, they flee in leaps to find shelter, often in rock crevices, and remain frozen until the danger has passed.

Aggression: Aggression is shown by raising the hair surrounding the dorsal gland

The rock dassie has long blackish hairs in the centre of the back

and releasing gland secretions. Other signs of aggression include baring and grinding the teeth, growling, snarling and biting. They may feign death if caught.

REPRODUCTION
Breed in the summer rainy season in the southern parts of their range; in East Africa, breed in either of the rainy seasons, but only once a year. 1–6 cubs, weighing 150–300 g each, are born after a gestation period of 7–8 months. Cubs are born with their eyes open and fully furred. They leave the nest within a few minutes of birth. Each cub is allocated its own teat and is not allowed to suckle from another. They take solid food at 1 week and are weaned at 3–6 months. Juveniles often join nursery crèches.

DIET
Predominantly grazers, feeding on a variety of grasses and herbs, favouring giant lobelia and certain *Senecio* spp. Grazing increases during the dry season. Browse a variety of forbs, shrubs and also fruit and berries. Water independent, obtaining enough moisture from food, but will drink when water is available.

HABITAT
Rocky outcrops, sea cliffs, boulder piles and erosion gulleys, provided these have bushes and trees for browse and cover. In the Kruger, found in rocky areas in the thorn veld, rugged veld, mopane shrubveld, mopane/bushwillow woodlands and the Lebombo Mountain bushveld habitats.

Yellow-spotted Hyrax/Dassie
Heterohyrax brucei

Ger: Buschschliefer; **Fre:** Daman de steppe; **Afr:** Geelkoldas; **Nde:** imbila.

Mass: ♂ 2,7–3,2 kg; ♀ 2,3–3,6 kg. **Head-and-body length:** ♂ 46–53 cm; ♀ 48–56 cm. **Distinguishing features:** A patch of long, blackish or whitish hair surrounding the dorsal gland in the centre of the back. Distinctive white patches above the eyes. **Life-span:** ± 10 yrs. **Predators:** Main predators include leopard, cheetah, jackal, caracal, serval and civet. Other predators include black eagle, rock python, mongooses and large snakes.

H

Front: 5 cm
Hind: 7 cm

DESCRIPTION

The coat is coarse with long, black tactile hairs scattered among the shorter hair. The overall body colour varies according to habitat. In higher-rainfall areas, the upperparts are brown to dark brown, tinged reddish with whitish flecks and the underparts are paler. The dorsal patch is buff or reddish. In arid regions, the upperparts are varying shades of grey, with or without a brownish tinge. The underparts are paler and the dorsal patch is yellowish. The soles of the feet are naked with soft, elastic pads that are moistened with sweat gland secretions. The moist soles function as suction pads, enabling the hyrax to climb trees and steep, smooth rock surfaces.

Scent glands: Dorsal.
Senses: Very good sight and hearing, good sense of smell.

DISTRIBUTION

In the Kruger, they are common in suitable habitat in the extreme northern parts of ecozones M and N, north of the Punda Maria and Pafuri roads, and along the eastern border as far south as Malonga Spring.

BEHAVIOUR

Predominantly diurnal, but may be active on moonlit evenings during the warm summer months; least active during the hotter hours of the day. They form harem clans of up to 25 individuals, comprising a dominant male, and several, usually related, females and their young. Several clans may share the same area, but core areas are defended as territories. Subordinate males remain on the periphery of the dominant male's territory. The home range covers 4–6 km^2 and is marked with communal dung and urine middens. The dung is distinctly bright white, and the urine leaves whitish stains on rock surfaces, which is caused by crystallized calcium carbonate.

They shelter in rock crevices and cavities, or in the burrows of other animals, including suricates and aardvarks. Yellow-spotted hyraxes may shelter and forage with or alongside Cape hyraxes. Hyraxes have an extremely low tolerance to cold temperatures, and therefore they conserve energy by basking in the sun or by huddling together.

Calls: Contact calls include twitters, whistles, chirrups, growls, grunts, yips and screams, and characteristic, long shrill calls, which are repeated for up to 5 minutes. Alarm calls include squeaks, shrieks and characteristic piping whistles.

Alarm signals: When alarmed, the hair surrounding the dorsal gland is raised and dorsal gland secretions are released. To escape danger, they flee in leaps to find

The yellow-spotted hyrax has distinctive white patches above the eyes

shelter, often in rock crevices, and remain frozen until the danger has passed.

Aggression: Aggression is shown by raising the hair surrounding the dorsal gland and releasing gland secretions. Other signs of aggression include baring the teeth, grinding the teeth, growling, snarling and biting. May feign death if caught.

REPRODUCTION

Breed in the summer rainy season in the southern parts of their range; in East Africa, breed in either of the rainy seasons, but only once a year. 2–6 cubs, weighing 250 g each, are born after a gestation period of 7–8 months. Cubs are born fully furred, with their eyes open. They leave the nest within a few minutes of birth. Each cub is allocated its own teat and is not allowed to suckle from another. They take solid food at 1–2 weeks, and are weaned at 3–6 months. Juveniles often join nursery crèches.

DIET

Browse mainly on a wide variety of forbs and shrubs, but also take fruits and berries. Graze various grasses and herbs. Grazing increases in the dry season. Water independent, obtaining enough moisture from food, but will drink when water is available.

HABITAT

Rocky outcrops, sea cliffs, boulder piles, and erosion gulleys, provided these have bushes and trees for browse and cover. In the Kruger, found in the alluvial plains and sandveld communities habitats, and marginally into the mopane shrubveld habitat.

Aardvark

Orycteropus afer

Ger: Ameisenbär; **Fre:** Orycterope; **Afr:** Erdvark; **Nde, Zul, Swa:** isambane; **Set, Sot:** thakadu; **Tsh:** thagalu; **Xit:** xomboni.

Status: IUCN: EN, VU 🌙 B

Mass: ♂ 40–70 kg; ♀ 40–70 kg. **Shoulder height:** ♂ 58–66 cm; ♀ 58–66 cm. **Head-and-body length:** ♂ 1,00–1,58 m; ♀ 1,00–1,58 m. **Tail length:** ♂ 44–63 cm; ♀ 44–63 cm. **Distinguishing features:** Heavy, powerful limbs. Hindquarters are longer than forequarters, resulting in a prominently arched back. Snout and erect ears are long and tubular. The tapering tail is thick and fleshy, and is dragged along the ground, leaving a distinct trail mark behind. **Life-span:** ± 18 yrs. **Predators:** Main threat is man: the flesh is considered a delicacy among indigenous people, and the snout and claws are used in medicines and as charms. Aardvark are killed by farmers because their burrows are said to cause damage to crops, roads and dams. Other predators include lion, spotted hyaena, leopard and pythons.

Front: 9 cm
Hind: 8 cm

DESCRIPTION

The skin is pinkish grey, often taking on the colour of the local soil, and thick, offering protection against insect bites, and is sparsely covered with yellow-grey or brownish-grey bristles. The hair on the limbs and base of the tail is darker. The head and tail are white-buff in females, darker in males. The chisel-shaped claws are specialized for digging, during which the dense bristles around the nostrils prevent soil from entering the nose, and the ears are folded closed. Aardvark are digitigrade (they walk on their toes).

Scent glands: Perineal, elbow and hip.

Senses: Poor sight, very good hearing and sense of smell.

DISTRIBUTION

Although patchily distributed, aardvark are common in savanna areas with termitaria in all the ecozones of the Kruger, except in ecozone M. They are generally less common in montane areas.

BEHAVIOUR

Predominantly nocturnal, but occasionally active during the day. Solitary, with males establishing home ranges of 2–4,7 km², females 4,4–4,6 km². Home ranges are marked with thick, yellowish perineal gland secretions.

Aardvark dig their own burrows. The more commonly used ones are temporary overnight shelters that are usually only used once and are simple structures, about 3 m long, with a single entrance. Permanent burrows are more complex, with many chambers that are about 1 m wide and 0,8 m high, and may be over 30 m long and have over 20 entrances. Aardvark enter and exit burrows head first, sealing the entrance with soil. They often bask in the morning sun in front of their burrows.

Calls: Contact calls include loud sniffs while foraging, and grunts. Alarm calls include bleating cries.

Alarm signals: Freeze, then flee with a series of leaps to get a head start on predators, followed by fast trotting. Dig very quickly to escape predators, easily faster than several men digging together.

Aggression: Sit on their haunches, while lashing out with the tail and claws; roll onto the back, lashing out with the claws and tail.

Aardvark feed on ants and termites and have a 45 cm-long tongue

REPRODUCTION

Breed all year. A single cub, weighing 1,3–2 kg, is born after a gestation period of 7 months. Birth takes place in a nesting chamber. Eyes are open at birth and it remains in the burrow for 2 weeks. It takes solid food at 3 months, is nursed to 4 months, and is fully independent at 6 months.

DIET

Feed mainly on ants and termites, but also take other insects, such as beetles, cockroaches and grasshoppers, as well as insect larvae and small rodents. The 45 cm-long, sticky tongue is used for lapping up ants and termites. Soil and gravel are ingested with the prey and aid digestion in the gizzard-like stomach. Aardvark have a sym-

biotic relationship with *Cucumis humifructus* (aardvark cucumber). They eat the fruit for its water content, and the dispersed seeds then germinate in their dung.

Water independent, obtaining enough moisture from their food, especially from the aardvark cucumber in arid regions, but will drink when water is available.

HABITAT

Favour sandy and clay soils in open woodland, scrubland and grassland savanna, particularly in areas with abundant termite mounds. Less common in mopane woodland with harder soils. Absent from rain-forest. Found in all the habitats of the Kruger, except the alluvial plains.

Spotted/Laughing Hyaena

Crocuta crocuta

Ger: Fleckenhyäne; **Fre:** Hyène tachetée; **Afr:** Gevlekte hiëna; **Nde, Xho, Zul, Swa:** impisi; **Nde:** ipisi enamabala; **Swa:** imphisi; **Xho:** isandawane, ingcuka-cheya; **Set, Sot:** phiri; **Sot:** sentawana, lefiritshwana; **Xit:** mhisi, xitsindziri; **Tsh:** phele.

Status: not endangered

Mass: ♂ 50–75 kg; ♀ 55–80 kg. **Shoulder height:** ♂ 70–85 cm; ♀ 70–90 cm. **Distinguishing features:** Forelegs are longer than hindlegs, resulting in the back sloping down to the hindquarters. Spotted hyaena are very vocal, their 'whoo-op' call is one of the characteristic sounds of the African night, and their eerie 'giggling' has given rise to their alternative name, laughing hyaena. **Life-span:** ± 15 yrs. **Predators:** Main predator is lion. Young also fall prey to black-backed jackal, leopard and wild dog.

Front: 12 cm
Hind: 10 cm

DESCRIPTION

The yellow-grey to reddish-brown coat is covered with black spots that tend to fade with age. The muzzle is black, and the bushy tail black-tipped. Newborns are almost black; 2-month-old juveniles are grey. The neck is strong and well developed, and the jaws and canines are massive. The teeth can exert pressure of 800 kg/cm², demolishing the flesh and bones of even the largest mammals with great ease. It is difficult to distinguish females from males as the external appearance of their genitalia closely resembles those of the male. Contrary to popular belief, however, they are not hermaphrodites (that is, they do not carry both male and female sexual organs). After they have given birth, females can be distinguished from males by their two black nipples. Spotted hyaena are high-stamina hunters, maintaining speeds of 50 km/h for up to 5 km.
Scent glands: Anal and digital.
Senses: Very good sight and hearing (can hear other predators feeding 10 km away), and well-developed sense of smell (can smell carrion 4 km away).

DISTRIBUTION

Found in all the ecozones of the Kruger, occurring at high densities in the central districts, particularly in the Satara, Nwanetsi, Kingfisherspruit and Tshokwane areas. Common in the Crocodile Bridge area.

BEHAVIOUR

Predominantly nocturnal, with most activity occurring during the night, dawn and dusk; occasionally active during the day. In the Kruger, however, they are equally active during the night and day. They form clans of 3–15 or more individuals, led by a dominant female. Territory ranges vary from 30–2 000 km², with only core areas defended as territories in large ranges. In the central districts of the Kruger, the territory range is 50–130 km². Territories are marked with dung middens, with whitish anal gland secretions pasted onto grass stalks, bushes, roots and rocks, usually near middens, and by ground pawing (depositing digital gland secretions). Hyaena eat the entire carcass (hair, hooves, horns, pelt, etc.). The result is that fresh dung pellets have a characteristic chalk-white colour. Females remain in the natal clan throughout their lives, males leave at 2 years of age. Caves (50–60 cm wide and 30–45 cm high), aardvark burrows, drain gulleys and boulder piles are used as dens. Hunting is done only when food is scarce, in a team effort.

Females can hardly be distinguished from males as their genitalia resemble those of males

Calls: Contact calls include groans, squeals, grunts, whines and chatters. 'Whoo-op' calls signify a food source has been found. Alarm calls include grunts, growls and squeals. High-pitched giggles are uttered when they are being chased, and they scream and yell when they flee.

Alarm signals: Bristle the hair on the neck, back and tail. When frightened, they tuck their tails between their legs and skulk away.

Aggression: Two or more hyaenas walking shoulder to shoulder with erect posture, ears cocked, and tails curled onto their backs signify that they will most likely mob-attack the intruder. An erect tail signals attack. Other signs of aggression include snarling, growling, chasing and biting.

REPRODUCTION

Breed all year, with a peak in the summer rainy season. 1–4 (average 2) cubs, weighing 1,5 kg each, are born after a gestation period of 3,5 months, with an average interval of 1,5 years between births. Cubs are born with their teeth developed, and with their eyes open. They are moved to communal dens at 2–6 weeks, take solid food at 5 months, are suckled up to 18 months, and join kills at 8 months. They suckle only from their own mother, but all nursing mothers take turns to protect the young. Unlike brown hyaenas, adults do not bring food to the nursery den. Adult coloration is attained at 4 months.

DIET

Carnivorous: scavengers and efficient team hunters, taking practically anything. Main prey in the Kruger Park are (in order of preference) impala, wildebeest, waterbuck, and kudu. Prey is disemboweled and more than 15 kg can be consumed during one meal. The parts of the carcass that are not digested (the hair, hooves and horns) are expelled as pellets. Excess food is occasionally cached in shallow scrapes, under bushes and in shallow water. They are high-stamina hunters, and are relentless in their pursuit of prey once they have tasted blood. Water dependent, drinking daily, but can go without water for up to one week.

HABITAT

Found in many habitats, but favour open grassland and open woodland savanna. Absent from rain-forests and true deserts. Occur in all the habitats of the Kruger.

Brown Hyaena/Strand Wolf

Hyaena brunnea

Ger: Braune Hyäne; **Fre:** Hyène brune; **Afr:** Bruin hiëna; **Nde:** impisi, ipisi enzotho; **Xho:** ingqawane, ingcuka; **Zul:** isidawana; **Set, Sot:** phiri; **Set:** letlonkana, tlonkana, phiritshwana; **Sot:** thamahane, phiribjokwane; **Swa:** imphisi; **Xit:** mhisi, mhisana; **Tsh:** thsivhingwi.

Status: IUCN: NT. CITES: App. II B

Mass: ♂ 35–50 kg; ♀ 35–45 kg. **Shoulder height:** ♂ 75–90 cm; ♀ 65–90 cm. **Distinguishing features:** A rare species with a whitish mantle over the shoulders and neck. Forelegs longer than hindlegs, resulting in the back sloping noticeably down to the hindquarters. Ears erect, pointed and 14 cm long. **Life-span:** ± 15 yrs. **Predators:** Main predators include lion and spotted hyaena.

Front: 9 cm
Hind: 7 cm

DESCRIPTION

Brownish-grey coat with dark brown stripes. Long, dark, coarse hair covers the back, extending from the neck to the base of the tail. There is a lighter, whitish mantle on the shoulders and neck. The tail is dark and bushy.

Scent glands: Digital and anal (only one anal scent gland, but there are two different scent emissions).

Senses: Very good sight, hearing and sense of smell.

DISTRIBUTION

Reported in ecozones E, L, N and P of the Kruger, but reports are rare and their permanent residency status is questionable. There have been occasional reports of sightings from the southern and central districts, but reports are more common from the western border, north of the Letaba River. Additional sightings have been reported at Chukamhila Hills and at Shantangalani near Klopperfontein.

BEHAVIOUR

Predominantly nocturnal, with most activity occurring at night, dawn and dusk; occasionally active during the day. Usually forage alone, but live in clans comprising several males, females and their young. The size of the territory depends on food availability, ranging from 15–500 km². Territories are defended against other clans but no aggression is shown towards nomads. Territories are marked by pasting two secretions from the anal gland onto grass stalks, bushes, roots and rocks, at 1 km intervals. The first secretion is white and is active for more than a month; the second one is black, is usually pasted higher on the plant stem, and lasts only for a short period. Territories are also marked by ground pawing (depositing digital gland secretions), and with communal dung middens. Dung middens are characteristically 1 m in diameter and 25 cm deep. In the course of a night's foraging, brown hyaena may travel up to 55 km over their territories.

Females remain in the natal clan, but males migrate to other clans or become nomads at 2 years of age. Females only mate with nomadic males. All the clan members may care for the young. Caves (50–60 cm wide and 30–45 cm high), aardvark burrows, and drain gulleys are used as dens.

Calls: Contact calls include howls and growls. Alarm calls include grunts, growls, yells and screams.

Alarm signals: Bristle the hair on the neck, back and tail. If frightened, tuck their tails between their legs and skulk away.

This hyaena is rare and its survival threatened

Aggression: Hair on the neck, back and tail is bristled, and the ears are cocked; grunt; growl; snarl; snort; ground pawing; chasing; and biting. Known to feign death.

REPRODUCTION

Breed all year. 2–3 cubs, weighing 800 g each, are born after a gestation period of 3 months. They are born in dens, with their eyes closed and their ears folded closed. The eyes open at 8–14 days and the ears are raised at 28 days. Cubs are moved to communal dens after 3 months and are suckled by any of the nursing females. They take solid food at 3–4 months, but suckle up to 10 months and are weaned at 15 months. All the members of the clan carry food to the nursery den.

DIET

Carnivorous scavengers that eat almost anything: antelope, birds' eggs, insects, reptiles, fish and mush-rooms. Commonly seen scavenging along the Namibian coastline. Main prey in the Kruger are (in order of preference) kudu, impala, waterbuck, and zebra. 7–8 kg of meat can be consumed during one meal, and excess food may be cached in a clump of grass or in a hole, around 30–100 m from the source. May eat vegetables and fruit, mainly hottentot melons, during the dry season for their water content. Water independent, obtaining enough moisture from their food, and from tsamma and other melons, but will drink when water is available.

HABITAT

Found in many habitats, but favour areas such as arid savanna, sub-desert and desert, provided that there is sufficient cover. In the Kruger, found in the thorn veld, mopane/bushwillow woodlands as well as the mopane shrubveld and sandveld communities habitats.

Aardwolf

Proteles cristatus

Ger: Erdwolf; **Fre:** Protèle; **Afr:** Aardwolf; **Nde, Zul:** isanci; **Nde:** inthuhu; **Zul:** isinci; **Xho, Swa:** ingci; **Xho:** inyongci; **Swa:** singci; **Set:** thukgwi, thuku, mmabudu, thukwi; **Sot:** thikgwi, thikhoi; **Xit:** xithugu; **Tsh:** tshivhingwi.

Status: CITES: App. III (Botswana)

 B

Mass: ♂ 9–12 kg; ♀ 9–12 kg. **Shoulder height:** ♂ 40–50 cm; ♀ 40–50 cm. **Distinguishing features:** Forelegs are longer than hindlegs. A 15–20 cm long, wiry, dark mane stretches along the neck and back, extending to the tail base. The tail is large and bushy with a black tip. **Life-span:** ± 10–12 yrs. **Predators:** Main predators include jackals. Other predators include virtually all carnivores their size or larger, and man (aardwolf are easily stunned by torchlight and frequently run over by cars).

 H

Front: 5 cm
Hind: 5 cm

DESCRIPTION

Pale buff to yellowish-white coat (often stained the colour of the local soil), with several brown to brown-black stripes down the sides of the body, and a long, dark mane along the back. The feet, bands on the upper legs, muzzle and tail tip are black. The large pointed ears are black on the outside and white on the inside. Unlike other hyaenas, aardwolf have small, weak, cone-shaped teeth. The spoor differs from other hyaenas (4 digits on all feet) – aardwolf have 5 digits on forefeet and 4 digits on hindfeet.
Scent glands: Anal.
Senses: Good sight, very good hearing and sense of smell.

DISTRIBUTION

Rare in the Kruger, occurring in ecozones A, B, E, L, N and P. Occur infrequently in the Pretoriuskop area, along the western border of the Park, and in the open grassland areas of the Lebombo Flats.

BEHAVIOUR

Predominantly nocturnal, but more active at dawn and dusk during the winter months, when diurnal harvester termites (*Hodotermes* spp) are their principal food source. Forage alone but monogamous pairs share territories with their young. Territories, ranging from 1–2 km², include up to 12 den sites and 3 000 termite mounds. They are marked with anal gland secretions pasted onto grass stalks, bushes, roots and rocks, and with dung middens; pastings are spaced about 50 m apart. The anal gland secretion is initially a yellowish orange, but oxidizes to black.

May dig their own burrows, but usually shelter in abandoned aardvark, porcupine and particularly springhare burrows, which they modify. Burrows (32 cm high, 42 cm wide on average, narrowing to 20 x 30 cm) are occupied for 6–8 weeks and may be reused.
Calls: Contact calls include whistles, howls and clucks. When frightened, they bark explosively, growl and roar.
Alarm signals and aggression: Raise the hair on the mane and tail to increase their apparent size; bite. When threatened, eject a strong-smelling fluid from their anal glands.

REPRODUCTION

Breed in the summer rainy season. 2–4 cubs, weighing 250–350 g each, are born after a gestation period of 3 months. They are born with their eyes open but are

An aardwolf may consume up to 300 000 termites in one night

helpless for the first few weeks. At 6–8 weeks they play outside the den, at 2–3 months they take solid food and at 3–4 months they are weaned. Both parents care for the young.

DIET

Carnivorous, feeding mainly on harvester termites (*Trinervitermes* and *Hodotermes* spp). Noxious chemicals squirted by the soldier ants prevent many other species from feeding on these termites. About 300 000 termites can be consumed during a nocturnal foraging session. The broad, sticky tongue is used to lap up the termites, and the hairless muzzle prevents termites from sticking to the face. Occasionally carrion, other insects, and rodents are taken. Aardwolf are water independent, obtaining enough moisture from termites, but during the winter season, when this food source is scarce, they walk long distances to find water.

HABITAT

Only found in habitats with *Trinervitermes* and *Hodotermes* termites. Favour dry open grassland, dry and open scrub, dry gravel plains, and open savanna woodland. Avoid forests. In the Kruger, found in the mixed bushwillow woodlands, mopane/bushwillow woodlands, sourveld, thorn veld, mopane shrubveld and sandveld communities habitats.

Lion

Panthera leo

Ger: Löwe; **Fre:** Lion; **Afr:** Leeu; **Nde, Xho, Zul:** ingonyama, ibhubezi; **Nde:** isilwane, indau; **Zul:** imbube; **Set, Sot:** tau; **Swa:** libhubesi, ingwenyama; **Xit:** nghala, n'shumba; **Tsh:** ndau.

Status: IUCN: VU. CITES: App. I

Mass: ♂ 160–250 kg (Kruger av. 181 kg); ♀ 110–180 kg (Kruger av. 126 kg). **Shoulder height:** ♂ 0,8–1,2 m; ♀ 0,8–1,0 m. **Distinguishing features:** Largest of Africa's three 'big cats'. Males have a long, thick mane surrounding the face and extending on to the shoulders and chest. Whisker spots are unique in each individual. **Life-span:** ♂ 12–16 yrs; ♀ ± 15 yrs. **Predators:** Main predator is man. Young fall prey to spotted hyaena, leopard, wild dog and other lions.

Front: 16 cm
Hind: 14 cm

DESCRIPTION

Upperparts vary from tawny to reddish tawny and reddish grey; the underparts are paler. The ears are black on the outside, as is the tasseled tip at the end of the long tail. Adult males have a long tawny to brownish-black mane; it is fully developed at 5 years and darkens with age. Cubs have lightly spotted coats.
Scent glands: Anal, chin and cheek.
Senses: Good eyesight, very good hearing and sense of smell.

DISTRIBUTION

Found in all the ecozones of the Kruger, but are more common in the southern half of the Park. They are particularly common in the eastern parts of the central and southern districts in the Satara, Tshokwane, Lower Sabie and Crocodile Bridge areas.

BEHAVIOUR

Most active at night and in the cooler daylight hours, although they can be active at any time. Usually spend 20 hours a day resting or sleeping. After a large meal they can spend up to 24 hours resting. Lion form prides of 3–35 members (average 15), comprising 1–8 adult males (often litter mates) and related females and their cubs. Females usually remain in the natal pride, while males leave the pride at between 2 and 4 years of age, with litter mates tending to form life-long coalitions. After taking over a pride, males may kill the cubs of their predecessors in order to bring females into oestrus. Large male coalitions have longer tenures than individuals or small coalitions. Territory size is determined by prey availability, and ranges from 20–400 km², or more. Males mark the territory with urine and dung, and both sexes roar to advertise their territory. Roars can be heard up to 5 km away. Both sexes defend the territory against same-sex intruders. Although pride members share territories, they do not always stay together in one group. When they reunite, they shake their heads, rub their cheeks against one another, and grunt.

On average, lion travel 8 km/day (occasionally up to 25–30 km/day) in search of prey. Lionesses usually do the hunting, while pride males are the first to eat at a kill; the cubs get the remains.
Calls: Contact calls include roars and grunts. Alarm calls include growls, snarls, and roars. A full roar begins with a single growl-like bark. This is followed by a series of short, hoarse, cough-like calls, the first 2–4 intensifying in amplitude, the ones that follow gradually subsiding. A series of extremely loud coughs serves as a warning to intruding humans.

Lion (right) and lioness (left). The whisker spots are unique for each individual

Aggression: Aggression is shown by staring fixedly at the intruder, crouching, with the head held low, forelegs set wide apart, and ears pinned back or twisted, showing the black on the back of the ears. An open-mouthed gape with teeth bared is a greater threat display. If the tail is swished rapidly from side to side, accompanied by growls or coughs, the lion is most likely on the verge of attack. Other signs of aggression include raking the claws and biting.

REPRODUCTION

Breed all year, with females in the same pride often synchronizing births. In the Kruger, the breeding peak is from Mar-Jul. 2–6 cubs, weighing 1,5–2 kg each, are born after a gestation period of 3,5 months, with an average interval of 2 years between births. Cubs are born in dens or in dense cover. They are blind at birth, but their eyes open after 3–11 days. They walk within 10–15 days, and join the pride in nursery crèches at 4–8 weeks. They take solid food at 3 months but suckle for up to 6 months from any nursing female. Adult coloration is attained by 3 months. Cubs remain with their mothers for 2 years.

DIET

Carnivorous, generally favouring zebra, giraffe, warthog and antelope, but will take practically anything, including fish, turtles, guinea fowl, and carrion. Roan are the favoured prey in the northeastern Kruger, and one pride in the Park specializes in porcupines. Carcasses may be dragged into cover and the entrails covered with soil to prevent detection by other predators. Average interval between kills is 3–4 days. Prey is caught by stalking and pouncing from about 15 m away. Males require 7 kg of meat per day, females 5 kg per day; males can consume 35 kg of meat during a single feeding session.

Lion are water independent, obtaining enough moisture from the blood of their prey, but will drink when water is available. In arid regions, they may eat tsamma melons for their moisture content.

HABITAT

Favour open woodland, thick bush and scrub, and open grassland savanna. Absent from true desert and rain-forest. Occur in all the habitats of the Kruger, but are particularly common in the central plains area where there is water and abundant game.

Leopard

Panthera pardus

Ger, Fre: Leopard; **Afr:** Luiperd; **Nde, Xho, Zul, Swa, Xit, Tsh:** ingwe; **Xho:** ihlosi; **Zul:** shikane; **Sot, Set:** nkwe; **Set:** sinkwe z inqwe.

Status: CITES: App. I

Mass: ♂ 35–80 kg (weights of more than 91 kg have been recorded in the Kruger); ♀ 28–60 kg. **Shoulder height:** ♂ 70–80 cm; ♀ 70–80 cm. **Distinguishing features:** Coat is covered in black rosettes and spots that are unique for each individual. **Life-span:** ± 12–15 yrs. **Predators:** Main predator is man. Young fall prey to lion, spotted hyaena, jackal and wild dog.

Front: 10 cm
Hind: 12 cm

DESCRIPTION

The upperparts are light tawny, covered in black rosettes, and the underparts are whitish. The colour of the coat varies according to habitat: leopard found in deserts are paler, those found in forests, darker. There are black spots on the face, legs, hindquarters and flanks, and black bands on the tail; the tail tip is white. Some individuals appear completely black, but the rosetting and spotting can be seen in certain light. This melanism (i.e. black pigmentation) is caused by a recessive gene that occurs more frequently in Asia, and in forest and mountain populations. Leopard can run at speeds of 60 km/h; they are also good swimmers and climbers, and often spend time in trees.

Scent glands: Anal, chin and cheek.

Senses: Very good sight, hearing, and sense of smell.

DISTRIBUTION

Found in all the ecozones of the Kruger, but are more common in ecozone H, particularly in the riverine habitats along the Sabie, Shingwedzi, N'waswitsontso and Luvuvhu rivers.

BEHAVIOUR

Diurnal and nocturnal; least active during the hotter hours of the day. In the Kruger, there is an activity peak at night for males and for females with cubs. Both males and females are solitary and defend a territory range. The size of the territory is determined by prey availability and habitat, ranging from 8–65 km², up to 490 km² in the Kalahari for males, and up to 390 km² in the Kalahari for females. Male territories may cross several female territories, but the ranges of neighbouring same-sex individuals do not overlap. Territories are advertised with rasping grunts, and are marked with urine and dung, and tree scratching.

Calls: The contact call is a rasping grunt (made when the leopard inhales and exhales), sounding like wood being sawed. Alarm calls include snarls and growls. The growl is a single growl-like bark followed by a series of short, hoarse, cough-like calls, the first 2–4 intensifying in amplitude, and the following calls gradually subsiding.

Alarm signals: When faced with direct aggression from large carnivores, leopard may seek shelter in trees.

Aggression: Wide-eyed stare, with ears cocked and turned outwards. Crouching with head held below shoulder level. Tail twitching. A greater threat is an open-mouthed gape with teeth bared and ears pinned back, while snarling, growling and grunting.

The rosetted and spotted pattern of the coat is unique for each individual

REPRODUCTION

Breed all year. 1–6 (average 3–4) cubs, weighing 0,5–0,6 kg each, are born after a gestation period of 3–3,5 months, with an average interval of 15 months between births. Cubs are born in caves, in hollow trees, or in dense cover. They are blind at birth, but their eyes open after 6–10 days. They remain hidden for 6 weeks, and are periodically moved to new hiding spots. At 6 weeks they take solid food. They are weaned at 3 months, but stay with the mother until about 22 months.

DIET

Carnivorous, eating anything from insects to antelope, including porcupines, but show a preference for antelope in the 20–80 kg range, and monkeys, jackals, peacocks and snakes. Main prey in the Kruger are impala, but most preferred prey are (in order of preference) bushbuck, reedbuck, waterbuck, and impala. Prey is caught by stalking and then pouncing on the victim, followed by a suffocating bite to the neck. Leopard are very strong,

and are capable of bringing down prey 3 times their size and weight. Large prey, such as giraffe juveniles that can weigh 125 kg, can be hauled into trees, out of reach of scavenging lion and hyaena. Before prey is consumed, the flank and rump is cleared of fur and feathers. Carcasses are disemboweled, and the entrails usually buried. Excess food is often cached in trees or in holes. Males eat an average of 3,5 kg daily, females 3 kg. The average interval between kills is 7 days.

Leopard are water independent, obtaining enough moisture from the blood of their prey, but will drink when water is available.

HABITAT

Found in most habitats with an annual rainfall of more than 50 mm, and along river courses in areas with less rainfall. Prefer areas of broken country with heavy cover, such as rocky outcrops and mountains. Occur in all the habitats of the Kruger, and are particularly common in the riverine vegetation of the riverine communities habitats.

Cheetah

Acinonyx jubatus

Ger: Gepard; **Fre:** Guépard; **Afr:** Jagluiperd; **Nde, Xho, Zul:** ihlosi; **Zul:** ingulule; **Set, Sot:** lengau; **Sot:** letlotse; **Swa:** sinkankanka, lihlosi; **Xit:** ndloti, xinkankanka; **Tsh:** sinkankanka, lihlosi.

Status: IUCN: VU. CITES: App. I

Mass: ♂ 35–65 kg; ♀ 25–55 kg. **Shoulder height:** ♂ 80–100 cm; ♀ 80–100 cm. **Distinguishing features:** Cheetah have a sleek 'greyhound' build. The legs are long, the head small and rounded. A characteristic black tear mark runs from the inner corner of each eye to the outer corner of the mouth. **Life-span:** ± 12 yrs. **Predators:** Man has the biggest negative impact on cheetah populations through habitat modification and eradication. Young fall prey to lion, spotted hyaena, jackal, leopard, wild dog and large birds of prey.

Front: 10 cm
Hind: 9 cm

DESCRIPTION

The upperparts are tawny, covered in black spots. The underparts, chin and throat are white. The chest and anterior belly are faintly spotted. The tail is spotted from the base to half its length, then banded, and ends in a white tip. Cubs have a 7–8 cm-long mantle of silver-grey hair, which extends from the back to the tail. Cheetah are the fastest land animals, capable of reaching 100 km/h in 3 seconds, and maintaining this speed for about 200–300 m. It is the only cat with non-retractable claws.
Scent glands: Anal, chin and cheek.
Senses: Very good sight, hearing, and sense of smell.

DISTRIBUTION

Occur in all the ecozones of the Kruger, but are only common in the southern and central districts, particularly in ecozones A and D between Skukuza and Pretoriuskop, and in ecozones G and F in the Tshokwane, Satara, Kingfisherspruit, Nwanetsi, Lower Sabie and Crocodile Bridge areas.

BEHAVIOUR

Diurnal; least active during the hotter hours of the day. Males are usually solitary, but may form small coalitions, usually with male siblings. They are territorial, defending an area of 70–80 km² (100–200 km² in the Kruger, up to 800 km² in Namibia), the size of the territory depending on prey availability. The territory is marked with urine, which is usually sprayed against large rocks and trees.

Females are solitary and non-territorial. The size of their home range is determined by prey availability, and usually ranges from 55–80 km² (100–200 km² in the Kruger, up to 1 500 km² in Namibia). Although the home ranges of neighbouring females may overlap, they avoid contact with each other.

Males travel about 7 km per day within their home range in search of prey, females about 4 km per day.
Calls: Contact calls include chirrups and purrs, and a loud 'yowl', audible over 2 km away, that sounds like a bird chirping or a dog yapping. Alarm calls include growls, snarls and coughs. They bleat when distressed.
Alarm signals: When faced with direct aggression from large carnivores, they may bluff, run and hide, or seek shelter in a tree.
Aggression: Wide-eyed stare, with ears cocked and turned outwards. Slow, stiff-legged approach, with head held below shoulder level. Tail twitching. A greater threat is an open-mouthed gape with teeth bared, with the ears pinned back, while

A distinctive tear mark runs from the inner corner of the eye to the corner of the mouth

growling, snarling, coughing and spitting. May lunge suddenly, alternating this with crouching and snarling with an open mouth. Other signs of aggression include ground slapping, slapping with the front paws and biting.

REPRODUCTION
Breed all year. 2–5 cubs, weighing 250–300 g each, are born after a gestation period of 3 months, with an average interval of 1,5 years between births. Cubs are hidden in dense cover or in burrows for 5–6 weeks. They are blind at birth, their eyes opening after 2–11 days. Solid food is taken by 1 month. Cubs are weaned at 3–6 months, but stay with the mother for about 15 months. The non-retractable claws are released at 5 months. Adult colouration is attained at 10–12 weeks, but traces of the mantle are present for up to 1 year.

DIET
Carnivorous, favouring small antelope under 60 kg, but also take warthog, hare, springhare and ground birds. Main prey in the Kruger is the impala, but most preferred prey are (in order of preference) reedbuck, waterbuck, and kudu. Prey is often dragged into cover to protect it against scavengers. Prey is caught by stalking for a short distance and then chasing at high speeds. Victims are knocked down with the front paws and killed by a suffocating bite to the neck. Cheetah require 2,8 kg of meat per day, and about 12 kg can be consumed during a single feeding session.

Cheetah are water independent, obtaining enough moisture from the blood of their prey, but will drink when water is available. In arid regions, tsamma melons are eaten for their relatively high water content.

HABITAT
Open savanna grasslands, light woodland, bush, scrub and desert fringes. Avoid forests and dense woodland. Occur in all the habitats of the Kruger, but are only common in the southeastern parts of the mixed bushwillow woodland and thorn thickets habitats, and in the delagoa thorn thickets, thorn veld and knobthorn/marula savanna habitats.

Caracal

Felis caracal

Ger: Wüstenkatze; **Fre:** Caracal; **Afr:** Rooikat; **Nde:** indabutshe, intwane; **Xho:** ingqawa, ngade; **Zul:** indabushe; **Set, Sot:** thwane; **Swa:** indzabushe; **Xit:** nandani; **Tsh:** thwani.

Status: CITES: App. II ☽ B

Mass: ♂ 12–19 kg; ♀ 8–13 kg. **Shoulder height:** ♂ 40–50 cm; ♀ 35–45 cm. **Distinguishing features:** Ears long and pointed, with distinctive 4–5 cm-long, black tufts at tips. Hindquarters more developed than the fore-quarters. **Life-span:** ± 12 yrs. **Predators:** Main predators include leopard and spotted hyaena. Young also fall prey to lion and jackal.

Front: 5 cm
Hind: 6 cm

DESCRIPTION

Tawny to reddish-brown upperparts, interlaced with silvery-grey hair; faintly spotted, white underparts. Colour varies according to habitat: in drier, semi-desert areas caracal are paler or greyer; in higher rainfall areas they are darker and redder. The face is marked with black and white patches above the eyes, on the inside corner of the eye, and on the upper lip and lower jaw; the chin is white. The black ears are generously sprinkled with silvery-white hair. Caracal are excellent climbers and jumpers, capable of leaping 4 m into the air.
Scent glands: Anal, chin, cheek and digital.
Senses: Good sight, very good hearing and sense of smell.

DISTRIBUTION

Found in suitable habitat in all the ecozones of the Kruger, but are more commonly seen in woodland areas near rocky outcrops.

BEHAVIOUR

Predominantly nocturnal, but may be active in the early morning and late afternoon in undisturbed areas. Solitary, but occasionally seen in pairs. Both sexes defend a territory of about 30–65 km². Male and female territories may overlap, but same-sex territories do not overlap. The territory is marked with urine.
Calls: Contact calls include barks, chirrups and meows. Cubs twitter. Alarm calls include snarls and growls.
Alarm signals: Threat is signified by flicking, twisting or turning the ears. May seek shelter in trees when threatened by large carnivores.
Aggression: Wide-eyed stare, with ears cocked and turned outwards. Slow, stiff-legged approach with head held below shoulder level. Tail twitching. A greater threat is an open-mouthed gape with teeth bared, and ears pinned back, while hissing and spitting.

REPRODUCTION

Breed all year, with a peak during the summer rainy season in the southern parts of their range. 1–4 (average 2) cubs, weighing 300 g each, are born after a gestation period of 80 days, with an average interval of 1 year between births. Cubs are born in nests that are lined with hair and feathers, in abandoned dens, in rock crevices or in dense vegetation. They are blind at birth, but open their eyes after 6–10 days, and raise their ears after 28 days. Cubs walk at 2–3 weeks, take solid food at 1 month, and are weaned at 4–6 months.

Distinctive 4–5 cm-long black tufts of hair occur at the tips of the ears

DIET

Carnivorous, feeding on small to medium-sized mammals, and favouring hyraxes, grysbok, duiker, rhebok, reedbuck, hares and rodents. Main prey in the Kruger are impala lambs, steenbok and hyraxes. They also take birds (particularly guinea fowl and francolin in the Kruger), reptiles and amphibians. Before prey is consumed, the fur is removed, but birds may be eaten with their feathers. Excess food may be cached in trees or dense bush. Prey is caught by stalking and then pouncing on the victim, or knocking it down with a sideways strike; capable of leaping into the air to bring down birds. Males eat an average of 500 g daily; females 315 g. Caracal are water independent, obtaining enough moisture from the blood of their prey, but will drink when water is available.

HABITAT

Most areas, preferring drier savanna, brush and woodland regions; avoid sandy deserts. Occur in all the habitats of the Kruger.

Serval

Felis serval

Ger: Servalkatze; **Fre:** Serval; **Afr:** Tierboskat; **Nde, Xho, Zul:** indlozi; **Nde, Xho:** inhlosi; **Nde:** inhlozi; **Xho:** ihlosi, ingwenkala; **Set:** tadi; **Sot:** phaha, tloli, tholi, qwako, tlodi; **Swa:** idloyi, indloti; **Xit:** ndloti; **Tsh:** didinngwe, dagaladzhie.

Status: CITES: App. II

Mass: ♂ 10–18 kg; ♀ 8–13 kg. **Shoulder height:** ♂ 45–65 cm; ♀ 45–65 cm. **Distinguishing features:** Noticeably long neck and legs. At a distance, serval may be mistaken for cheetah. Comparative differences are: serval have a spotted and striped coat, a short tail, large rounded ears, and the tear stripe does not reach the corner of the mouth; cheetah have a spotted coat (no stripes), a long tail, small rounded ears, and the tear stripe reaches the corner of the mouth. **Life-span:** ± 12 yrs. **Predators:** Main predators include leopard, spotted hyaena and wild dog.

Front: 4 cm
Hind: 4 cm

DESCRIPTION

Colour varies according to habitat, with serval in moister areas being darker, and those in drier areas having bolder markings. The coat is yellow-tan and has black spots, blotches and bars on the neck, shoulders, legs and tail, and spots of varying sizes on the flanks and legs; the whitish underparts are also spotted. 4 black stripes extend from the back of the neck across the shoulder blades. A distinctive black 'tear mark' runs from the inner corner of each eye, ending before the outer corner of the mouth. The large rounded ears are white on the front surface and black on the back surface, with a white or yellowish patch in the centre. The black-banded tail has a black tip. Serval are excellent climbers, swimmers and jumpers, making leaps 4 m long or 3 m high.

Scent glands: Anal, chin, cheek and digital.

Senses: Very good sight, hearing, and sense of smell.

DISTRIBUTION

Occur in suitable habitat in all the ecozones of the Kruger, but are more commonly found in the Pretoriuskop area and on the plains of the northern Lebombo Flats.

BEHAVIOUR

Diurnal and nocturnal; least active during the hotter hours of the day. Usually solitary, but sometimes found in pairs. Home ranges cover 10 km² or more, but only core areas are defended as territories. Home ranges of males may overlap with those of several females, but the ranges of neighbouring same-sex individuals do not overlap. Serval remain faithful to their home range. Ranges are marked with urine and dung, and by rubbing chin and cheek gland secretions onto grass stems and the ground. The dry scats are characteristic, being pale grey in colour, agglutinated with rodent hair, and containing a powdery, pale grey mixture. Serval travel about 2 km per day over their home range in search of prey.

Calls: The contact call is a high-pitched 'how, how, how'. Cubs meow. Alarm calls include hisses, snarls and growls.

Alarm signals: When faced with direct aggression from large carnivores, serval will crouch and duck into cover, or may retreat up a tree. They flee by running in leaps and bounds with the tail held high.

Aggression: Wide-eyed stare, with ears cocked and turned outwards. Tail twitch-

The coat has stripes as well as spots

ing. Slow, stiff-legged approach with head held below shoulder level. A greater threat is signified by an open-mouthed gape, with teeth bared, ears pinned back and head nodding, while hissing, spitting, growling or barking. Prodding with a straightened foreleg also shows aggression.

REPRODUCTION

Breed all year, with a peak in the rainy season. 1–3 cubs, weighing 250 g each, are born after a gestation period of 67–77 days, with an average interval of 1–1,5 years between births. Cubs are born in caves, in abandoned burrows or in dense cover. They are blind at birth but their eyes open at 10 days. Solid food is taken at 1 month; they are weaned at 4–5 months.

DIET

Carnivorous, taking small mammals (particularly rodents), reptiles, birds, fish, and snakes. Able to kill small antelope, and in the Kruger, impala lambs, duikers and steenbok have been recorded as prey items. Prey is sometimes disemboweled, and excess food may be cached. Hunt up to as many as 15 times per day, leaping 4 m long or 3 m high to pounce on prey, with 50 per cent of attempts being successful.

Serval are water independent, obtaining enough moisture from the blood of their prey, but will drink when water is available.

HABITAT

Tall grassland savanna with permanent water, found particularly in areas associated with reed beds and marshes; also occur in brush near forest. Absent from desert or rain-forest habitats. Occur in all the habitats of the Kruger, occurring more commonly in the sourveld and Lebombo Mountain bushveld habitats.

African Wild Cat

Felis lybica

Ger: Wildkatze; **Fre:** Chat granté; **Afr:** Vaalboskat; **Nde:** igola, ipaka ye-Afrika; **Xho, Zul, Swa:** imbodla; **Xho:** ingada, ichathaza; **Zul:** impaka; **Swa:** imphaka, ligoya, ingcwa; **Set:** phagê, phahê, tibê; **Sot:** qwabi, tsetse, setsetse; **Xit, Tsh:** goya; **Xit:** mphaha; **Tsh:** gowa, phaha.

Status: CITES: App. II $\quad$ B

Mass: ♂ 3,5–6,5 kg; ♀ 3,0–5,5 kg. **Shoulder height:** ♂ 25–35 cm; ♀ 25–35 cm. **Distinguishing features:** Being an ancestor of the domestic cat, the African wild cat is very similar in appearance to the domestic tabby cat. It can be distinguished by the rusty brown tint on the back of the ears, distinct markings on the front legs (4–5 black bands on the upper legs, usually 2 broad black bands on the lower legs), and the noticeably longer legs with black-soled feet. **Life-span:** ± 12 yrs. **Predators:** Main predators include lion, leopard and spotted hyaena. Other predators include virtually all other carnivores their size or larger.

Front: 4 cm
Hind: 4 cm

DESCRIPTION
The coat is tawny brown to grey, with faint tabby stripes and spots. The colour varies according to habitat: it is paler in drier areas, and darker in moister areas. There is a reddish tint on the chest and belly, and a reddish to rusty brown tint on the back of the ears. The chin and throat are white; the tail is ringed with black and has a black tip.

Scent glands: Anal, chin, cheek and digital.
Senses: Good sight, very good hearing and sense of smell.

DISTRIBUTION
Found in all the ecozones of the Kruger, but less common in the southern districts south of the Sabie River.

BEHAVIOUR
Predominantly nocturnal; occasionally seen basking in the sun outside burrows during the day. Solitary, with males defending a territory range of 2 km² or more, and females defending only a core area of about 0,5–1 km². Male and female territory ranges may overlap, but same-sex territories do not overlap. The territory is marked with urine, tree scratching, and with cheek and chin gland secretions. Shelters include abandoned springhare and aardvark burrows, old termite mounds, cavities under the roots of trees, and thick underbrush.

Wild cats interbreed successfully with domestic cats, which may lead to the extinction of their currently pure genetic form.

Calls: Contact calls include meows. Alarm calls include hisses, spits and growls.
Alarm signals: When threatened, may seek refuge in trees or holes.
Aggression: Wide-eyed stare, with ears cocked and turned outwards. Tail twitching. Slow, stiff-legged approach with head held below shoulder level. A greater threat is an open-mouthed gape, with teeth bared and ears pinned back, while hissing, spitting and growling. Chasing intruders also signifies aggression.

REPRODUCTION
Breed in summer. 1–8 (average 2–4) cubs, weighing 80–135 g each, are born after a gestation period of 68 days. They are born in hollowed trees, caves, burrows, or in dense vegetation. Their eyes open at 10 days. They are nursed for 1 month and are

The rusty tint at the back of the ears and the bands on the legs are characteristic

weaned at 2–3 months. At 3 months, cubs accompany their mother on hunting trips. Adult coloration is attained at 5 months.

DIET
Carnivorous, feeding mostly on rodents, but also take birds, reptiles, amphibians, insects, spiders, frogs, fish, young antelope and hares. Since they can only catch small prey, they hunt as often as 10–20 times per day. They are water independent, obtaining enough moisture from the blood of their prey, but will drink when water is available.

HABITAT
Found in a variety of habitats with sufficient cover, such as underbrush, stands of tall grass or rocky hillsides. Avoids deserts and rainforests. Found in all the habitats of the Kruger.

African Wild Dog   *Lycaon pictus*

Ger: Afrikanischer Wildhund, Hyänenhund; **Fre:** Cynhyène; **Afr:** Wildehond; **Nde:** iganyana, iketsi leKapa; **Xho:** ixhwili; **Zul:** inkentshane, inkontshane; **Set, Sot:** lekanyana; **Set:** leteane, letlhalerwa; **Sot:** mokoto, tlalerwa; **Swa:** budzatja, budzatje, inkentjane; **Xit:** hlolwa; **Tsh:** dalerwa, litalerwa la kapa.

Status: IUCN: EN   ☼ B

Mass: ♂ (east) 20–25 kg, (south) 20–35 kg; ♀ (east) 20–25 kg, (south) 20–35 kg. **Shoulder height:** ♂ 60–75 cm; ♀ 60–75 cm. **Distinguishing features:** Owes its alternative name 'painted dog' to the rich brown, yellow, yellow-brown, black and white mottling pattern of its coat, which is unique for each individual. Other distinguishing features include the large, round ears and a very strong body odour. **Life-span:** Seldom more than 10 yrs. **Predators:** Main predators include lion and spotted hyaena (about 60 per cent of young are killed by these two predators). Other predators include leopard.

Front: 8 cm
Hind: 8 cm

DESCRIPTION

The shaggy coat is mottled with brown, yellow, yellow-brown, black and white splotches. The muzzle is black, and a black line runs from the muzzle up the forehead to between the ears. The tail has a white tip. Pups are black and white with no yellow splotches. African wild dog are high-stamina hunters, pursuing prey at 40 km/h, with short bursts of over 60 km/h for up to 5 km.

Scent glands: Digital, anal, inguinal and corners of the mouth.

Senses: Very good sight, hearing and sense of smell.

DISTRIBUTION

Occur in suitable habitat in all the ecozones of the Kruger. Common in the southern parts of the Park, in the Skukuza, Pretoriuskop, Stolsnek, Malelane and Kingfisherspruit areas; in the central districts of the Park, between the Sabie River and Tshokwane, and in the Kingfisherspruit area south of the Olifants River; in the western parts of the Park, in mopane woodland habitat; and in the northern parts of the Park, east and west of Punda Maria.

BEHAVIOUR

Predominantly diurnal, with some moonlight activity. Wild dogs form nomadic packs of up to 30 individuals (usually 10–15); the average group size in the Kruger is 10. Packs are comprised of a dominant male and female, their young and siblings. Only the dominant pair reproduces. The role of other adults is to provide food and care for the young of the dominant pair. The Kruger supports one of the four remaining populations in Africa, containing about 250 individuals.

Home ranges vary according to distribution, from 250 km², up to 2 000 km² in the Serengeti; the average range in the Kruger is 250 km². Ranges of neighbouring packs may overlap, and only the core area around the den is defended. Only the dominant pair marks the home range with urine and anal gland secretions.

Packs may travel about 50 km² per day within their home range, and will only remain in one place within their home range when a new brood arrives. Shelters include abandoned burrows.

Females, not males, migrate from the natal pack, and survival rates increase if several female siblings migrate together.

The pattern of the coat is unique for each individual

There is a characteristic greeting ceremony before each hunt, with mutual sniffing and muzzle-licking, chirping, chattering and twittering. The hunt is led by a subordinate member of the pack, and once the pack has isolated the prey, it is pursued and killed by the hunt leader. Youngest pack members eat first, subordinates last, and the dominant pair at any time. Nursing mothers depend on other adults to gorge themselves and regurgitate meat for the pups.

Calls: Contact calls include chirps, chatters, twitters and yelps. 'Hoos' are used as long-range contact calls, and can be heard up to 4 km away. The alarm call is a short, deep, growling bark. Pups whine.

Alarm signals: The marbled coat pattern of wild dogs allows pack members to blend together, making it difficult for predators to judge pack numbers and to select individual pack members for attack.

Aggression: Stalking gait with ears pinned back or cocked, and tail carried low. Pack members mob-attack intruders with their tails carried stiffly upward. With efficient team interaction, even hyaenas can be warded off.

REPRODUCTION

Breed all year, with a peak just after the rainy season. 2–19 (average 6–10) pups, weighing 300 g each, are born after a gestation period of 73 days, with an average interval of 1 year between births. Pups are born blind and naked in abandoned burrows or in holes in the ground lined with grass and leaves. Their eyes open at about 2 weeks. They take regurgitated meat from any adult at 3 weeks, and are weaned at 10 weeks. Adult coloration is attained at 6–8 weeks. Pups leave the burrow to join the pack at about 3 months.

DIET

Carnivorous, favouring antelope in the 15–45 kg range. Other prey include the juveniles of wildebeest, hartebeest, tsessebe, kudu, zebra and buffalo. Preferred prey in the Kruger are (in order of preference) impala, kudu, waterbuck, and reedbuck. Small prey are killed by dismemberment, larger prey by disembowelment. Wild dogs are water independent, obtaining enough moisture from their food, but will drink when water is available.

HABITAT

Semi-arid desert, open plains, open savanna woodland, and open bush. Avoid forest and woodland with thick underbrush and tall grass cover. Occur in all the habitats of the Kruger.

Black-backed/Silver-backed Jackal

Canis mesomelas

Ger: Schabrackenschakal; **Fre:** Chacal á chabraque; **Afr:** Rooijakkals; **Nde, Zul:** ikhanka; **Nde:** ipun-gutjha enzima; **Zul:** impungushe, inkanka; **Xho:** impungutye; **Set, Sot:** phokojwe; **Set:** phokojê; **Sot:** phokobje, phokojoe; **Swa:** impungutje, imphungushe, jakalasi; **Xit:** mhungubya, phungubya, hun-gudzwa, jajaja; **Tsh:** phungubwe, phunguhwe, phunguhwe i re na mutana mutswu.

Mass: ♂ 6–14 kg; ♀ 6–10 kg. **Shoulder height:** ♂ 35–45 cm; ♀ 35–45 cm. **Distinguishing features:** Characteristic white-flecked, black saddle, broadest at the neck and narrowing towards the base of the tail. **Life-span:** ± 12 yrs. **Predators:** Main predators include leopard and cheetah. Young also fall prey to lions, hyaenas and eagles.

Front: 6 cm
Hind: 6 cm

DESCRIPTION

In the eastern parts of the distributional range, the face, flanks and legs are grey-brown; in the southern parts of the range, they are reddish brown. The black back saddle is flecked white. The underparts are white or have a rusty tinge. The lips are white, and the tail is fringed with black.

Scent glands: Digital, anal, inguinal and corner of the mouth.

Senses: Very good sight, hearing and sense of smell (can smell carrion 1 km away).

DISTRIBUTION

Occur in ecozones A, B, D, E, F, G, I, J, K, L, O and P of the Kruger, but are only common in the central savanna districts.

BEHAVIOUR

Predominantly nocturnal, but may be diurnal in undisturbed areas, with activity peaks during the cool hours of the early morning and late afternoon. Usually sighted alone, but occasionally family packs are seen foraging together. Life-long monogamous pairs share a territory range, which they both defend. The size of the territory varies according to distribution, ranging from 2,5–20 km². It is marked with urine. Often siblings remain in the parental territory and co-operate in rearing the young, which contributes substantially to an increase in survival rates.

Shelters include self-dug burrows, abandoned (usually springhare and aardvark) burrows that are modified, dens, termite mounds and thick underbrush.

Calls: The contact call is a characteristic 'nyaaaaa' howl that ends with 3–4 short yaps. Pups whine. Alarm calls include snarls, growls, yelps and persistent sharp yaps. When they are distressed, a shrill chattering sound is uttered.

Alarm signals: Generally flee to the nearest cover.

Aggression: Direct stare with ears cocked and snarling. A greater threat is arching the back, bristling the hair on the back and tail, lowering the ears with the ears pinned back and the teeth bared, whilst snarling and growling. The tail is whipped from side to side, but is erect during attack.

REPRODUCTION

Breed in the dry winter season. 3–6 pups, weighing 200–250 g each, are born after a gestation period of 60–65 days. Pups are born in dens, burrows or dense thickets. They are blind at birth, with their eyes opening at about 10 days. They feed on regurgitated meat until 2 months and are weaned at 2–3 months. At 3 months they

The black saddle on the back differentiates this species from the side-striped jackal

start foraging. Pups leave the family territory at 6–8 months or remain in it to assist their parents in raising the next litter.

DIET

Omnivorous scavengers, feeding on anything dead, and also take insects, rodents, reptiles, small antelope, hares, springhares, fruit and wild melons. They are particularly fond of ostrich eggs. Larger prey, such as wildebeest calves, are hunted in packs. In the Kruger, the main prey is impala; wildebeest calves and small antelope such as steenbok and oribi are also occasionally taken. Black-backed jackals are water independent, obtaining enough moisture from their food, but will drink when water is available.

HABITAT

Found in many habitats, including bush, grassland savanna and light forest. In the eastern part of its distributional range, where it overlaps with the golden jackal, *Canis aureus*, the black-backed jackal occurs predominantly in *Acacia/Commiphora* woodland. In the Kruger, black-backed jackals are associated with savanna woodlands and grasslands with some scrub cover. They are found in mixed bushwillow woodlands, mopane/bushwillow woodlands, mopane shrubveld, tree mopane savanna, stunted knobthorn savanna, knobthorn/marula savanna, thorn thickets, delagoa thorn thickets, Lebombo Mountain bushveld, rugged veld, thorn veld and the sourveld habitats of the Kruger.

Side-striped Jackal

Canis adustus

Ger: Streifenschakal; **Fre:** Chacal aux flancs rayés; **Afr:** Witkwasjakkals; **Nde:** ikhanka, igowa, ipungutjha enemida; **Xho:** udyakalashe; **Zul:** impungushe; **Set, Sot:** phokojwe; **Set:** rantalàje; **Swa:** inkalwane, jakalasi, imphungushe; **Xit:** mhungubye, hlathi; **Tsh:** dabe.

Status: not endangered	☽ B

Mass: ♂ 7–12 kg; ♀ 7–12 kg. **Shoulder height:** ♂ 40 cm; ♀ 40 cm. **Distinguishing features:** As the common name aptly describes, side-striped jackals have a side stripe on each flank. The band is lighter in colour than the coat and is edged in black. **Life-span:** ± 12 yrs. **Predators:** Main predators include lion, leopard and spotted hyaena. Young also fall prey to eagles.

Front: 5 cm
Hind: 5 cm

DESCRIPTION

The coat is greyish and has a lighter coloured band, which is edged in black, along each flank. The underparts are paler. The legs are brownish grey. The tail is predominantly black and usually has a broad white tip. The snout is blunter and smaller, and the ears more round than in other jackals.

Scent glands: Digital, anal, inguinal and corners of the mouth.

Senses: Very good sight, hearing and sense of smell.

DISTRIBUTION

Widespread within the Kruger, occurring in ecozones A, B, D, E, F, G, I, J, L, N, O and P, but are not common. Mostly associated with the grassland flats of the far northern regions, the *Combretum* woodlands of the southern regions, and the tall grasslands of the Pretoriuskop area.

BEHAVIOUR

A predominantly nocturnal animal, but may be active in the early morning and early evening. Usually solitary or in pairs, but tend to hunt in packs. The territory range (0,5–2,5 km²) is marked with urine and dung. They shelter in self-dug burrows, in abandoned (usually springhare and aardvark) burrows that they modify, in dens, in termite mounds and in thick underbrush.

Calls: Contact calls include explosive 'bwaa' barks, repetitive 'nya' barks, hoots as well as yips, cackles and howls. Pups whine. Alarm calls include growls, snarls, yelps, screams and persistent sharp yaps. They emit a shrill chattering when distressed.

Alarm signals: Generally flee to cover.

Aggression: Direct stare, cocked ears, snarling. A greater threat is signified when it arches the back, bristling the hair on the back and tail, lowering the head with the ears pinned back and the teeth bared, while snarling and growling. The tail is whipped from side to side. Attack with the bushy tail erect.

REPRODUCTION

Breed in the dry winter season. 3–6 pups, weighing 200–250 g each, are born after a gestation period of 60–65 days. Pups are born in breeding chambers in abandoned burrows, in dens or in dense thickets. They are blind at birth but their eyes open at 10 days. They feed on regurgitated meat up to 2 months and are weaned at 2–3 months. They begin foraging at 3 months.

A characteristic white band marks each flank

DIET

Omnivorous scavengers, feeding on anything they find dead. Apart from carrion, they forage for insects, insect larvae, lizards and other small reptiles, rodents, snakes, small antelope (including calves). They will also catch fish in shallow waters and hunt down birds by dashing and leaping into the air. Fond of ostrich eggs. Also take fruit, maize and other organic matter. Water independent, obtaining enough moisture from their food, but will drink when water is available.

HABITAT

Broad-leaved deciduous woodland, woodland savanna and forest mosaics, all with a good water supply; avoid open savanna grassland; not found in forests. In the Kruger Park, they are found in the mixed bushwillow and mopane/bushwillow woodlands, mopane shrubveld, tree mopane savanna, knobthorn/marula savanna, thorn thickets, delagoa thorn thickets, Lebombo Mountain bushveld, rugged veld, thorn veld, sourveld and sandveld communities habitats.

Bat-eared Fox

Otocyon megalotis

Ger: Löffelhund; **Fre:** Otocyon; **Afr:** Bakoorvos; **Nde:** unga; **Xho:** impungutye; **Zul, Swa:** udlamhlo-shana; **Swa:** imphungushe; **Set, Sot:** motlhose; **Sot:** thlose phokojwe e ditsebe tsa mankgane; **Xit:** xilwa-na-ndzawo, xilwanandau; **Tsh:** phunguhwe i re na ndevhe khulwane.

Status: not endangered

 B

Mass: ♂ 3–5,5 kg; ♀ 3–5,5 kg. **Shoulder height:** ♂ 35–40 cm; ♀ 35–40 cm. **Distinguishing features:** Very large ears are rimmed with black on the upper inner portion, and are black on the back surface. The eye mask is black, and the tail is bushy. **Life-span:** ± 5 yrs, up to 10 yrs. **Predators:** Main predators are lion, leopard, spotted hyaena, cheetah and man. Bat-eared foxes are hunted extensively by man in Botswana for their fur. Young also fall prey to black-backed jackal and birds of prey.

Front: 5 cm
Hind: 5 cm

DESCRIPTION

The upperparts are grizzled grey-brown, and the underparts are tawny grey. The lower legs and tail tip are black. The muzzle is dark and there is a pale band on the forehead. Cubs have sparse grey underfur. Bat-eared foxes are very good diggers, equipped with 20 mm-long claws on the forefeet. The large ears aid in lowering body temperature.

Scent glands: Digital, anal, inguinal and corners of the mouth.
Senses: Good sight, very good hearing and sense of smell.

DISTRIBUTION

Occur in ecozone L within the Kruger, north of the Letaba River.

BEHAVIOUR

Predominantly nocturnal, with some early morning and evening activity; least active in the hotter hours of the day. May become predominantly diurnal in the cold winter months in certain regions. Family packs of up to about 6 individuals are formed, comprising a life-long monogamous pair and their offspring. Relations between pack members are maintained through mutual grooming. The territory range varies according to distribution, ranging from 0,7–5 km². Territories are marked by spraying urine directly onto bushes and grass, and with dung. Territory ranges of neighbouring packs may overlap, with different families foraging together on common ground.

Shelters include self-dug burrows, and abandoned springhare and aardvark burrows that are modified. The burrows contain several entrances and chambers, and average 1 m deep and 3 m long.

Calls: Almost 10 contact calls recorded, including a repetitive 'who-who-who', chirps, woofs, growls, snarls and yaps. A high-pitched bark is a rallying call. The alarm call is a short bark.

Alarm signals: Groups scatter in all directions, escaping predators by running in zigzags using their tails as rudders to rapidly change direction, and by darting down holes.

Aggression: Direct stare with the ears cocked and snarling. A greater threat is signified when the bat-eared fox arches its back, bristling the hair on the back and tail, lowering the head with the ears pinned back and teeth bared, while snarling and growling.

Mother and pup

REPRODUCTION

Breed in the summer rainy season. 3–6 pups, weighing 100–140 g each, are born after a gestation period of 60–70 days. Pups are born blind in burrows; their eyes open at 8–10 days. They leave the den at 2–3 weeks. They take solid food at 1 month and are weaned at 10 weeks. Adult coloration is attained at 4–5 weeks.

DIET

Omnivorous, feeding on termites, especially harvester (*Hodotermes* spp) ants; other insects such as locusts and beetles, millipedes, scorpions and spiders. Also take rodents, birds, eggs, frogs, toads, lizards, carrion and many kinds of fruits. Water independent, obtaining enough moisture from their food, but will drink when water is available.

Note the large ears and the black eye mask

HABITAT

Prefer short or overgrazed open grassland and open *Acacia* woodland, but in the Kruger, found in savannas and grasslands with some scrub cover. Avoid dense woodland, forest and mountainous terrain. Occur in the eastern grassland plains and mopane shrubveld habitats of the Kruger.

African Civet

Civettictis civetta

Ger: Afrikanische Zibetkatze; **Fre:** Civette d'Afrique; **Afr:** Afrikaanse siwet; **Nde:** insimba; **Xho:** inyhwagi; **Zul:** iqaqa; **Set:** tshipalore; **Sot:** tsaparangaka; **Swa:** lifungwe, imphicamadloti; **Xit:** fungwe; **Tsh:** dhatshatsha, dzhatshatsha, dzamatamanga, dzambaranwaha, dzambarananga, linyanganwaha.

Mass: ♂ 9–20 kg; ♀ 7–18 kg. **Shoulder height:** ♂ 35–40 cm; ♀ 27–32 cm. **Head-and-body length:** ♂ 65–90 cm; ♀ 65–90 cm. **Tail length:** ♂ 40–50 cm; ♀ 40–50 cm. **Distinguishing features:** A black dorsal crest extends from forehead to tail. The back is noticeably arched, and the head is held close to the ground when walking. **Life-span:** ± 10–12 yrs. **Predators:** Main predator is the spotted hyaena.

Front: 5 cm
Hind: 5 cm

DESCRIPTION

The coarse, shaggy coat is grey to grey-brown with black blotches and bands on the body and tail. The black and white facial mask consists of a black eye mask extending down to the cheeks, a pale forehead, and a white muzzle. The limbs are black. The tail is black on top, banded below and ends in a black tip. Juveniles are dark brown with faint markings.
Scent glands: Perineal.
Senses: Very good sight, hearing and sense of smell.

DISTRIBUTION

Occur commonly in suitable habitat in all the ecozones of the Kruger.

BEHAVIOUR

Nocturnal, and usually solitary. Well-defined paths and roads are followed within the home range. Whether home ranges are defended as territories is unknown. Rocks, trees and stumps along paths and roads within the home range are marked with the thick, yellowish perineal gland secretion. The tail is characteristically held upright when marking. Roads and paths are also marked with communal dung middens. Shelters include hollows, abandoned burrows, termite mounds and thick vegetation.
Calls: Contact calls include coughs and meows. Alarm calls include hisses, growls, spits and explosive coughs.
Alarm signals: Stare at the intruder from a sitting position with the crest flattened, then slink off to cover, or freeze motionless and lie flat. Flee with sudden changes in direction.
Aggression: The hair on the dorsal ridge is raised. Head darting. Hissing, spitting, screaming. An objectionable odorous liquid is discharged from the perineal glands to deter predators.

REPRODUCTION

African civets breed in the summer rainy season. 1–4 (average 2) cubs, weighing 600 g each, are born after a gestation period of 60–72 days. Cubs are born in abandoned springhare and aardvark burrows, in termite mounds, or in dense vegetation, and remain hidden for 1 week. They are blind and fully furred at birth; their eyes open at 8–10 days. They take solid food at 1 month, and are weaned at 3–4 months.

Civets are nocturnal and solitary

DIET

Omnivorous, feeding on rodents, insects, fruits and berries as well as small newborn antelope, birds, frogs, small reptiles, snakes, eggs, roots and other vegetable matter, and grass. Water independent, obtaining enough moisture from their prey and food, but will drink when water is available.

HABITAT

A habitat requirement is dense undergrowth near permanent water. They occur in suitable habitat in woodland and light forest as well as in brush. Also found in marshy areas. Not found in subdeserts or deserts. Found in all the habitats of the Kruger, favouring areas near permanent water, especially palm thickets.

Large-spotted Genet

Genetta tigrina

Ger: Großfleckige Ginsterkatze; **Fre:** Genette à grandes taches; **Afr:** Rooikolmuskejaatkat; **Nde, Zul, Swa:** insimba; **Xho:** inyhwagi; **Set, Sot:** tshipa; **Set:** tshipa-thokolo; **Sot:** tsipa e matheba a maholo; **Xit:** msimba-mangovo, nsimba; **Tsh:** tsimba.

Status: not endangered

Mass: ♂ 2,0–3,2 kg; ♀ 2,0–2,5 kg. **Head-and-body length:** ♂ 50–55 cm; ♀ 50–55 cm. **Tail length:** ♂ 40–54 cm; ♀ 40–54 cm. **Distinguishing features:** The tail is black-tipped (white-tipped in *G. genetta*). **Life-span:** ± 8 yrs. **Predators:** Main predators include large owls. Other predators include leopard and cheetah.

Front: 3 cm
Hind: 3 cm

DESCRIPTION

The smooth, soft coat is pale buff-grey in drier areas, reddish brown in moister areas, with black-rust spots, bars and bands. Two distinct bands extend from the inner edges of the ears to the front of the shoulders, two less distinct bands extend from the back of the neck to the flanks. There are spots and bars on the back, and smaller spots on the flanks and legs. The underparts are paler. The black and white facial markings are distinctive, comprising white patches below the eyes, white stripes extending from the inner corner of the eye to the forehead, dark whisker spots, and a white chin (the chin is blackish in *G. genetta*). The tail has 8–11 dark bands and ends in a black tip. Large-spotted genets are agile climbers and can leap distances of 3–4 m.

Scent glands: Perineal and anal.
Senses: Very good sight, hearing and sense of smell.

DISTRIBUTION

Occur in ecozones D, E, F, I, K, N, M, O and P of the Kruger; and are more common in the northern parts of the Park.

BEHAVIOUR

Nocturnal and solitary. The male home range covers 5 km²; the female home range 0,25–1 km². Home ranges of neighbouring same-sex or opposite-sex individuals may overlap, and are marked with urine, communal dung middens and perineal gland secretions. Females remain faithful to their home range.

Large-spotted genets are partly terrestrial and partly arboreal. Shelters include hollow logs, tree cavities, rock crevices, boulder piles, and abandoned burrows and termite mounds.

Calls: Contact calls include coughs, meows and purrs. Alarm calls include hisses, cough-spits, growls and screams. They 'churr' when distressed.
Alarm signals: Discharge an odorous liquid from the anal glands. Flee for cover in bounding leaps, often finding shelter in trees or in holes in the ground.
Aggression: Open-mouthed gape, head darting, snapping, and biting. Discharge an odorous liquid from the anal glands to deter predators, while hissing, spitting, and screaming.

REPRODUCTION

Breed annually in the summer rainy season in the southern parts of their distributional range, and biannually at the beginning and end of the wet season(s) elsewhere

Distinguishing features are the black-tipped tail and the white chin

in Africa. 1–5 (average 1–3) cubs, weighing 100 g each, are born after a gestation period of 70–77 days. They are born in leaf-lined nests, in abandoned burrows, termite mounds, rock crevices, hollow trees and logs. They are blind and fully furred at birth; their eyes open at 8–10 days. Solid food is taken at 6 weeks, and they are weaned at 2 months. By 6 months they are independent and catch and kill prey.

DIET

Carnivorous, feeding on small rodents, insects (especially beetles), lizards and other small reptiles, snakes, bats, frogs, fish, birds, eggs and fruit. They are water independent, obtaining enough moisture from their prey and food, but will drink when water is available.

HABITAT

Well-watered country: riverine habitats, moist woodland and forest, grassy savannas, swamps, and reed beds. In the Kruger, found in the mopane/bushwillow woodlands, thorn thickets, thorn veld, tree mopane savanna, stunted knobthorn savanna, knobthorn/marula savanna, Lebombo Mountain bushveld, alluvial plains and sandveld communities habitats.

Small-spotted Genet

Genetta genetta

Ger: Kleinfleckige Ginsterkatze; **Fre:** Genette commune; **Afr:** Kleinkolmuskejaatkat; **Nde, Swa:** insimba; **Xho:** inyhwagi; **Zul:** insimba enamabala; **Set, Sot:** tshipa; **Sot:** tsipa e matheba a masesane; **Xit:** nsimba-maxanatsi; **Tsh:** tsimba.

Status: not endangered

Mass: ♂ 1,5–3 kg; ♀ 1,5–3 kg. **Head-and-body length:** ♂ 38–57 cm; ♀ 41–51 cm. **Tail length:** ♂ 43–51 cm; ♀ 38–52 cm. **Distinguishing features:** A black dorsal crest and black lower hindquarters (both not found in *G. tigrina*). The tail is white tipped (black tipped in *G. tigrina*). **Life-span:** ± 8 yrs. **Predators:** Main predators include large owls. Other predators include leopard and cheetah.

Front: 3 cm
Hind: 3 cm

DESCRIPTION

The smooth, soft coat is pale buff-grey, with black-rusty spots, bars and bands. 2 distinct bands extend from the inner edges of the ears to the front of the shoulders; 2 less distinct bands extend from the back of the neck to the flanks. There are spots and bars on the back in some populations, and smaller spots on the flanks and legs. The underparts are white-grey, and the lower hindquarters are black in some populations. The black and white facial markings are distinctive: white patches below the eyes, white stripes from the inner corner of the eye to the forehead, dark whisker spots, and a blackish chin (chin is white in *G. tigrina*). The tail is nearly as long as the body and has 8–11 dark bands, ending in a white tip. Small-spotted genets are agile climbers.
Scent glands: Perineal and anal.
Senses: Very good sight, hearing and sense of smell.

DISTRIBUTION

Found in suitable habitat in all the ecozones of the Kruger. Occur in higher densities in the southern parts of the Park.

BEHAVIOUR

Nocturnal and solitary. Home ranges averaging 0,5–1 km² may overlap with the ranges of neighbouring same-sex or opposite-sex individuals. They are marked with urine, communal dung middens and with perineal gland secretions.

Small-spotted genets are partly terrestrial and partly arboreal. Shelters include hollow logs, tree cavities, rock crevices, boulder piles, and abandoned burrows and termite mounds.
Calls: Contact calls include coughs and meows. Alarm calls include hisses, cough-spits, growls, whines and screams. They 'churr' when distressed.
Alarm signals: Raise the black dorsal crest. Discharge an objectionable odorous liquid from the anal glands. Flee for cover, often finding shelter in trees or in holes in the ground.
Aggression: Open-mouthed gape, head darting, snapping, and biting. Discharge an objectionable odorous liquid from the anal glands to deter predators, while hissing, spitting and screaming.

REPRODUCTION

Breed annually in the summer rainy season in the southern parts of their distributional range, and biannually at the beginning and end of the wet season(s) elsewhere in

Distinguishing features are the black dorsal crest, the white-tipped tail and the blackish chin

Africa. 2–4 cubs, weighing 100 g each, are born after a gestation period of 70 days. Cubs are born in leaf-lined nests, abandoned burrows, termite mounds, rock crevices, hollow trees and in logs. They are blind and fully furred at birth; their eyes open at 8–10 days. Solid food is taken at 6 weeks; they are weaned at 2 months. By 6 months they are independent.

DIET

Carnivorous, feeding on small rodents, insects, lizards and other small reptiles, snakes, spiders, scorpions, bats, frogs, fish, birds as well as eggs and fruit. Water independent, obtaining enough moisture from their prey and food items, but will drink when water is available.

HABITAT

Found in a variety of drier habitats, including dry scrubland savanna, open savanna woodland, forest fringes, and are found particularly in rocky terrain with cover. Occur in all the habitats of the Kruger Park – although they are usually associated with drier areas, they aslo occur in savanna areas with much higher rainfall.

Banded Mongoose

Mungos mungo

Ger: Zebramanguste; **Fre:** Mangouste rayée; **Afr:** Gebande muishond; **Nde:** usikibhoror; **Zul:** ubuhala, ubuhaye; **Set:** letototo, ramoswe; **Sot:** letodi; **Swa:** lichacha; **Xit:** nkala; **Tsh:** tshihoho, tzwikitowe.

Mass: ♂ 1–2 kg; ♀ 1–2 kg. **Head-and-body length:** ♂ 30–45 cm; ♀ 30–45 cm. **Tail length:** ♂ 15–30 cm; ♀ 15–30 cm. **Distinguishing features:** 10–12 blackish transverse bands on the back, extending from beyond the shoulders to the tail base. **Life-span:** ± 12 yrs. **Predators:** Main predators include birds of prey and large snakes. Other predators include leopard, jackals, hyaenas and serval.

Front: 3 cm
Hind: 3 cm

DESCRIPTION

The long, stiff coat is grizzled grey to grey-brown, with 10–12 blackish transverse bands on the back, which extend from beyond the shoulders to the tail base. The banding is less pronounced towards the underparts. The feet are black, and the bushy tail has a black tip.

Scent glands: Cheek and anal.

Senses: Very good sight, hearing and sense of smell.

DISTRIBUTION

Widely distributed in suitable habitat in all the ecozones of the Kruger.

BEHAVIOUR

Diurnal. Form packs of 5–40 individuals, comprising 3–4 breeding pairs and their off-spring. The home range is 0,4–1,3 km², up to 15 km² in the Serengeti. It is marked with cheek gland secretions, with whitish anal gland secretions, and with communal dung and urine middens. When foraging, the pack moves together in the same general direction, but each member forages alone while keeping in constant contact with other pack members; a number of pack members act as sentries. They cover about 2 km within their home range during a day's foraging. Shelters include rock crevices, burrows, and hollow trees or logs, but they prefer old termite mounds containing several entrances.

Calls: Contact calls include twitters. Alarm calls include chatters and chirps.

Alarm signals: Freeze. Bristle the hair on the back and neck to appear larger. The group may bunch together with the young in the centre, creating the effect of one large animal, with some pack members sitting on their hind haunches to investigate the source of the disturbance. Flee for cover, often darting down holes.

Aggression: Bristle the hair on the back and neck to appear larger. Stiff-legged approach. Mob-attack, with members of the pack bunched together, and those at the front rising onto their hindlegs, while snapping, biting, spitting, growling, screeching, and screaming.

REPRODUCTION

Breed all year. Females within the pack tend to synchronize breeding. 1–5 cubs, weighing 20 g each, are born after a gestation period of 60 days. Cubs are born in nests of grass and leaves, in maternity chambers in burrows, in termite mounds, caves, rock crevices, hollow trees and logs. They are blind at birth and sparsely furred, with darkly pigmented skin; their eyes open at 8–10 days. They suckle from

There are 10–12 transverse bands on the back

any lactating female, and all adults care for the young. Cubs leave the nest at 3–4 weeks and are weaned at 5 weeks. They attain adult coloration at 6 weeks.

DIET
Carnivorous, feeding mainly on insects such as beetles, crickets, grasshoppers, termites and ants. They also take rodents, lizards, snakes, toads, spiders, scorpions, centipedes, birds, eggs, berries and fruits. Water independent, obtaining enough moisture from food, but will drink when water is available.

HABITAT
Woodland savanna and woodlands with adequate cover. Avoid forests; absent from deserts. Found in all the habitats of the Kruger, favouring savannas, thickets and scrub thickets with termite mounds.

Dwarf Mongoose

Helogale parvula

Ger: Zwergichneumon, Zwergmanguste; **Fre:** Mangouste naine; **Afr:** Dwergmuishond; **Nde:** iduha; **Sot:** motswitswane; **Tsh:** matswi.

Mass: ♂ 230–340 g; ♀ 210–340 g. **Head-and-body length:** ♂ 18–28 cm; ♀ 18–28 cm. **Tail length:** ♂ 14–19 cm; ♀ 14–19 cm. **Distinguishing features:** Dwarf mongoose are easily distinguishable from other mongoose by their diminutive size. **Life-span:** ± 10 yrs. **Predators:** Main predators include birds of prey, snakes and black-backed jackal. Other predators include large grey mongoose, slender mongoose and ratel.

Front: 2 cm
Hind: 2 cm

DESCRIPTION

Colour varies greatly according to distribution and subspecies, from grizzled tan to dark brown to dark greyish brown. The inner portions of the lower legs are darker and the outer portions are paler. The tail is darker than the body. Dwarf mongoose are good diggers. The soles of their feet are naked.

Scent glands: Cheek and anal.

Senses: Very good sight, hearing and sense of smell.

DISTRIBUTION

Commonly found in all the ecozones of the Kruger, except C. Common on granitic soils in the western parts of the Park.

BEHAVIOUR

Diurnal, being most active in the morning and late afternoon; not active in cold, overcast or wet weather. They form packs of up to 35 individuals, comprised of a dominant female, her mate (who is ranked second in the hierarchy), and their offspring. The alpha female may also mate with other males. The subordinates care for and feed the young. The pack members forage together, with a number of pack members acting as sentries. Social relations between pack members are maintained through mutual grooming.

The territory range of 0,35–1,6 km² includes 10–30 termite mounds and regularly used paths. Territory ranges of neighbouring packs overlap, resulting in termite mounds and paths being shared between neighbours. When two packs meet where ranges overlap, disputes are usually won by the larger pack. The territory is marked with cheek and anal gland secretions, and with communal dung middens that are usually located near the dens.

Rock crevices, hollow trees or logs, burrows, and particularly termite mounds are used as shelters. At the beginning and end of each day they bask in the sun near their burrows.

They have a symbiotic relationship with the hornbill: the mongoose expose insects during their foraging activities and, in return, the hornbills warn the mongoose against predatory birds. Mongoose have been observed waiting at their burrows, reluctant to leave until the hornbills arrive.

Calls: Contact calls include chirps, chirrups and twitters. Young emit peeps. Alarm calls include churrs ('tchrr') and shrieks. They also respond to the hornbill's 'wok-wok-wok' call, warning them against predatory birds.

Alarm signals: Freeze. Bristle the hair on the back and neck to appear larger. The

group may bunch together with the young in the centre, creating the illusory effect of one large animal. Some pack members sit on their hind haunches in order to investigate the source of the disturbance. They also flee for cover, usually darting down holes.

Aggression: Aggression is generally only seen in dominance displays, and involves mounting, hip slamming, slashing out at the opponent's neck while rolling or sitting on their hind haunches. However, packs may mob-attack predators: the pack bunches together with the mongooses at the front rising onto their hindlegs, while snapping, biting, spitting, and screeching.

REPRODUCTION

Breed all year. 1–6 (average 4) cubs are born after a gestation period of 53 days. Up to 4 litters may be produced annually, with an average interval of 9–26 weeks between births. Cubs are born in burrows, termite mounds, caves, rock crevices, and in hollow trees and logs. They are blind at birth and fully furred. They leave the nest when they are approximately 3 weeks old, and are weaned at 6–7 weeks.

Territories include 10–30 termite mounds

DIET

Carnivorous, feeding mainly on insects, such as beetles, crickets, grasshoppers and termites, but also take rodents, lizards, grubs, snakes, spiders, scorpions, centipedes, small birds, eggs, berries and fruit. Water independent, obtaining enough moisture from their food, but will drink when water is available.

HABITAT

Grassland and woodland savanna, brush, scrub and thickets; favouring areas with numerous termite mounds. Occur in all the habitats of the Kruger, except the Malelane Mountain bushveld.

Selous' Mongoose

Paracynictis selousi

Ger: Selous-Manguste, Trugmanguste; **Fre:** Mangouste de Selous; **Afr:** Kleinwitstertmuishond; **Nde:** iduhwa, ubuchakide; **Zul:** insengane; **Set:** kgano.

Mass: ♂ 1,4–2,2 kg; ♀ 1,3–1,9 kg. **Head-and-body length:** ♂ 35–48 cm; ♀ 35–48 cm. **Tail length:** ♂ 29–44 cm; ♀ 30–37 cm. **Distinguishing features:** Very similar in appearance to white-tailed mongoose, but only a small portion of the tail tip is white; in the white-tailed mongoose over four fifths of the tail is white. The muzzle is noticeably pointed. When walking, the head and body are held low and the tail horizontal. **Lifespan:** ± 12 yrs **Predators:** Main predators are birds of prey.

Front: 3 cm
Hind: 3 cm

DESCRIPTION

The coat is grizzled grey or tawny grey with a dense underfur, which shows as a reddish tint on the flanks, thighs and chest. The body and legs are noticeably long. The feet are dark brown-black. The bushy tail has a white tip. The prominent ears are spaced widely apart and are rounded.

Scent glands: Anal.

Senses: Good sight, very good hearing and sense of smell.

DISTRIBUTION

The Selous' mongoose is a rare species in the Kruger Park (and in South Africa, where only a handful of specimens has been recorded). It has only been reported in ecozone L, in the Shingwedzi area.

BEHAVIOUR

Nocturnal and predominantly solitary. The home range is marked with anal gland secretions, and with urine and dung middens. Shelters include self-dug burrows in softer, sandy soils, and abandoned burrows (particularly aardvark, porcupine and springhare burrows) in harder soils. Burrow entrances are usually hidden under a bush or at the base of a termite mound, but occasionally they are also in the open. Burrows are usually two-tiered structures that have two or more entrances and may be up to 1,5 m deep, with a series of passages and chambers.

Calls: Alarm calls include screams, barks and growls.

Alarm signals: Freeze. Bristle the hair on the back and neck to appear larger. Sit on the hind haunches to investigate the source of the disturbance, then flee for cover, usually darting down any hole.

Aggression: Bristle the hair on the back and neck to appear larger. Staring, crouching with open-mouthed gape, rushing, snapping, and biting. An objectionable odorous liquid is discharged from the anal glands in order to deter predators.

REPRODUCTION

Breed in the summer rainy season. 1–4 cubs are born after a gestation period that is presumed to be 60 days. Cubs are born in chambers within the burrow system. They are blind at birth and fully furred. Their eyes open at 3 weeks, and they are weaned at 1 month.

This mongoose has distinctive brown-black feet

DIET

Carnivorous, feeding mainly on invertebrates, and favouring beetles, larvae, termites and grasshoppers. Also take rodents, lizards and other reptiles, snakes and occasionally birds and their eggs. Water independent, obtaining enough moisture from their food, but will drink when water is available.

HABITAT

Open *Acacia* scrub, open mopane woodland and short grasslands, all with well-drained sandy soils. Often found in cattle pens, digging for dung beetle larvae. Not found in desert, semi-desert or forest. In the Kruger, reported only from one section of the mopane shrubveld habitat.

Meller's Mongoose

Rhynchogale melleri

Ger: Meller-Manguste; **Fre:** Mangouste de Meller; **Afr:** Meller se muishond.

Status: not endangered

Mass: ♂ 1,7–2,7 kg; ♀ 2,4–2,8 kg. **Head-and-body length:** ♂ 44–50 cm; ♀ 44–50 cm. **Tail length:** ♂ 30–40 cm; ♀ 30–40 cm. **Distinguishing features:** Distinctive, long cowlicks of fur on the throat. **Life-span:** ± 12 yrs. **Predators:** Main predators are birds of prey.

Front: 3 cm
Hind: 4 cm

DESCRIPTION

The coarse, shaggy coat is grizzled tawny brown. The lower limbs are darker than the rest of the body. The tail is black, brown or white. The muzzle is broad and blunt, and the wide upper lip is swollen in appearance, and covered in short fine hair. There are distinctive cowlicks of fur on each side of the throat, with the hair running in the opposite direction to the fur on the rest of the body. White-tailed specimens can be confused with Selous' mongoose or white-tailed mongoose. Meller's mongoose can be easily distinguished because it characteristically lacks a central vertical slit on the front of the rhinarium. The feet have only short claws, resulting in this mongoose scratching for food because it is not a good digger.

Scent glands: Anal.
Senses: Very good sight, hearing and sense of smell.

DISTRIBUTION

This mongoose is rare in the Kruger, occurring marginally in the southwest sections of the Park in ecozones A, B, C, D and E, marginally in the northern parts of ecozone L, and in ecozone N in the Punda Maria area.

BEHAVIOUR

Nocturnal and solitary. An extremely wary mongoose that lives in seclusion and is very rarely seen. The home range includes dense cover with abundant termite mounds, and is marked with anal gland secretions, and urine and dung middens.

Calls: Alarm calls include screams, barks and growls. Possibly also uses long-range contact calls (hollow sinuses on the forehead are thought to act as resonators).
Alarm signals: Freeze. Bristle the hair on the back and neck to appear larger. Flee for cover, often darting down holes.
Aggression: Bristle the hair on the back and neck to appear larger. Staring, crouching with open-mouthed gape, rushing, snapping, and biting. An odorous liquid is discharged from the anal glands to deter predators.

REPRODUCTION

Breed in the summer rainy season. 1–3 cubs are born after a gestation period that is presumed to be 60 days. Cubs are born in burrows, termite mounds, caves and in rock crevices. They are blind at birth and fully furred. Their eyes open at 3 weeks, and they are weaned at 1 month.

DIET

Carnivorous, feeding mainly on harvester (*Hodoterme*) and *Macroterme* termites, which are the principle food source. Also take grasshoppers, beetles, worms, cen-

Distinctive cowlicks of fur mark each side of the throat

tipedes, snakes, frogs and fruit. Water independent, obtaining enough moisture from food, but will drink when water is available.

HABITAT
Open woodland and grassland savanna with abundant termite mounds and dense cover; they are particularly found in wide and shallow well-watered valleys. Most recordings are from moist Miombo woodlands. However, in the Kruger, they occur in montane and grassland areas and in *Combretum* woodland. Found in the Malelane Mountain bushveld, sourveld, mixed bushwillow woodlands, thorn thickets and thorn veld habitats of the Kruger, and marginally in the sandveld communities and mopane shrubveld habitats.

Large Grey/Egyptian Mongoose

Herpestes ichneumon

Ger: Große graue Manguste; **Ger, Fre:** Ichneumon; **Afr:** Grootgrysmuishond; **Zul:** inhlangala; **Set:** leswekete, tshagane.

Mass: ♂ 2,5–4 kg; ♀ 2,5–4 kg. **Head-and-body length:** ♂ 45–60 cm; ♀ 45–60 cm. **Tail length:** ♂ 45–60 cm; ♀ 45–60 cm. **Distinguishing features:** There is a narrow strip of naked skin around the eyes. Characteristically moves in a trot with the body held low and the head down. This gave rise to its scientific name 'ichneumon' from the Greek, meaning 'tracker'. **Life-span:** ± 12 yrs. **Predators:** Main predators are birds of prey.

Front: 5 cm
Hind: 5 cm

DESCRIPTION

The coat is usually grizzled grey-brown; occasionally it is grizzled reddish brown with yellow speckles. The lower legs and feet are black and are almost concealed by the long fur on the body. The body is low slung, long and slender. The tapered, long tail ends in a black-tasselled tip. Large grey mongoose are good diggers and swimmers.

Scent glands: Anal.

Senses: Very good sight, hearing and sense of smell.

DISTRIBUTION

This mongoose is rare in the Kruger, having been reported to occur south of the Olifants River, marginally in ecozones E, F and G.

BEHAVIOUR

Predominantly diurnal, with most activity occurring in the early morning and late afternoon. In Africa, they usually occur solitarily or in pairs. Elsewhere, packs have been reported comprising a dominant male, and 2–3 females and their young. Older siblings act as babysitters for the young.

Territories contain regularly used paths that are marked with anal gland secretions, which are pasted at communal sites on rocks near the paths. Territories are also marked with communal urine and dung middens.

Rock crevices, burrows, hollow trees or logs, holes in the ground and thick bush are used as shelters. In the morning, they are often seen basking in the sun outside their shelters.

Calls: Contact calls include whoos ('o-o-o'), hoots, clucks and chatters. Alarm calls include screams, growls and high-pitched cackles.

Alarm signals: Bristle the hair on the back and neck to appear larger. Freeze, then lie flat or flee to cover, often darting down holes. Readily take to water when threatened.

Aggression: Bristle the hair on the back and neck to appear larger. They stare at the intruder, while crouching with an open-mouthed gape, and lashing with the tail. Other signs of aggression include rushing, snapping, biting, growling, cackling, hissing, and spitting.

REPRODUCTION

Breed in the summer rainy season. 1–4 cubs are born after a gestation period of 60 days. They are born in burrows, caves, rock crevices, in hollow trees and logs

This mongoose has the ability to kill poisonous snakes such as cobras

or in thickets. They are blind at birth and fully furred; their eyes open at 3 weeks. Cubs suckle from any lactating female. They take solid food at 1 month and leave the nest at 6 weeks. They are weaned at 10 weeks but may remain with their mother for up to 1 year.

DIET
Carnivorous. Known for its ability to kill snakes, including poisonous ones such as the cobra. Also take birds, small mammals, rodents, insects, lizards, spiders, scorpions, centipedes, reptiles, frogs, fish, crabs, crayfish, eggs and fruit. Water independent, obtaining enough moisture from their food, but will drink when water is available.

HABITAT
Areas with dense undergrowth near water: lake fringes, swamps, reed beds and dams. Common in flat, grassy areas of floodplains. In the Kruger, found marginally in the central knobthorn/marula savanna, thorn veld and delagoa thorn thickets habitats.

Slender Mongoose

Galerella sanguinea

Ger: Roteichneumon, Rote Manguste; **Fre:** Mangouste rouge à queue noire; **Afr:** Swartkwasmuishond; **Nde:** iwobo; **Zul:** uchakide; **Set:** ramotsibodise, kganwe; **Sot:** kgano; **Swa:** chakidze; **Xit:** mangovo; **Tsh:** khohe, khoke.

Status: not endangered

Mass: ♂ 500–800 g; ♀ 375–550 g. **Head-and-body length:** ♂ 28–34 cm; ♀ 26–32 cm. **Tail length:** ♂ 24–30 cm; ♀ 23–27 cm. **Distinguishing features:** Eyes are olive-green in young up to 6 months of age, and red in adults. The tail is characteristically arched over the back when darting across terrain. Walk with the nose close to the ground, the back arched, and the tail trailing with only the tip turned up. **Life-span:** ± 12 yrs. **Predators:** Main predators are birds of prey.

Front: 4 cm
Hind: 4 cm

DESCRIPTION

The long-haired coat is fine and silky. The colour varies according to habitat, being greyer in drier areas; and dark brown in moister areas, speckled with yellowish orange-brown. The lower legs, feet and tail tip are black. The digits of all feet splay readily, and the claws are short and sharply curved, which makes slender mongoose very agile climbers. They can scale trees at the speed of a squirrel.

Scent glands: Cheek and anal.

Senses: Good sight, very good hearing and sense of smell.

DISTRIBUTION

A common species throughout Kruger, occurring widely in suitable habitats in all the ecozones of the Park.

BEHAVIOUR

Predominantly diurnal, being most active in the morning and late afternoon; not active in cold, overcast or wet weather. Predominantly solitary. The male territory range of 0,5 km² may cross several female territories, but the territories of neighbouring same sex-individuals do not overlap. Territories contain regularly used paths and are marked with cheek and anal gland secretions, and with urine and dung middens.

Rock crevices, burrows, hollow trees or logs, termite mounds, holes under floors in outbuildings and holes in stone walls are used as shelters. They are fond of basking in the morning sun before setting off to forage.

Calls: Contact calls include 'whoos', chirps and whistles. Alarm calls include screams.

Alarm signals: Bristle the hair on the back and neck to appear larger, while threatening with an open-mouthed gape. Freeze, sitting on the hind haunches to investigate the source of the disturbance, then flee for cover with tail raised, often darting down holes or up trees. When chased, gallop with sudden changes in direction (often by bounding off trees).

Aggression: Bristle the hair on the back, neck and tail to appear larger. Staring, crouching with open-mouthed gape, and teeth bared; rushing, snapping, biting, snarling, growling, and spitting. An odorous liquid is discharged from the anal glands to deter predators.

The long coat is fine and silky

REPRODUCTION

Breed in the summer rainy season. 2–4 cubs are born after a gestation period of 60 days. Up to 3 litters may be produced annually. Cubs are born in burrows, termite mounds, rock crevices, and in hollow trees and logs. They are blind at birth and fully furred; their eyes open at 3 weeks. They take solid food at 1 month. Cubs leave the nest at 1 month, and are weaned at 2–3 months.

DIET

Carnivorous, feeding mainly on insects, but also take rodents, lizards, skinks and other reptiles, snakes (including cobras and mambas), frogs, spiders, scorpions, centipedes, small birds and birds' eggs, fruits and berries. Water independent, obtaining enough moisture from their food, but will drink when water is available.

HABITAT

Slender monogoose have a wide habitat tolerance, occurring in savanna, woodland, forest, thickets, brush and scrub, preferring areas of dense cover close to water. Also found in papyrus and forest swamps. They are not found in desert habitats. Occur in all the habitats of the Kruger Park.

Water/Marsh Mongoose

Atilax paludinosus

Ger: Sumpfichneumon, Sumpfmanguste; **Fre:** Mangouste des marais; **Afr:** Kommetjiegatmuishond; **Nde:** imvuzi; **Xho:** umhlangala; **Zul:** umvuzi; **Set:** tshagane; **Sot:** motswitswi; **Swa:** liduha.

Status: not endangered

Mass: ♂ 2,5–5 kg; ♀ 2,5–5 kg. **Head-and-body length:** ♂ 46–64 cm; ♀ 46–64 cm. **Tail length:** ♂ 31–53 cm; ♀ 31–53 cm. **Distinguishing features:** Long and shaggy coat. The muzzle is distinctly blunt. **Life-span:** ± 12 yrs. **Predators:** Main predators are birds of prey. Others include lion, hyaenas, leopard, crocodile and pythons.

Front: 5 cm
Hind: 5 cm

DESCRIPTION

The long-haired, shaggy coat is grizzled dark brown or black to reddish brown. The fur on the legs is short and sleek. Water mongoose are good swimmers, often submerging themselves, leaving only the nose exposed. The palms of the feet are naked.
Scent glands: Cheek and anal.
Senses: Good sight, very good hearing and sense of smell.

DISTRIBUTION

A rare mongoose species in the Kruger, occurring in ecozone H, and marginally in suitable habitat in ecozones L and N. Most reports are from the Sabie River, but there have also been reports from along the Olifants, Luvuvhu and Madzaringwe rivers.

BEHAVIOUR

Predominantly nocturnal, but they may be active at dawn and dusk. Predominantly solitary. Home ranges are marked with cheek gland secretions, with black anal gland secretions that turn creamish with age, and with urine and dung middens. Home ranges include well-defined paths that run along shore lines. Abandoned burrows, termite mounds, and thick vegetation are used as shelters.
Calls: Contact calls include grunts, snorts, meows, purrs and bleats. Alarm calls include screams, barks and growls.
Alarm signals: Bristle the hair on the back and neck to appear larger. Often flee to water when threatened, fully submerging themselves, leaving only the nose exposed.
Aggression: Bristle the hair on the back and neck to appear larger. Staring, crouching with open-mouthed gape, rushing, snapping, and biting. To deter predators, an objectionable odorous liquid is discharged from the anal glands while backing away or rolling in a ball.

REPRODUCTION

Breed in the summer rainy season. 1–3 cubs, weighing 125 g each, are born after a gestation period that is presumed to be 60 days. Cubs are born in nests made of grass, reeds and sticks, in burrows, termite mounds, and in hollow trees and logs. They are blind at birth and fully furred. Their eyes and ears open at 3 weeks, and they are weaned at 1 month.

DIET

Carnivorous, feeding mainly on crustaceans such as crabs, mussels, snails, but also take fish, frogs, eggs, birds, insects, rodents, lizards, snakes and fruit. Water inde-

The water mongoose is a rare species in the Kruger Park

pendent, obtaining enough moisture from their food, but will drink when water is available.

HABITAT

A variety of damp habitats: rivers, swamps, mangroves, river deltas, marshes, dams, dense riverbank vegetation, all with tall grasses or reed beds for cover. Found in the riverine communities habitats of the Kruger Park. Water mongoose are also found occuring marginally in the sandveld communities and northern parts of the mopane shrubveld habitats, in suitably damp areas.

White-tailed Mongoose

Ichneumia albicauda

Ger: Weißschwanzichneumon, Weißschwanzmanguste; **Fre:** Mangouste à queue blanc; **Afr:** Witstertmuishond; **Nde:** ubuchakide; **Xho:** ingqwalashu; **Zul:** gqalashu; **Set:** lese la motlhaba, tshagane; **Swa:** liduha; **Xit:** tlolota; **Tsh:** mutsherere.

Status: not endangered 🌙

Mass: ♂ 3–5,2 kg; ♀ 3–5 kg. **Head-and-body length:** ♂ 45–70 cm; ♀ 45–70 cm. **Tail length:** ♂ 35–48 cm; ♀ 35–48 cm. **Distinguishing features:** The tail is distinctive, being white for four fifths of its length at the terminal end. When walking or trotting, the head and shoulders are held closer to the ground than the tail. **Life-span:** ± 12 yrs. **Predators:** Main predators are birds of prey.

Front: 4 cm
Hind: 5 cm

DESCRIPTION

The long-haired coat is grizzled brownish black. The face is grizzled grey. It has an almost fox-like appearance. The legs are almost black, and the tail is white for four-fifths of its length. They are good diggers. The hindfeet are larger than the forefeet.
Scent glands: Anal.
Senses: Good sight, very good hearing and sense of smell.

DISTRIBUTION

Common south of the Olifants River in ecozones A, B, D, E, F, G, H and I of the Kruger, and occur marginally into the northern parts of ecozones L and P.

BEHAVIOUR

Nocturnal, retiring before dawn. Solitary, with the home range covering 0,8–1,2 km², and extending up to 8 km² in poorer habitat areas. Anal gland secretions and dung middens and urine are used to mark ranges. Females may share their home range with offspring, and their ranges may overlap male home ranges. Home ranges of neighbouring same-sex individuals do not overlap. Abandoned porcupine and aardvark burrows, termite mounds and holes under roots are used as shelters. 2–3 different shelters within the home range may be used during a single month.
Calls: Contact calls include whimpers and grunts. Alarm calls include screams, shrieks, growls, barks and explosive grunts.
Alarm signals: Freeze, then stand high on their legs to locate the source of the disturbance, but do not sit on their hind haunches as other mongoose do. Flee for cover, often darting down holes.
Aggression: Bristle the hair on the back, neck and tail to appear larger. Stand erect, high on their legs, with the tail waving and arched over the back, staring with open-mouthed gape, rushing, snapping, biting, growling, and barking. An objectionable odorous liquid is discharged from the anal glands to deter predators.

REPRODUCTION

Breed in the summer rainy season. 1–4 cubs are born after a gestation period of 60 days in burrows, caves, crevices, and in hollow trees and logs.

DIET

Carnivorous, feeding mainly on insects, especially harvester termites and ants, and dung beetles. Also take rodents, lizards, snakes, spiders, scorpions, centipedes

The white tail (white for four-fifths of the tail) is characteristic

birds, eggs, berries and fruit. Water independent, obtaining enough moisture from their food, but will drink when water is available.

HABITAT
Well-watered grassland savanna, woodland savanna, grassy areas in cleared forest and cultivated areas, all with thick cover. In the Kruger Park, they are found in the mixed bushwillow woodlands, knobthorn/marula savanna, sourveld, thorn veld, thorn thickets and delagoa thorn thickets habitats. White-tailed mongoose occur marginally in the southern parts of the Lebombo Mountain bushveld and riverine communities habitats; and marginally in the northern parts of the mopane shrubveld and the mopane/bushwillow woodlands habitats.

Cape Clawless Otter

Aonyx capensis

Ger: Fingerotter, Kapotter; **Fre:** Loutre à joues blanches; **Afr:** Groototter; **Nde, Xho, Zul:** intini; **Zul:** umthini; **Set:** lenyebi, lenyedi, nyedi; **Sot:** qibi, thene; **Swa:** ntsini; **Tsh:** nivho, tshiphu.

Mass: ♂ 16–28 kg; ♀ 13–20 kg. **Head-and-body length:** ♂ 70–92 cm; ♀ 70–92 cm. **Tail length:** ♂ 40–70 cm; ♀ 40–70 cm. **Distinguishing features:** The powerful tail is flattened underneath. Hindfeet are webbed about halfway; the webbing between the dexterous fingers of the forefeet is barely noticeable unless the digits are separated. Forefeet are clawless; third and fourth digits on hindfeet have nails. When walking on land, the back is arched. **Life-span:** ± 10 yrs. **Predators:** Main predators include crocodile, and man: Cape clawless otters are widely hunted for their pelts. Young also fall prey to large birds of prey and large snakes.

Front: 5 cm
Hind: 5 cm

DESCRIPTION

The coat is tan to dark brown with paler underparts. There are whitish markings on the face, chest and throat. The belly is white. The ears and nose can be closed under water. The flattened underside of the tail allows for propulsion and directional changes in the water.

Scent glands: Anal.

Senses: Very good sight, hearing and sense of smell.

DISTRIBUTION

Found in ecozone H of the Kruger, being common in the adjoining areas and in all the perennial and some of the seasonal rivers. Also found in swamps and dams throughout the Kruger.

BEHAVIOUR

Predominantly nocturnal, but they may be active during the afternoon and early evening in undisturbed areas. Solitary, or found in pairs or family clans. The home range is up to 14 km long, and includes a water body, its banks and undergrowth, and several holts (i.e. holes in the ground) dispersed across the range. Urine and dung middens that are located close to the water's edge and anal gland secretions are used to mark the home range. Cape clawless otter shelter in holts during the day, under rocks and driftwood, and in dense reed beds and vegetation.

Calls: Contact calls include chirps, growls, squeals, whistles, mews, moans and screaming wails. The alarm call is a snort.

Alarm signals: Run to water for refuge.

Aggression: Like ratel, Cape clawless otter are considered fearless. Their tough, loose skin allows them to 'turn in their skin' and bite their attacker viciously whilst gripping tightly, growling and snarling. They are also known to attack people.

REPRODUCTION

Breed all year, with a peak in the dry winter season. Peak breeding season in the Kruger is Mar-Apr. 1–2 cubs are born after a gestation period of 2 months in holes or in nests in dense vegetation, but mainly in holts. They are blind at birth, and weigh 260 g at 1 week. At 1 month, their eyes open, and they leave the nest. They are weaned at 3–4 months, but remain with their mother for 1 year.

The nose and ears can be closed under water

DIET

Carnivorous, favouring crabs. Also take crayfish, shellfish, fish, molluscs, frogs, snails, snakes, other amphibians, insects, small mammals and birds. They are finicky eaters, following elaborate cleansing routines for washing their prey before eating, and for washing themselves after meals. Being semi-aquatic, they are water dependent, requiring water daily.

HABITAT

Areas near permanent water, with sufficient cover. A fresh water supply must be available. Occur in the riverine communities habitats of the Kruger.

Honey Badger/Ratel

Mellivora capensis

Ger: Honigdachs; **Ger, Fre, Afr:** Ratel; **Nde:** ulinda; **Zul, Swa:** insele; **Set:** matswani, matshwane; **Sot:** magôgê; **Xit:** xidzidzi; **Tsh:** tshiselele.

Mass: ♂ 8–14,5 kg; ♀ 7–13,5 kg. **Shoulder height:** ♂ 23–30 cm; ♀ 23–30 cm. **Head-and-body length:** ♂ 65–75 cm; ♀ 65–75 cm. **Tail length:** ♂ 18–25 cm; ♀ 18–25 cm. **Distinguishing features:** A white, whitish-grey, or greyish-brown mantle extends from the top of the head to the tail. Powerful and sturdy short legs. Tail is held erect when walking, and the normal gait is a trot. **Life-span:** ± 20 yrs. **Predators:** Main predators include leopard and lion. Other predators include jackals and foxes.

Front: 8 cm
Hind: 8 cm

DESCRIPTION

The thick black coat has a sparse underfur. Adults have a white, whitish-grey, or greyish-brown mantle that extends from the top of the head to the tail; those of juveniles are rusty brown. The eyes and ears are small, and the ears can be closed while digging or raiding beehives. The skin is very thick and loose, especially around the neck, offering ratels great resistance to bites and enabling them to turn around in their skin to bite their attacker. They are good climbers and diggers, and have knife-like 35 mm claws on the forefeet. The soles are naked.

Scent glands: Anal.
Senses: Good sight, very good hearing and sense of smell.

DISTRIBUTION

Common in all the ecozones of the Kruger.

BEHAVIOUR

Diurnal and nocturnal, but mainly active at dawn, dusk and at night; they may be diurnal in undisturbed areas. Solitary or found in monogamous pairs. The male home range is about 200 km², the female home range about 70 km². Female ranges may overlap male ranges but the ranges of neighbouring same-sex individuals do not overlap. Dung middens and anal gland secretions are used to mark home ranges. In captivity, males have displayed territorial behaviour, but whether or not they are territorial in the wild is still unknown. They travel 35 km over their home range in the course of a day's foraging. Self-dug or abandoned holes in the ground, burrows, caves, hollow tree trunks, and hollow stumps or logs are used as shelters.

Calls: The contact call is a grunt. Alarm calls include hisses, growls, screams and roars.
Alarm signals: Bristle the fur on the neck and back, arch the back and emit an objectionable odour from the anal gland to deter predators.
Aggression: Renowned for their fearless temperament. They have a very loose and tough skin and can 'turn around' in their skin to bite their attacker. They have been known to attack wildebeest, waterbuck, buffalo and people, generally attacking and biting the scrotum. There have even been reports of ratel attacking cars and steel traps from which they have freed themselves. May feign death when caught.

REPRODUCTION

Breed all year with a peak in the summer rainy season. 1–4 (average 2) cubs, weighing 115 g each, are born after a gestation period of 6 months, in a nest lined with

A distinctive whitish-grey mantle extends from the top of the head to the tail

grass and leaves. They are blind at birth, with naked pink skin; the skin is mottled grey at 1 week. The mantle is distinctive at 24 days. Their eyes open at 3–4 weeks. Adult coloration is attained at 6 weeks. They emerge from their burrows at 2–3 months.

DIET
Omnivorous, feeding on honey, insects, lizards, rodents, birds, carrion, snakes, scorpions, spiders, frogs, turtles, tortoises, plants, roots, fruits, berries and eggs. Favour honey, and have a symbiotic relationship with the honey guide bird, which guides them to beehives. Water independent, obtaining enough moisture from their food and from dew, but will drink when water is available.

HABITAT
All major habitats, avoiding deserts and dense forests. Occur in all the habitats of the Kruger, but are not common in forested areas.

Striped Polecat/Zorilla

Ictonyx striatus

Ger: Zorilla; Fre: Zorille commun; Afr: Stinkmuishond; Nde, Zul: iqaqa; Zul: ingangakazana; Set, Sot: nakedi; Swa: licaca; Tsh: thuri.

Mass: ♂ 0,6–1,5 kg; ♀ 0,42–0,90 kg. **Head-and-body length:** ♂ 27–43 cm; ♀ 25–40 cm. **Tail length:** ♂ 24–30 cm; ♀ 25–26 cm. **Distinguishing features:** 4 characteristic white stripes extend from the back of the neck to the base of the tail. Move about with a characteristic trot, with the back arched and the tail held horizontally. **Life-span:** ± 10–12 yrs. **Predators:** Main predators include virtually all carnivores their size or larger, and birds of prey.

Front: 3 cm
Hind: 4 cm

DESCRIPTION

The black fur is long and silky. Four white stripes extend from the back of the neck to the base of the tail. The face is marked with white. The ears have white tips. The tail is white, flecked with black. Juveniles are grey. The rounded muzzle is pointed, the ears are round. They are good diggers, swimmers and climbers. The soles of the feet are naked.
Scent glands: Anal.
Senses: Very good sight, hearing and sense of smell.

DISTRIBUTION

Striped polecat are rare within the Kruger, occurring marginally in ecozones A, C, D, I, L, N and P. Sightings are more common in the south in the Lebombo Mountain area, in the central district between the Letaba and Olifants rivers, and in the north in the Punda Maria and Pafuri areas.

BEHAVIOUR

Nocturnal, usually foraging alone. Anal gland secretions are used to mark the home range, and only a core area of the home range is defended as a territory. Striped polecat shelter in self-dug burrows in soft soils; or in abandoned burrows, in rock piles, in crevices in walls, under logs and in holes under tree roots.
Calls: Contact calls include a high-pitched yapping. Alarm calls include growls and screams.
Alarm signals and aggression: Flee for cover. When threatened, bristle the fur on the neck and back, appearing twice as large, then turn their back to the attacker with the tail raised vertically or curled over the back, and the back arched, squirting anal gland secretion into the attacker's face. May feign death when caught.

REPRODUCTION

Breed in the summer rainy season in South Africa. 1–3 cubs, weighing 10–15 g each, are born after a gestation period of 36 days, with an average interval of 1 year between births. Cubs are born nearly hairless with pink skin. They are totally helpless for 1 week, but can crawl by 2 weeks. Juvenile coloration is attained by 3 weeks. Their eyes open at 4–6 weeks, and they are weaned at 2–3 months.

DIET

Carnivorous, favouring insects such as dung beetles, larvae, grasshoppers and crick-ets. Also take rodents, birds, eggs, lizards, frogs and snakes. The larger prey items are

Four characteristic white stripes stretch from the back of the neck to the tail

immobilized by being repeatedly bitten over the body, until they can be held with the front paws, and then bitten on the head or neck. Water independent, obtaining enough moisture from their food, but will drink when water is available.

HABITAT

Open grassland (favouring short grasslands), savanna woodland, forest, deserts along drainage lines with some cover, and steppe areas. Avoid moist forest. In the Kruger, they tend to be absent from forest and occur more commonly in areas where there is rocky cover. They have been reported to occur in the thorn thickets and Malelane Mountain bushveld habitats, marginally in the sandveld communities habitats, in the central parts of the mopane shrubveld and mopane/bushwillow woodlands habitats, and in the southernmost parts of the mixed bushwillow woodlands and Lebombo Mountain bushveld habitats of the Kruger.

Chacma Baboon

Papio ursinus

Ger: Tschakma Pavian; **Fre:** Babouin Chacma; **Afr:** Kaapse bobbejaan; **Nde:** indwangula, ifene yakapa; **Xho, Zul, Swa:** imfene; **Set, Sot:** tshwene; **Xit:** mfenhe; **Tsh:** pfene la kapa.

Mass: ♂ 25–45 kg; ♀ 14–20 kg. **Shoulder height:** ♂ 50–75 cm; ♀ 40–60 cm. **Head-and-body length:** ♂ 0,8 m–1,1 m; ♀ 0,5–0,8 m. **Tail length:** ♂ 60–85 cm; ♀ 55–61 cm. **Distinguishing features:** The first third of the distinctive tail extends straight up, the last two thirds fall sharply, as if broken or snapped. The buttocks have large, hairless, violet-brown callosities – they are widely separated in females, but meet in the middle, below the anus, in males. When females are in oestrus, this area becomes swollen and takes on a bright, deep red colour. **Life-span:** ± 20–30 yrs. **Predators:** Main predators include leopard, lion and spotted hyaena. Other predators include cheetah, jackals and pythons.

H

Front: 11 cm
Hind: 15 cm

DESCRIPTION

The coarse hair is olive grey-brown to dark grey-brown. The hands and feet are a dark brownish black, and the muzzle is dark. In males, the hair on the neck is very long. Infants are black with pink faces. Two subspecies occur in the Kruger. The majority (*P.u. orientalis*) are a darker grey-brown; specimens from the northern Pafuri area (*P.u. griseipes*) are more yellow in colour. Adult males have large, prominent canine teeth. While foraging, chacma baboons store their food in large cheek pouches.

Scent glands: None present.

Senses: Very good sight, hearing and sense of smell.

DISTRIBUTION

Occur widely and commonly in all the ecozones of the Kruger, with dense population concentrations occurring on the Luvuvhu and Limpopo floodplains.

BEHAVIOUR

Diurnal, being least active during the hotter hours of the day. Spend most of their time on the ground, but sleep in trees or on steep cliffs at night. Associate in troops that usually have about 30 members, but numbers can increase to 100 or more. Troops comprise one or more dominant males, subordinate males, and females and their young. The size of the home range varies according to habitat, water availability and troop size, ranging from 4–40 km². Home ranges of neighbouring troops may overlap. Home ranges are not defended as territories but troops avoid contact with one another. Troops travel 2,5–14,5 km over their home range in the course of a day's foraging.

A strict hierarchy is maintained within the troop: the dominant male(s) rank highest, and all males outrank females. A hierarchy system is also maintained among same-sex individuals. Dominant males always travel at the front of the group, and may kill a female if she encourages other males. Females stay in the natal troop, males move from troop to troop. Social relations between troop members are maintained through mutual grooming, often performed up to several hours a day.

Troops often associate with herds of other animals, acting as watch-dogs. They very commonly associate with impala and bushbuck, which feed on fruits dropped by the baboons.

Baboons are omnivorous – they feed on almost anything

Calls: Over 30 vocalizations have been recorded. Contact calls include chatters, grunts, growls, shrieks and a distinctive 'wa-hoo' bark. Alarm calls include a short, sharp yak.

Alarm signals: When startled, they shrug their shoulders, wipe their muzzles and grin. When threatened, will flee to trees if they are nearby, otherwise troop members will gather together, with the leaders and males on the outside, the males being the first to approach the intruder.

Aggression: Threat is displayed with a direct stare. A greater threat is raising the eyebrows, showing the contrasting white eyelids, and an open-mouthed gape or yawn, both of which display the long canines. The hair may be bristled. Other threat displays include slapping the hands and feet on the ground, throwing dirt, shaking branches, snarling, squealing, and screaming. If these fail, attack may follow. Baboons are known to take on lions.

REPRODUCTION
Breed all year. A single infant, weighing 750–950 g, is born after a gestation period of 6 months. The mother seeks cover to give birth, often with other females keeping watch. The infant clings to its mother's underside almost immediately, while she holds it with one arm. At 5–6 weeks, the infant rides on her back, clinging to her with all its limbs. By 3 months, it sits upright on her back. At 4–6 months it starts playing with other juveniles. It is weaned at 6–8 months.

DIET
Omnivorous, feeding on almost anything: grass, bulbs, fruits, flowers, leaves, seeds, tubers, lichens, mushrooms, lizards, rodents, insects, spiders, scorpions, small mammals, fish, birds and eggs. Fond of marula berries. Will dig for corms and rhizomes. In the Kruger, baboons have been reported killing small mammals, such as the lambs of impala, duiker, bushbuck and nyala, as well as hares. Water dependent, drinking daily. They will dig for water in dry riverbeds.

HABITAT
Rocky regions and open woodland with a water supply. Occur in all the habitats of the Kruger.

Vervet/Green Monkey

Cercopithecus a. pygerythrus

Ger: Südafrikanische Grüne Meerkatze; **Fre:** Vervet; **Afr:** Blouaap; **Nde, Xho, Zul, Swa:** inkawu; **Nde:** ikgabu ehlaza; **Swa:** ngobiyane, ingobiyane; **Set, Sot:** kgabo; **Set:** kgatla; **Sot:** khabo; **Xit:** nkawu, hacha, ritoho, ritohwe; **Tsh:** thoho, thobo.

Status: not endangered

Mass: ♂ 3,5–9,0 kg; ♀ 3,5–5,5 kg. **Head-and-body length:** ♂ 50–65 cm; ♀ 38–62 cm. **Tail length:** ♂ 60–75 cm; ♀ 48–65 cm. **Distinguishing features:** Adult males have a distinct pale blue scrotum; that of the alpha male has the deepest coloration. **Life-span:** ± 15–20 yrs. **Predators:** Main predators include lion, leopard, spotted hyaena, cheetah, jackals and serval. Other predators include large eagles, pythons, crocodile and baboon.

H

Front: 6 cm
Hind: 8 cm

DESCRIPTION

Coarse, longish hair covers the torso. The colour varies according to distribution: grizzled silver-grey to a yellowish reddish green. The underparts are whitish. The black face is rimmed with whitish hair, and the eyelids are pink. The upper surfaces of the hands and feet are covered with short black hair. Infants are black with a pink face. The tail is well developed, and is used for balance; it is not adapted for grasping, seizing, etc. Vervet monkeys are good swimmers.
Scent glands: Chest.
Senses: Very good sight, hearing and sense of smell.

DISTRIBUTION

Common and widespread throughout all the ecozones of the Kruger, with high densities occurring in the riparian growth along waterways, and in woodland and forest near water.

BEHAVIOUR

Diurnal. Not strictly arboreal; time is spent both on the ground and in trees, but they sleep in trees at night. They usually form troops consisting of under 20 members, but occasionally larger groups are encountered. Troops are comprised of a dominant male, with subordinate males, females and young. The dominant male does not exercise tight control over the troop. Troops are territorial, defending a range of 0,1–1 km². Females stay in the natal troop, males move from troop to troop.

Social relations between troop members are maintained through mutual grooming, often performed up to several hours daily. Troops often associate with samango monkey troops.
Calls: Over 35 vocalizations have been recorded. Contact calls include chirps, grunts, chatters and barks. Alarm calls include a low, loud bark and screams. Different calls signify different threats, for example, a short tonal call – leopard, low staccato grunt – eagle, high-pitched chutter – snakes.
Alarm signals: Generally flee to trees when threatened.
Aggression: The more the tail is looped over the back, the more confident the monkey is. Threat is displayed with a direct stare. A greater threat is raising the eyebrows to show the contrasting pink eyelids, and an open-mouthed gape. Other threats include shaking branches, jumping up and down, slapping the ground and/or branches, bobbing the head up and down, lunging forward and striking. Dominant males may give a 'red, white and blue' display to a subordinate male:

Mother suckling her offspring

holding the tail erect whilst strutting in front of the other male, displaying its blue scrotum, red perianal region and white fur between the scrotum and perianal region. Males may attack small predators.

REPRODUCTION
Breed all year, but in the Kruger there is a definite summer peak. A single infant, weighing 300–400 g, is born after a gestation period of 5 months. The infant clings to its mother's underside almost immediately, while she holds it with one arm. At 5–6 weeks, the infant rides on her back, clinging to her with all its limbs. By 3 months it rides upright, and at 4 months it starts playing with other juveniles. Adult coloration is attained at 3 months, and the infant is weaned at 6 months.

DIET
Omnivorous, feeding on fruit, leaves, seeds, roots, flowers, insects, birds, small reptiles and eggs. Water dependent, drinking regularly when water is available. Water requirements vary according to distribution: from drinking every few days, to very rarely when enough moisture is obtained from food and dew.

HABITAT
Woodlands, woodland savanna and forest-grassland mosaics, favouring *Acacia*-dominated woodland adjacent to grasslands and riverine areas. Occur in all the habitats of the Kruger, primarily in savanna, forest-savanna transition and riparian growth areas.

Samango/Blue Monkey

Cercopithecus n. mitis

Ger: Diadem Meerkatze; **Fre:** Cercopithèque à diadème; **Afr:** Samango-aap; **Nde, Zul, Swa:** insimango; **Nde:** ikgabu; **Xho:** intsimango; **Set:** tshwene; **Xit:** ndlandlama; **Tsh:** dulu.

Status: not endangered

Mass: ♂ 8–12 kg; ♀ 3,5–5,2 kg. **Head-and-body length:** ♂ 48–70 cm; ♀ 43–52 cm. **Tail length:** ♂ 78–87 cm; ♀ 66–74 cm. **Distinguishing features:** Tail is well adapted for an arboreal lifestyle. **Life–span:** ± 15–20 yrs. **Predators:** Main predators include leopard and python (and the golden cat outside of southern Africa). Other predators include crested and crowned eagles.

H

Front: 7 cm
Hind: 9 cm

DESCRIPTION
Longish, coarse hair covers the torso. The colour varies according to distribution: grizzled blue-grey to reddish blue-grey. The blue-black face is rimmed with grizzled bluish-grey hair. The limbs and tail are brown-black. The upper surfaces of the hands and feet are covered with short black hair. Eastern populations have white lips and a white throat. Infants are black with a pink face.
Scent glands: None present.
Senses: Very good sight, hearing and sense of smell.

DISTRIBUTION
Occur marginally in the extreme northern parts of ecozones H, L, M and N of the Kruger, along the banks of the Luvuvhu River at Pafuri.

BEHAVIOUR
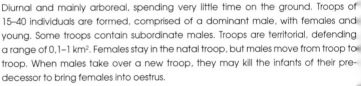
Diurnal and mainly arboreal, spending very little time on the ground. Troops of 15–40 individuals are formed, comprised of a dominant male, with females and young. Some troops contain subordinate males. Troops are territorial, defending a range of 0,1–1 km². Females stay in the natal troop, but males move from troop to troop. When males take over a new troop, they may kill the infants of their predecessor to bring females into oestrus.

Social relations between troop members are maintained through mutual grooming, often performed up to several hours daily. Samango monkeys often sun themselves in the morning for up to an hour before setting off to forage.

Troops often associate with troops of other primates, such as black and white colobus monkeys, red-tail monkeys, mangabeys (in rain-forests) and vervet monkeys (in savannas).

Calls: A wide range of contact calls has been recorded, including croaks, grunts growls and deep booms uttered by males as a rallying call. Alarm calls include a 125 Hz low, but loud 'pyow' bark, which is usually given by the dominant male. The call is followed by a series of after-pulses. All members chirp and click to signal alarm.

Alarm signals: Generally flee to trees when threatened by a ground predator, and scurry to the ground to escape avian predators.

Aggression: Threat is displayed with a direct stare. A greater threat is raising the eyebrows to show the contrasting pink eyelids, and an open-mouthed gape. Other threats include shaking branches, jumping up and down, slapping the ground and/or branches, bobbing the head up and down, lunging forward and striking.

Mother and infant – note the long hair cover

REPRODUCTION

Breed in the summer rainy season. A single infant, weighing 400 g, is born after a gestation period of 4,5 months, with an average interval of 2 years between births. The infant clings to its mother's underside almost immediately, while she holds it with one arm. At 5–6 weeks the infant rides on her back, clinging to her with all its limbs. By 3 months it rides upright, and at 4 months it starts playing with other juveniles. Adult coloration is attained at 2 months. The infant is weaned at 6 months.

DIET

Omnivorous, feeding on fruit, leaves, seeds, flowers, sprouts, buds, gum, insects and small mammals. Water dependent, drinking regularly.

HABITAT

Rain-forests, secondary forests, woodlands and woodland savanna. Not strictly arboreal. In the Kruger, found in the gallery forests of the mopane shrubveld, alluvial plains, sandveld and riverine communities habitats.

Thick-tailed Bushbaby

Otolemur crassicaudatus

Ger: Riesengalago; **Fre:** Galago à queue épaisse; **Afr:** Bosnagaap; **Nde:** impukunyoni; **Zul:** sinkwe; **Xit:** xidweta.

Mass: ♂ 0,9–1,6 kg; ♀ 0,9–1,45 kg. **Head-and-body length:** ♂ 27–47 cm; ♀ 27–47 cm. **Tail length:** ♂ 36–45 cm; ♀ 35–45 cm. **Distinguishing features:** Dark rings around eyes. The bushy tail is longer than the body. Move on all fours, instead of hopping along like other bushbabies. In torchlight, the eyes characteristically shine red. **Life-span:** ± 4 yrs. **Predators:** Main predators include civet, genets and large owls. Other predators include serval, African wild cats and snakes.

H

Front: 3 cm
Hind: 5 cm

DESCRIPTION

The woolly coat is long, soft, and thick. The upperparts are grey-brown or brown and the underparts paler. There are dark rings around the eyes, and the dark grey ears are naked. There are flattened discs of soft, thickened skin on the tips of all the digits and on the palms of the hands. Each digit has a nail except the second digit on the feet, which is equipped with a claw. Thick-tailed bushbabies are very good jumpers, leaping as far as 2,5 m and as high as 2 m in one jump. The head can be rotated almost 180 degrees.

Scent glands: Chest, lips, cheeks and perineal.

Senses: Very good sight, hearing and sense of smell.

DISTRIBUTION

Occur sparsely in forested areas of ecozones B, C, D, F, N and M of the Kruger.

BEHAVIOUR

Nocturnal, with an activity peak during the first 2 hours after sunset. Arboreal. They forage alone but sleep in unrelated groups of 6–7 individuals. Both sexes are territorial, with males holding a territory of 0,2 km², and females 0,07 km². The territory range of males may cross those of several females, but the territories of neighbouring males do not overlap. During the non-breeding season, subordinate males may be tolerated in the dominant male's territory. The territory ranges of neighbouring females may overlap. Females tend to remain in the same territory, while males tend to move annually.

Territories are marked by urine washing: bushbabies lean to one side and urinate over their feet, then lean to the other side and repeat the process, thereby leaving urine scent on all their feet. Territories are also marked with lip, cheek, perineal and oily, yellowish chest gland secretions.

Thick-tailed bushbabies sleep in broad-leaved nests in dense vegetation, tree forks, hollow trees, and in old birds' nests. A large amount of time is spent on mutual grooming before setting off to forage.

Calls: Contact calls include squeaks, clicks, croaks and barks. Alarm calls include squeaks, shrill whistles, chirps, chatters, yaps, yells, moans and mournful screaming cries, similar to that of a human baby (hence the common name).

Alarm signals: When excited, rub the short, horny combs on the outer edge of the soles of the feet against substrates, producing a grating sound. Great leaps of flight are made to escape predators.

Aggression: Eyes wide and staring, ears cocked, open-mouthed gape with teeth

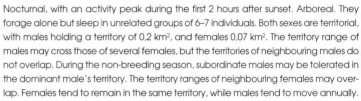

A distinguishing feature is the dark ring surrounding each eye

...pared, growling and spitting. May stand on the hind-
...egs with hands raised, ready to grab and bite.

REPRODUCTION

...reed in the summer rainy season. 2–3 infants, weigh-
...ng 45 g each, are born in a leafy nest after a gesta-
...ion period of 4,3 months. At birth, their eyes are open
...and they are fully furred; within an hour they can
...crawl. After staying in the nest for 2 weeks, the infants
...are transported in their mother's mouth or ride
...around on her back. At 25 days, they follow their
...mother everywhere. Solid food is taken at 1 month,
...and they are weaned at 2,5–3 months.

DIET

Omnivorous, feeding mainly on fruits and flowers, but
also take insects, seeds, gum, small birds, lizards and
eggs. Water independent, obtaining enough moisture from their food.

HABITAT

Dense forest (*Miombo*, coastal and montane), bushland and woodland savanna, favouring trees with
little grass around them. In the Kruger, found in the
forested areas of the Malelane Mountain bushveld,
thorn thickets, knobthorn/marula savanna, sourveld,
alluvial plains and sandveld communities habitats.

Lesser Bushbaby

Galago moholi

Ger: Moholigalago; **Fre:** Galago moholi; **Afr:** Nagapie; **Nde:** impukunyoni; **Set:** mogwele; **Sot:** maselale-ntlwë; **Xit:** mhimbi; **Tsh:** tshimondi.

Mass: ♂ 150–230 g; ♀ 150–180 g. **Head-and-body length:** ♂ 9–20 cm; ♀ 8–20 cm. **Tail length:** ♂ 20–26 cm; ♀ 19–25 cm. **Distinguishing features:** Dark rings around the eyes and a white stripe on the nose. The bushy tail is longer than the body length. Due to the long upper hindquarters, these bushbabies move with a kangaroo-like gait. In torchlight, the eyes characteristically shine red. **Life–span:** ± 4 yrs. **Predators:** Main predators include virtually all carnivores their size or larger, and birds of prey. Other predators include snakes.

H

Front: 3 cm
Hind: 5 cm

DESCRIPTION

The woolly coat is long, soft, and thick. The upperparts are grey to grey-brown and the tail is darker. The underparts are paler than the upperparts. The limbs and feet are yellowish. There are dark rings around the eyes and a white nose stripe. There are flattened discs of soft, thickened skin on the tips of all the digits and on the palms of the hands. Each digit has a nail except the second digit on the feet, which is equipped with a claw. Lesser bushbabies are very good jumpers, leaping as far as 5–7 m in one jump. The head can be rotated almost 180 degrees.

Scent glands: Chest, lips, cheeks and perineal.

Senses: Very good sight, hearing and sense of smell.

DISTRIBUTION

Although not common, lesser bushbabies are widely distributed in the woodland and woodland savanna regions of ecozones A, D, E, G, H, J, K, L, N and O of the Kruger.

BEHAVIOUR

Nocturnal, with an activity peak during the first 2 hours after sunset. Arboreal. They forage alone but sleep in unrelated groups of 6–7 individuals. Both sexes are territorial. Males hold a territory range of 0,1–2,3 km², females 0,04–1 km². The territory range of males may cross those of several females, but the territories of neighbouring males do not overlap. During the non-breeding season, subordinate males may be tolerated in the dominant male's territory. The territory ranges of neighbouring females may overlap. Females tend to remain in the same territory, while males tend to move annually.

Territories are marked by urine washing: bushbabies lean to one side and urinate over their feet, then lean to the other side and repeat the process, thereby leaving urine scent on all their feet. Territories are also marked with lip, cheek, perineal and oily, yellowish chest gland secretions.

Lesser bushbabies sleep in broad-leaved nests in dense vegetation, tree forks, hollow trees, and in old birds' nests. A large amount of time is spent on mutual grooming before setting off to forage.

Calls: Contact calls include croaks, clicks, squeaks, coos and barks. Alarm calls include sobs, chatters, rasps, grunts, shrill whistles, yaps, wails and mournful screaming cries, similar to that of a human baby (hence the common name).

A distinguishing feature is the white stripe on the nose

Alarm signals: When excited, rub the short, horny combs on the outer edge of the soles of the feet against substrates, producing a grating sound. Great leaps of flight are made to escape predators.

Aggression: Eyes wide and staring, ears cocked, open-mouthed gape with teeth bared, and ready to bite. May mob-attack.

REPRODUCTION

Breed biannually, at the beginning and end of the summer rainy season. 2 infants, weighing 9–12 g each, are born in a leafy nest after a gestation period of 4 months. At birth, their eyes are open and they are fully furred; within an hour they can crawl. After spending 2 weeks in the nest, the infants are transported in their mother's mouth or ride around on her back. At 25 days, they follow her everywhere. They take solid food at 1 month, and are weaned at 2,5–3 months.

DIET

Omnivorous, feeding mainly on insects (1–2 g daily), favouring grasshoppers, and on tree sap and gum. Also take fruits, seeds, flowers, small birds and eggs. Water independent, obtaining enough moisture from their food.

HABITAT

Open savanna woodland, especially *Acacia* woodland; bushland; riverine habitats; favouring trees with little grass around them. In the Kruger, the lesser bushbaby are particularly associated with *Acacia* savannas, especially *A. tortilis* and *A. welwitschii*. Occur in the mixed bushwillow woodlands, tree mopane savanna, stunted knobthorn savanna, sourveld, rugged veld, mopane shrubveld, thorn veld, thorn thickets, delagoa thorn thickets, and the riverine and sandveld communities habitats of the Kruger Park.

Cape Pangolin/Scaly Anteater

Manis temminckii

Ger: Schuppentier; **Fre:** Pangolin de Temminck; **Afr:** letermagog; **Nde:** inkakha; **Set, Sot:** kgaga; **Swa:** imfinyezi; **Xit:** xikwaru; **Tsh:** khwara.

Status: IUCN: NT, CITES: App. II

☽ B

Mass: ♂ 15–18 kg; ♀ 15–18 kg. **Head-and-body length:** ♂ 35–60 cm; ♀ 35–60 cm. **Tail length:** ♂ 31–45 cm; ♀ 31–45 cm. **Distinguishing features:** Unmistakable as they resemble an enormous pine cone with their large brown, overlapping scales. The head is very small and pointed. **Life-span:** ± 20 yrs. **Predators:** Main predator is man. The flesh is considered a delicacy among indigenous populations. The claws and scales are used in medicines and as charms. If worn around the neck, pangolin scales are thought to prevent malaria. The Cape pangolin is known as 'bwana mganga' or 'bwana doctor' in East Africa because every part of the body is said to have healing properties. Pangolin are often killed by electric fences. Other predators include leopard, lion, pythons and hyaena.

F

H

Front: 3 cm
Hind: 6 cm

DESCRIPTION

Large, brown, overlapping scales cover the head and sides of the body and extend down the back to just before the tip of the tail. The face, throat, belly and inner surfaces of the limbs lack scales and are sparsely covered with dark fur. The scales are derived from the dermis and are composed of agglutinated hairs. Pangolin walk on their well-developed hindfeet with the forefeet tucked under the chin, the tail lifted off the ground and the back distinctly arched. The tongue is longer than the head and body length. Part of the tongue folds back into a throat pouch when it is not extended. Pangolin have no teeth. The nostrils and ears can be closed, preventing sand, ants and termites from entering while the animal forages. Pangolin are good swimmers and strong diggers. The 3 middle claws of the forefeet are sharply curved; the central claw is the longest at 4,5 cm.
Scent glands: Anal.
Senses: Poor sight, good hearing and very good sense of smell.

DISTRIBUTION

Widely but patchily distributed, occurring in all the ecozones of the Kruger, wherever termitaria are found.

BEHAVIOUR

Predominantly nocturnal, but they may be active during the day. Solitary, with home ranges of 1,3–8 km² defended as territories. The male territory range may overlap those of several neighbouring females, but the territory ranges of neighbouring same-sex individuals do not overlap. Territory ranges are marked with anal gland secretions, and with dung and urine.

Although capable of digging, Cape pangolin prefer to shelter in abandoned aardvark and springhare burrows, abandoned hyaena dens, and caves and piles of debris. Every few weeks they move within their territory range, allowing ants and termites to rebuild their nests. They may travel up to 6 km over the territory range in the course of a night's foraging.
Calls: Contact calls include snorts, grunts, puffs and hisses. Alarm calls include snorts.
Alarm signals: Freeze at the slightest disturbance. If threatened, roll into a tight ball and raise the scales.

The large brown scales covering the body render this species unmistakable

Aggression: If the attacker attempts to unroll it, the pangolin lashes out with the tail, using it as a club and attempting to inflict cuts on its attacker with the razor sharp scales. A stream of objectionable, odorous anal gland secretion may be squirted at the attacker.

REPRODUCTION

Breed during the dry winter season. A single cub, weighing 300–400 g, is born after a gestation period of 4,5 months. The cub is brown and covered with soft scales that do not overlap. The scales start to harden after a few days. At about 1 month, the mother starts carrying the cub on her back and tail. At 3 months, the cub is weaned and starts taking solid food; at 5 months it is independent. Females may adopt the orphaned young of other females.

DIET

Insectivorous, consuming 140–200 g of ants and termites daily, favouring *Trimerviterme, Macroterme, Microterme, Odontoterme, Mictroceroterme, Amiterme* and *Ancistroterme* spp. Ingested soil and gravel aid digestion in the gizzard-like stomach. Water dependent, drinking regularly.

HABITAT

Many habitats, favouring sandy soils in woodland, savanna and grasslands, avoiding forest and true sandy desert. Occur in all the habitats of the Kruger, wherever termitaria occur.

Scrub Hare

Lepus saxatilis

Ger: Buschhase; **Fre:** Lièvre des buissons; **Afr:** Kolhaas; **Nde, Xho:** umvundla; **Zul:** unogwaja; **Set:** mmutlwa; **Sot:** mofuli; **Swa:** logwatja; **Xit:** mpfundla; **Tsh:** muvhuda, khomu.

Status: not endangered ☽ B

Mass: ♂ 2,5–4 kg; ♀ 2–4,5 kg. **Head-and-body length:** ♂ 39–50 cm; ♀ 40–51 cm. **Tail length:** ♂ 11–17 cm; ♀ 15–17,5 cm. **Distinguishing features:** Unlike the Cape hare, the underparts are all white. As in all rabbits and hares, the hindlegs are well developed. **Life-span:** ± 5 yrs. **Predators:** Main predators include virtually all carnivores their size or larger, birds of prey, snakes and monitors.

Front: 2 cm
Hind: 3 cm

DESCRIPTION

The fur is soft and silky. It is variable in colour, but is generally greyish brown with black flecking. The chest is paler than the upperparts, and the underparts are white. The legs and sides are reddish brown. The black, fluffy tail is white underneath. The length of the ears is approximately 11–15 cm. When they are erected, a network of radiating veins on the inner surface aids the hare in lowering its body temperature. Scrub hare are very fast runners, reaching speeds up to 70 km/h.

Scent glands: Anal and inguinal. Males also have chin glands.

Senses: Good sight (360 degree vision), very good hearing, and good sense of smell.

DISTRIBUTION

Occur commonly and widely in suitable habitat in all the ecozones of the Kruger, except in mountainous regions.

BEHAVIOUR

Predominantly nocturnal, but they may be active in the early morning and late afternoon, particularly in overcast weather. Activity increases on warmer nights, and they lie up in wet weather. Scrub hare are solitary. Male and female home ranges may overlap, but home ranges of neighbouring same-sex individuals do not overlap. Only core areas within the ranges are defended as territories. Home ranges are marked with dung and urine, and with anal, inguinal and chin gland secretions. Regular trails are followed within the home range.

During the day, scrub hare lie up in scratched-out depressions, called forms, in bush or thickets, with their ears resting on their backs.

Calls: Contact calls include loud chirps, growls, grunts and bleats. Alarm calls include screams and squeals.

Alarm signals: Stamp the ground with the hindfeet. Freeze, then dart away in leaping bounds, fleeing in zigzags, with the ears held back over the body.

Aggression: Drumming the ground with the forefeet, stamping the ground with the hindfeet, grinding the teeth and growling. Rearing up and boxing with the forefeet. If caught, will bite and kick with the hindfeet.

REPRODUCTION

Breed all year, with a peak in the summer rainy season. 1–3 leverets, weighing 70–100 g each, are born after a gestation period of 42 days, in forms on bare

The all-white underparts are a distinguishing feature of this species

ground, or in a nest heap in clumps of grass or under bushes. At birth, they are fully furred with their eyes open, and are able to move independently. They are weaned at 1 month.

DIET
Graze grasses, including leaves, stems and rhizomes, and also take herbs. Prefer green grasses. Water independent, obtaining enough moisture from their food and dew, but will drink when water is available.

HABITAT
Savanna woodland, grassland with brush and/or scrub cover. Absent from open grassland, forest or desert. Occur in all the habitats of the Kruger, usually being associated with grasslands and savannas with some cover. Also common in mopane savannas.

Juvenile

Cape Hare

Lepus capensis

Ger: Kaphase; **Fre:** Lièvre du Cap; **Afr:** Vlakhaas; **Nde, Xho:** umvundla; **Zul:** unogwaja; **Set:** mmutlwa; **Sot:** mofuli; **Swa:** logwatja; **Xit:** mpfundla; **Tsh:** muvhuda, khomu.

Front: 2 cm
Hind: 3 cm

DESCRIPTION

The fur is soft and silky. The upperparts are buffish grey-brown, interspersed with black or red-brown hairs. The colour varies geographically, with northern species tending to be paler. The chest is paler than the upperparts, and the lower limbs are greyish buff. The nose and cheeks are buff, and there is a reddish-grey to reddish-brown tinge on the throat. The black, fluffy tail is white underneath. The ears are 8,5–13 cm long. When they are erected, a network of radiating veins on the inner surface aids in lowering body temperature. Cape hare are very fast runners, reaching speeds up to 70 km/h.

Scent glands: Anal and inguinal. Males also have chin glands.

Senses: Good sight (360 degree vision), very good hearing, and good sense of smell.

DISTRIBUTION

Only a few specimens have been recorded in the Kruger, all occurring in the extreme eastern parts of ecozone N. They have been recorded near Shingomeni north of Shingwedzi Rest Camp, and at N'wambiya Pan.

BEHAVIOUR

Predominantly nocturnal, but they may be active in the early morning and late afternoon, particularly in overcast weather. Solitary, with male home ranges covering 0,65 km², and those of females 0,83 km². Male and female home ranges may overlap, but those of neighbouring same-sex individuals do not. Only core areas within the home range are defended as territories. Home ranges are marked with dung and urine, and with anal, inguinal and chin gland secretions. Regular trails are followed within the home range.

During the day, Cape hare lie up in scratched-out depressions, called forms, with their ears resting on their backs.

Calls: Contact calls include soft grunts and bleats. Alarm calls include screams.

Alarm signals: Stamp the ground with the hindfeet. Freeze, with the ears pinned to the body, then dart away at the last minute in leaping bounds, fleeing in zigzags, with the ears raised. When in extreme distress, they will seek refuge in aardvark and springhare burrows.

Aggression: Drumming the ground with the forefeet, stamping the ground with the hindfeet; grinding the teeth and growling. Other signs of aggression include rising on the hindlegs and slashing out with the claws on the front feet, while kicking with the hindfeet and biting.

This species can be distinguished because the underparts are not all-white

REPRODUCTION

Breed all year, with a peak in the summer rainy season. 1–5 (average 2–3) leverets, weighing 90–150 g each, are born after a gestation period of 42 days, in forms on bare ground, or in a nest heap in clumps of grass or under bushes. At birth, they are fully furred with their eyes open, and are able to move independently. They are weaned at 1 month.

DIET

Graze grasses, herbs, leaves and stems, showing a preference for short-cropped grasses. Water independent, obtaining enough moisture from their food and from dew, but will drink when water is available.

HABITAT

Prefer dry, open habitats such as open grasslands, grassy plains with some light brush/scrub cover and steppe areas and subdesert. Avoids heavily wooded areas. In the Kruger, only a few specimens have been recorded, these being in the sandveld communities habitats in the western border areas of the Kruger Park.

Natal Red Rock Rabbit
Pronolagus crassicaudatus

Ger: Natal-Rothase; **Fre:** Lièvre roux de Natal; **Afr:** Natalse rooi klipkonyn.

Status: not endangered B

Mass: ♂ 2,5–3 kg; ♀ 2,5–3 kg. **Head-and-body length:** ♂ 46–56 cm; ♀ 46–56 cm. **Tail length:** ♂ 3,5–11 cm; ♀ 3,5–11 cm. **Distinguishing features:** A characteristic grey-brown to grey-white band extends from the chin along the lower jaw to the nape of the neck. As in all rabbits and hares, the hindlegs are well developed. **Life-span:** ± 5 yrs. **Predators:** Main predators include virtually all carnivores their size or larger, birds of prey and snakes.

Front: 2 cm
Hind: 3 cm

DESCRIPTION

The thick, rather harsh woolly coat is grizzled reddish brown on the upperparts and flanks. The underparts are grey and grizzled reddish brown. The forehead and sides of the face are grey, and the chin is greyish white. A grey-brown to grey-white band extends from the chin along the lower jaw to the nape of the neck. The ears are 7,5–8,5 cm long. When they are erect, a network of radiating veins on the inner surface aids in lowering body temperature. The flesh is reported to have a rank urine odour. The reddish-brown tail is short and not bushy in comparison to other hares and rabbits.

Scent glands: Anal and inguinal. Males also have chin glands.

Senses: Good sight (360 degree vision), very good hearing, and good sense of smell.

DISTRIBUTION

Occur in the extreme northern parts of ecozones L, M, N and O of the Kruger, being confined to the mountainous and hilly country north of the Punda Maria and Pafuri roads, and between the Luvuvhu and Limpopo rivers. They have also been observed at Legogote, near White River, outside the Park.

BEHAVIOUR

Predominantly nocturnal, but occasionally active during the day. They usually forage alone but congregations may be seen in rich grazing areas. Often move to higher elevations to graze. The home range is marked with dung middens that are found on flat surfaces between rock crevices, with dung and urine scattered throughout the home range, and with anal, inguinal and chin gland secretions.

They lie up in forms in rock crevices, under ledges or boulders, deep within boulder crevices or in dense low vegetation, never venturing far from their rocky habitat.

Calls: Contact calls include grunts. Alarm calls include shrill cries and screams.

Alarm signals: Flee to seek cover under grassy bushes, rocky ledges and boulders, or dart down holes.

Aggression: If caught, will bite and kick with the hindfeet.

REPRODUCTION

Breed all year. 1–2 kittens, weighing 70–100 g each, are born after a gestation period of 1 month, in nests within the burrows. The nests are lined with the mother's hair and with plant material. Kittens are weaned at 1 month.

A distinctive grey-white band extends from the chin, along the jaw, to the neck

DIET

Graze grasses, weeds and herbs, showing a strong preference for short-cropped grasses. Water independent, obtaining enough moisture from their food and from dew, but will drink when water is available.

HABITAT

Rocky areas with scattered brush, grass and trees: on plains, steep grassy hills and mountains, even in dry riverbeds. In the Kruger, found marginally in the mopane shrubveld, tree mopane savanna, alluvial plains and sandveld communities habitats.

South African Hedgehog

Atelerix frontalis

Ger: Südafrikanischer Igel; **Fre:** Hérisson sud-Africain; **Afr:** Suid-Afrikaanse krimpvarkie; **Nde, Zul:** inhloni; **Xho:** intloni, umahau; **Set, Sot:** tlhong; **Set:** setlhong; **Swa:** indvundvwane; **Xit:** xihloni, nhloni, xitlhoni; **Tsh:** tshitoni, thoni.

Status: not endangered

Mass: ♂ 290–480 g; ♀ 280–450 g. **Head-and-body length:** ♂ 140–250 mm; ♀ 140–250 mm. **Tail length:** ♂ 15–50 mm; ♀ 15–50 mm. Specimens from Zimbabwe are generally larger and heavier than those from Botswana, Namibia and South Africa. **Distinguishing features:** Banded spikes extend over the head, back, rump and tail. Distinctive white band of hair across the forehead, extending to just beyond the ears. **Life-span:** ± 5 yrs. **Predators:** Main predators include man (the spines and meat are used in traditional medicines), the eagle owl and raptors.

Front: 1–2 cm
Hind: 2 cm

DESCRIPTION

The face, legs and tail are covered in short, dark hair. Banded spikes extend over the head, back, rump and tail. They can reach speeds of up to 7 km/h. They have 5 digits on their hindfeet.

Scent glands: None present.

Senses: Poor sight, good hearing, very good sense of smell.

DISTRIBUTION

This hedgehog is rare within the Kruger, only occurring in ecozone B. It is confined to the higher-lying grassed areas around Pretoriuskop, and at Mlangeni and Kambeni.

BEHAVIOUR

Diurnal and nocturnal, but predominantly active at dawn or dusk; in cool weather they may be seen throughout the day. Usually solitary, but pairs or family groups may forage together. The home range covers 220 m².

They shelter in thick vegetable debris, in bushes, under logs, in termite mounds holes in the ground and in rock crevices; their shelters change daily as they move over the home range.

They are very active in the spring to summer months (from August onwards), with the onset of the rains. During the winter (from May to August), when food is scarce they become torpid, slowing their metabolism and becoming inactive.

Calls: Contact calls include sniffs, snorts, spits and chatters. Alarm calls include a high-pitched scream.

Alarm signals and aggression: When threatened, roll up into a tight ball, pulling the spiny skin on their backs over their head and legs, presenting a mass of spines to the attacker, while snorting and growling.

REPRODUCTION

Breed in the summer rainy season. 1–11 (average 4) cubs, weighing 7,5–10,5 g each are born after a gestation period of 5 weeks. Cubs are born in nests lined with debris or in holes lined with dry leaves. At birth, they are blind and naked, with the spines just visible beneath the skin; spines start appearing after 24 hours, and their eyes open at 10 days. At 4–6 weeks the spines are shed and replaced by adult spines. Cubs are weaned at 4–6 weeks.

The banded spikes extend over the head, back, rump and tail

DIET

Although classified as an insectivore, the diet is omnivorous. The bulk of the diet consists of insects, favouring beetles, termites, grasshoppers and moths. Centipedes, millipedes, earthworms, snakes, frogs, lizards, mice, birds' eggs, carrion, vegetable matter, fungi and wild fruits are also taken.

Water independent, obtaining enough moisture from their food and from dew, but will drink regularly when water is available.

HABITAT

South African hedgehogs have a wide habitat tolerance, occurring in grassland, open thornveld, rocky outcrops, and bush and scrub savanna. They favour open dry areas, especially overgrazed areas, with patches of grass cover. Their distribution is limited to areas with an annual rainfall of 300–800 mm. They are absent from deserts or high-rainfall areas. Occur in the sourveld habitat of the Kruger.

Golden Moles

Golden moles are endemic to Africa south of the Sahara. There are 7 genera and 18 species, 15 occurring in southern Africa. 2 genera, each with 1 species, are found in the Kruger National Park. Very little is known about the habits of golden moles due to their subterranean existence.

Ger: Goldene Maulwürfe; **Fre:** Taupe dorée; **Afr:** Gouemolle.

Species: Yellow Golden Mole, *Calcochloris obtusirostris;* Juliana's Golden Mole, *Amblysomus julianae.*

Status: *A. julianae* – IUCN: CR. *C. obtusirostris* – Rare. ☽ B

Mass: ♂ 20–30 g; ♀ 20–30 g. **Head-and-body length:** ♂ 10–11 cm; ♀ 10–11 cm. **Tail length:** No tail present.
Distinguishing features: The body is torpedo-shaped. The eyes and ears are not visible, and the nose is blunt.
Life-span: Unknown. **Predators:** Main predators include snakes, raptors, large owls and other birds of prey.

■ *C. obtusirostris*
■ *A. julianae*

DESCRIPTION

The dense coat has a distinctive sheen to it. Yellow golden moles are golden yellow-brown, with yellowish underparts. The sides of the face are yellow with a yellowish band across the top of the snout. Juliana's golden moles are rich reddish brown with paler underparts.

The digits on the hindfeet of golden moles are webbed, an adaptation which enables them to push back soil while tunnelling.

Scent glands: Apart from a strong musky smell being emitted, no other data has been found as to the location or presence of scent glands.

Senses: Sensitive to vibrations but do not respond to sound or light.

DISTRIBUTION

C. obtusirostris occurs marginally in the northeastern parts of ecozone N of the Kruger, being restricted to the Nyandu and Machayi sandveld plateau.

A. julianae occurs in ecozones B, C and E of the Kruger, being restricted to the granitic soils north and south of the Pretoriuskop and Numbi roads, and extending southwards to the Matjulwana Valley and northwards to the Numbi Kop foothills.

BEHAVIOUR

Predominantly nocturnal, but some activity has been reported in the early morning and late afternoon. Golden moles are solitary, subterranean dwellers that move about in subsurface runs, which are visible on the surface as raised lines of arched soil. The subsurface runs lead off from chambers located at the base of trees. They are not permanent, with new tunnels being built continually. Burrows may be up to 200 mm deep for *C. obtusirostris*, and the burrow system may be over 200 m long in some species.

Golden moles may undergo periods of torpor in winter.

Calls: Contact calls include chirps and squeaks. Alarm calls include high-pitched squeaks.

Alarm signals: When disturbed, they may back up along a run, but more commonly, will tunnel deeply, moving away from the source of disturbance. When above ground, they dart quickly down burrows.

Juliana's golden mole

Aggression: No signs of aggression have yet been recorded.

REPRODUCTION
Breed in the summer rainy season. 1–2 cubs, weighing 4,5 g each, are born after an unknown gestation period, in side-chambers of the tunnel system, in ball-shaped nests made of dried grass. The skin is naked and pink at birth.

DIET
Insectivorous, feeding on insects, but beetle larvae, earthworms and other invertebrates are also taken. Food is usually consumed underground. *C. obtusirostris* is fond of tenebroid larvae, termites such as *Hodotermes* spp, and also of burrowing lizards.

Golden moles are water independent, obtaining enough moisture from their food and from dew.

HABITAT
Golden moles are found in light, sandy soil, alluvial soil or dune soil. They avoid hard clay soils. *C. obtusirostris* is found in light sandy soils, coastal sands, riparian sandy alluvium and also in dry, sandy river beds. *A. julianae* is found in sandy soils in grassland, bush savanna and woodland savanna.

C. obtusirostris occurs marginally in the northeastern parts of the sandveld communiies habitats of the Kruger, and is restricted to the Kalahari-like sands of the area. *A. julianae* occurs marginally in the sourveld, Malelane Mountain bushveld and thorn veld habitats of the Kruger.

Shrews

The southern African region supports 4 genera and 16 species of shrews, all belonging to the subfamily *Crocidurinae*. 2 genera and 6 species are found in the Kruger National Park, 5 species belonging to the genus *Crocidura*. The ranges given for physical characteristics and distribution are overall ranges for *Suncus* and *Crocidura* spp.

Ger: Spitzmäuse; **Fre:** Musaraignes; **Afr:** Skeerbekke; **Zul:** nqawunqawu.

Species: Greater Dwarf Shrew, *Suncus lixus;* Swamp Musk Shrew, *Crocidura mariquensis;* Tiny Musk Shrew, *Crocidura fuscomurina;* Reddish-grey Musk Shrew, *Crocidura cyanea;* Peters' Musk Shrew, *Crocidura silacea;* Lesser Red Musk Shrew, *Crocidura hirta.*

Status: not endangered

Mass: ♂ 3,5–40 g; ♀ 3,5–40 g. **Head-and-body length:** ♂ 45–140 mm; ♀ 45–140 mm. **Tail length:** ♂ 30–90 mm; ♀ 30–90 mm. **Distinguishing features:** Shrews can be distinguished from mice and rats by their narrow skulls with long, narrow, pointed muzzles, and by their very small eyes and ears. **Life-span:** ± 1,5 yrs. **Predators:** Main predators include birds of prey and snakes.

DESCRIPTION

Colour varies according to species and even subspecies, but the coat is generally grizzled grey-brown, with paler underparts. The tail is brown and is paler underneath. Shrews are hosts for the plague virus, which can be transmitted to humans via infected fleas.

Scent glands: On the flank between the forelegs and hindlegs.

Senses: Very good sight, hearing and smell.

DISTRIBUTION

C. fuscomurina and *C. hirta* occur throughout the Kruger in ecozones B, D, E, F, G, H, M, N and P. *C. mariquensis* has been reported only in ecozone N, on the swampy ground around the Matukwale Dam in the Punda Maria area. *C. cyanea* is found in ecozones H and N, occurring in the Malelane area, on the northern banks of the Crocodile River at Crocodile Bridge, and in the northern Punda Maria and Pafuri districts. *C. silacea* is found in ecozones H and N, occurring near Skukuza on the banks of the Sabie River, on the banks of the Luvuvhu River at Pafuri, and south of Pafuri at Matshitshindzudzi. *S. lixus* is found in ecozones B, D, I and N, occurring in the Pretoriuskop, Skukuza, Nwanetsi, Xilowa and Malahlapanga areas.

BEHAVIOUR

Diurnal and nocturnal. Generally solitary. Home ranges are defended strongly as territories. The territory range includes regularly used trails. *C. mariquensis* utilizes the runways of *Otomys* spp and *D. incomtus* for foraging purposes.

Nests are constructed of soft plant material. *C. hirta* constructs cup-shaped nests, *C. mariquensis* ball-shaped ones.

Calls: Contact calls include twitters, chatters and squeaks. The young churr softly. Alarm calls include piercing squeaks.

Alarm signals: A musky odour is emitted from the flank glands.

Aggression: Open-mouthed gapes. Rising on the back legs and slashing out at

Lesser red musk shrew

their opponent's head and neck with the teeth, sparring with the teeth, snapping and kicking, fighting, chasing, screaming and squeaking.

REPRODUCTION

Breed in the summer rainy season. 1–9 (average 2–5) cubs are born after a gestation period of about 2,5 weeks. The birth weight is 1,5 g. Cubs are born in nests with soft plant material, in clumps of grass on slightly elevated patches of ground. They are naked and blind at birth; their eyes open at 2 weeks. Adult coloration is attained at 10 days. Cubs take solid food at 3 weeks and are weaned at 3–4 weeks. In *Crocidura* spp, caravanning is common from 8–18 days. The mother is followed by her young, with the first cub gripping onto her rump, and the following cubs gripping onto each other's rumps, forming a trail behind her.

DIET

Insectivorous, feeding on insects. As a result of their very high metabolism, shrews have a very low toler-

ance to food deprivation and require food on a regular basis. Some arid-adapted species can survive without drinking water for a couple of months, but certain forest species die very quickly if they do not drink regularly.

HABITAT

Variety of habitats; from arid or semi-deserts with an annual rainfall of less than 100 mm to moist forest with an annual rainfall of 1 500 mm. Often associated with moist, damp areas along riverbanks, reed beds, swamps and riverine habitats. All species occur in the sandveld communities habitats of the Kruger. Additionally, *C. cyanea* and *C. silacea* occur in the riverine communities habitats; *S. lixus*, *C. hirta* and *C. fuscomurina* in the sourveld, thorn thickets, and Lebombo Mountain bushveld habitats, with *C. hirta* and *C. fuscomurina* also occurring in the thorn veld, knobthorn/marula savanna, delagoa thorn thickets habitats, and the riverine habitats of mopane/bushwillow woodlands.

Four-toed Elephant Shrew

Petrodromus tetradactylus

Ger: Vier-zehige Elefantenspitzmaus; **Fre:** Rat à trompe tétradactyle; **Afr:** Bosklaasneus.

Mass: ♂ 160–200 g; ♀ 200–280 g. **Head-and-body length:** ♂ 180 mm; ♀ 190 mm. **Tail length:** ♂ 150–180 mm; ♀ 150–180 mm. **Distinguishing features:** Long and tubular snout. Eyes are ringed with white, with a black patch behind them. The rump is almost hairless at the base of the tail. Feet are black, with naked soles. **Life-span:** Presumed to be ± 3–4 yrs as per other elephant shrews. **Predators:** Main predators include birds of prey and snakes. Other predators include virtually all carnivores their size or larger.

DESCRIPTION

The soft, thick fur is tawny grey with paler underparts. The eye rings are white, as are the upper lip, chin and throat. The eyes are very large and the ears are long. The hindlegs are long and powerful for hopping and jumping. They are distinguished from other elephant shrews because they only have 4 digits on the hindfeet (other elephant shrews have 5 digits on the hindfeet).
Scent glands: Chest and underside of tail.
Senses: Very good sight, hearing and sense of smell.

DISTRIBUTION

Occur in ecozones L, N and O of the Kruger, being restricted to the Punda Maria and Pafuri districts.

BEHAVIOUR

Predominantly diurnal, but some nocturnal activity has been reported; most active in the early morning and evening. In the Kruger, however, they are reported to be largely nocturnal. Although they maintain separate sleeping quarters and forage alone, pairs may share the same territory range, which they defend against same-sex intruders. The territory range includes distinct runs with bare 'landing' patches which mark the landing and take-off points of the elephant shrews as they move in jumps along the runs. The runs are marked with secretions from the chest gland and the gland beneath the tail, and with dung piles.

Nests of dried leaves on the forest floor, in patches of dense underbrush holes under tree roots, the underside of logs, the inside of hollow logs, shallow burrows, rock crevices and holes in termite mounds are used as shelters. Abandoned rodent holes are also often occupied.
Calls: Contact calls include squeaks, purrs, chirps and screams. Alarm calls include a shrill, high-pitched squeak.
Alarm signals: Stamp the hindfeet. Jump straight up in the air before hopping, jumping away or running on all fours. They drum the ground with their hindfeet when stressed, producing a 'purring' sound.
Aggression: Tapping of hindfeet. 'Strutting' to display the contrasting colours of the underparts and legs. Fight with canines aimed at their opponent's rump. Chasing.

REPRODUCTION

Breed all year with a peak in the summer rainy season. 1–2 cubs, weighing approximately 32 g each, are born after a gestation period of 2 months. Cubs are well

Four-toed elephant shrews have only 4 digits on the hindfeet, not 5

developed at birth – their eyes are open, and they can run independently within a few hours.

DIET

Four-toed elephant shrews are insectivorous; they feed on a variety of insects ranging from beetles, termites, ants, crickets to grasshoppers, spiders and earthworms. They may also feed on different plant materials.

HABITAT

Forests, thickets and woodlands with dense undergrowth; scrub. They are not found in areas with an annual rainfall of less than 700 mm. In the Kruger, they are particularly associated with *Androstachys johnstonii* communities. They occur in the tree mopane savanna and sandveld communities habitats of the Kruger, and very marginally in the mopane shrubveld habitats.

Rock Elephant Shrew
Elephantulus myurus

Ger: Felsen Elefantenspitzmaus; **Fre:** Rat à trompe des roches; **Afr:** Klipklaasneus.

Status: not endangered B

Mass: ♂ 60 g; ♀ 60 g. **Head-and-body length:** ♂ 90–135 mm; ♀ 90–135 mm. **Tail length:** ♂ 130–150 mm; ♀ 130–150 mm. **Distinguishing features:** Long and tubular snout. Eyes are ringed with white. The upper sur-face of the feet is whitish; and the soles on the hindfeet are naked and black. **Life-span:** Presumed to be ± 3–4 yrs as per other elephant shrews. **Predators:** Main predators include birds of prey and snakes. Other predators include virtually all carnivores their size or larger.

DESCRIPTION

The soft, thick fur is greyish brown with pale, greyish underparts. The eye rings are white. The ears are buff-brown on the back surface with a fringe of white hair on the inner margin. The eyes are very large and the ears are long. The hindlegs are long and powerful for hopping and jumping.

Scent glands: Chest, underside of tail, behind the ears, and in the corners of the mouth.

Senses: Very good sight, hearing and sense of smell.

DISTRIBUTION

Occur in ecozones I, L and N of the Kruger. Confined to the Lebombo Moun-tains north of Olifantspoort, and the hilly country north of the Punda Maria and Pafuri roads.

BEHAVIOUR

Predominantly diurnal with an activity peak at dawn, but some nocturnal activity has been reported. They characteristically tend to stay under the cover of rocks, or overhanging bushes and trees. Although they maintain separate sleeping quar-ters and forage alone, pairs may share the same territory range (0,02–0,06 km²), which they defend against same-sex intruders. The territory range includes well-worn trails, which are marked with secretions from the chest gland and the gland beneath the tail, and with dung piles.

Rock elephant shrews are very fond of basking in the morning sun for up to 2 hours before setting off to forage. They may become torpid in winter months in low temperatures.

Calls: Contact is established with squeaks and by tapping the hindfeet. Alarm calls include high-pitched squeaks and screams.

Alarm signals: Drum the hindfeet. Jump straight up in the air before hopping/ jump-ing away or running on all fours.

Aggression: Bristling the fur. 'Strutting' to display the contrasting colours of the underparts and legs. Fighting, with the canines aimed at their opponent's rump. Chasing.

REPRODUCTION

Breed all year, with a peak in the summer rainy season. 1–2 cubs, weighing 8 g each, are born after a gestation period of 49–56 days. They are well developed at birth, with their eyes open, and can run independently within a few hours.

A distinguishing feature is the whitish upper surface of the feet

DIET
Insectivorous, feeding on insects such as beetles, termites and ants; spiders and earthworms.

HABITAT
Rocky regions and/or piles of boulders, in drier areas with plenty of crevices for cover. They are occasionally found on flat ground, providing there is sufficient cover in the form of boulders and rocky outcrops. Often found within meters of *E. brachy-rhynchus*; the latter inhabits flat, sandy soils. Occur in rocky regions in the Lebombo Mountain bushveld, mopane shrubveld and sandveld communities habitats of the Kruger.

Short-snouted Elephant Shrew   *Elephantulus brachyrhynchus*

Ger: Kurznasige Elefantenspitzmaus; **Fre:** Rat à trompe à museau court; **Afr:** Kortneus klaasneus.

Status: not endangered   ))B

Mass: ♂ 30–52 g; ♀ 30–52 g. **Head-and-body length:** ♂ 100–110 mm; ♀ 100–110 mm. **Tail length:** ♂ 90–135 mm; ♀ 90–135 mm. **Distinguishing features:** Long and tubular snout. Eyes are ringed with white. Feet are whitish yellow and the soles on the hindfeet are brown and naked. **Life-span:** Presumed to be ± 3–4 yrs as per other elephant shrews. **Predators:** Main predators include birds of prey and snakes. Other predators include virtually all carnivores their size or larger.

DESCRIPTION
The fur is soft and thick. The colour varies geographically, with northern populations being reddish yellow, interspersed with black hairs; eastern populations being greyish; and southern populations being fawn-brown to brown. The underparts are paler in all populations. The eye rings and the upper lip are white. There is a whitish-yellow patch of hair behind the ears, at their base. The eyes are very large and the ears are long. The hindlegs are long and powerful for hopping and jumping.
Scent glands: Chest, underside of tail, and behind the ears.
Senses: Very good sight, hearing and sense of smell.

DISTRIBUTION
Occur in sandy soils in suitable habitat in ecozones B, I, L, M, N and P of the Kruger.

BEHAVIOUR
Predominantly diurnal, but some nocturnal activity has been reported. Their activity levels decrease in overcast weather and in rainy weather they are inactive. Although they maintain separate sleeping quarters and forage alone, pairs may share the same territory range (0,02–0,06 km²), which they defend against same-sex intruders. The territory range includes well-worn trails, which are marked with secretions from the chest gland, the gland beneath the tail, and the gland behind the ears (through sand rolling), and with dung piles. Abandoned rodent holes are often used as shelters.
Calls: Contact is established with squeaks and by tapping the hindfeet. Alarm calls include high-pitched squeaks and screams.
Alarm signals: Jump straight up in the air before hopping/jumping away or running on all fours. May freeze and remain motionless until the threat has passed.
Aggression: Bristling the fur. 'Strutting' to display the contrasting colours of the underparts and the legs. Fight with the canines aimed at their opponent's rump. Chasing.

REPRODUCTION
Breed all year, with a peak in the summer rainy season. 1–2 cubs, weighing about 8 g each, are born after a gestation period of 49–56 days. They are well developed at birth, with their eyes open, and can run independently within a few hours.

DIET
Insectivorous, feeding on insects such as beetles, crickets, grasshoppers, termites and ants. Also take spiders, earthworms, seeds and fruit.

A distinguishing feature is the naked, brown soles of the hindfeet

HABITAT

Short-snouted elephant shrews live in flat, open grass-land savanna offering dense grass cover, with shrubs, scattered trees and sandy soil. They are often within metres of *E. myurus*, which inhabits the rocky terrain of the region. In the Kruger Park, these shrews are found in sandy soils in the mopane/bushwillow woodlands, mopane shrubveld, Lebombo Mountain bushveld, sourveld, sandveld communities and alluvial plains habitats.

South African/Cape Porcupine   *Hystrix africaeaustralis*

Ger: Südafrikanisches Stachelschwein; **Fre:** Porcépique sud-Africain; **Afr:** Kaapse ystervark; **Zul, Swa:** ingungubane, inungu; **Set, Sot:** noko; **Xit, Tsh:** nungu.

Status: IUCN: NT   ☽ B

Mass: ♂ 12–27 kg; ♀ 12–27 kg. **Shoulder height:** ♂ 26–30 cm; ♀ 26–29 cm. **Head-and-body length:** ♂ 75–100 cm; ♀ 75–100 cm. **Tail length:** ♂ 10–17 cm; ♀ 10–17 cm. **Distinguishing features:** Distinctive black and white banded spines and quills cover upper body and flanks. A crest of black and white hair extends from the forehead to the shoulders. **Life-span:** ± 10–12 yrs. **Predators:** Main predators include leopard and hyaena. Other predators include large predatory birds and pythons. In the Kruger, at least one pride of lions specializes in porcupines.

Front: 8 cm
Hind: 10 cm

DESCRIPTION

Black and white banded spines up to 50 cm, and quills up to 30 cm long, cover the upperparts and flanks. The rest of the body, except the ears, is covered with coarse, black hair. A crest of erectile black and white hair, up to 50 cm long, extends from the forehead to the neck and shoulders. The rump is covered with short bristles. At the end of the tail is a rattle of hollow quills, over 6 cm long and 6 mm in diameter. Quills are composed of fused hairs. Porcupines are good swimmers and can climb if necessary. Porcupines are plantigrade (flat-footed).
Scent glands: None present.
Senses: Poor sight, good hearing, very good sense of smell.

DISTRIBUTION

Occur commonly and widely in suitable habitat in all the ecozones of the Kruger.

BEHAVIOUR

Predominantly nocturnal, but they may be seen in the daytime basking in the sun at their burrow entrances. They are either solitary or occur in family clans comprising a monogamous dominant breeding pair and their offspring. The home range average is 4 km², only part of which is defended as a territory. The home range is marked with urine and communal dung middens. Although clan members forage alone, they share trails and runs within the home range. They may travel up to 15 km over the home range in the course of a night's foraging.

Rock caves, self-dug burrows, or abandoned springhare and aardvark burrows are used as shelters. Burrow entrances may be 10 m apart and the main tunnels may be up to 20 m long. The nesting chamber is about 2 m deep, and is situated in the centre of the burrow system.
Calls: Contact calls include grunts, snuffles and piping calls. Alarm calls include growls and snarls.
Alarm signals: The bristles, quills and crest are erected, doubling the porcupine's apparent size. The tail quills are rattled at intervals, producing a whizzing, rattling sound.
Aggression: Stamp the ground with the hindfeet, and grunt. If approached, porcupines attack sideways and backwards. The quills are loose and easily removed sticking into the attacker. They are not shot out as commonly believed, and are not barbed in this species.

Distinctive black-and-white spines, up to 50 cm long, cover the upper body and flanks

REPRODUCTION

Breed all year, with a peak in the summer rainy season. 1–3 cubs, weighing 300–440 g each, are born after a gestation period of 3 months, with an average interval of 1 year between births. Cubs are born in nests of grass and leaves, in maternity chambers inside dens. Their eyes open at birth or within the first few hours after birth. Cubs are haired, and their spines are soft and less than 3 cm long. They leave the den at 1–2 weeks, take solid food at 2–4 weeks, and are weaned at 2–3 months.

DIET

Omnivorous, taking bulbs, roots, tubers, wild fruits (especially fig, marula, mobola plum and sausage tree fruits), seeds, bark (often ring-barking trees as they feed on the succulent tissue), agricultural crops and carrion. They chew bones for their calcium and phosphorus content. In the Kruger, they particularly ring-bark wild mango, *Cordyla africana*, as well as *Erythrina* spp, *Ficus* spp, *Spirostachys africanus* and also *Trichilia emetica* along the Limpopo River.

Water independent, obtaining enough moisture from their food, but will drink when water is available.

HABITAT

Most habitats, favouring broken country with rocky terrain in dry regions, grasslands and adjoining forest margins. Not found in the Namib Desert coastal strip or in forests. Occur in all the habitats of the Kruger.

Springhare

Pedetes capensis

Ger: Springhase; Fre: Lièvre sauteur; Afr: Springhaas; Nde: umahelane; Zul: indlulane, isandlulane; Set: tshipô; Sot: tshipjane; Swa: ndlulwane; Tsh: khadzimutavha.

Status: IUCN: VU

Mass: ♂ 3–4 kg; ♀ 3–4 kg. **Shoulder height:** ♂ 30 cm; ♀ 30 cm. **Head-and-body length:** ♂ 35–45 cm; ♀ 35–45 cm. **Tail length:** ♂ 35–50 cm; ♀ 35–50 cm. **Distinguishing features:** Resemble a small kangaroo, as a result of the powerful, well-developed hindlegs and tiny forelegs. The bushy tail tassel has a black tip. In torchlight, the eyes characteristically shine red. Only one eye shines at a time (bobbing up and down as the animal moves), distinguishing it from other nocturnal species. **Life-span:** ± 7 yrs. **Predators:** Main predator is man: the meat is popular with indigenous populations, the skins are used for water and other storage containers, and the tail sinews are used as thread. Other predators include virtually all carnivores their size or larger, birds of prey, snakes and monitors.

2 cm

5 cm

DESCRIPTION

The coat is reddish tan-buff with whitish-yellow underparts. The head and upper surface of the tail are darker than the body. The chin is white. A white patch extends from the inside of each thigh to the back. The tail tassel has a black tip. Springhare hop along in kangaroo-like fashion, and may leap 2 m in one bound. They are very good diggers, and their burrows are often used by many other species. The ears are 7–9 cm long, and the ears and nose can be closed while they dig, preventing sand and insects from entering.

Scent glands: Perineal.

Senses: Good sight, very good hearing and sense of smell.

DISTRIBUTION

In the Kruger, springhare are nowhere common. They occur mainly in the sandveld portions of ecozones L, M, N, O and P north of the Olifants River. The distribution south of the Olifants River extends marginally into parts of ecozones A, D, E, I and J, and again into sandveld areas at Kingfisherspruit, Girivana and Nsasane, and west of Tshokwane at the lower Vutomi loop, and along the eastern border in the Pumbe sandveld.

BEHAVIOUR

Nocturnal, usually remaining in their burrows during wet weather. They are solitary, but may occasionally be seen foraging in loose communities of up to 40 individuals in high-density areas. The home range covers 0,5–1 km². Springhare never venture far from their burrows, always grazing within a 400 m area around their home.

Springhare shelter in self-dug burrows that can be up to 50 m long. On average, there are 9 entrances to the burrows, and the average depth is 1 m. Burrow tunnels average 25 cm in height and 10–25 cm in width.

Calls: Contact calls include grunts and piping calls. Alarm calls include bleats.

Alarm signals: Flee with a kangaroo-like hopping gait, darting down their burrows, sealing the entrances behind them.

Aggression: Will kick with the hindlegs, cutting deeply with the hind claws, and will bite if caught.

Springhare resemble small kangaroos due to their powerful hindlegs and tiny forelegs

REPRODUCTION

Breed all year. A single cub (rarely 2), weighing 240–300 g, is born in the burrow after a gestation period of 80 days. It is blind at birth, but fully furred; the eyes open at 3 days. At 6–7 weeks, when weaning is complete, the cub leaves the burrow for the first time.

DIET

Herbivorous, feeding mainly on grasses, but also take stems, leaves, roots, tubers, corms, herbs, sprouts, and occasionally grasshoppers and beetles. Water independent, obtaining enough moisture from food and from dew. Drink rarely, even when water is available.

HABITAT

Flat, open overgrazed or short grassland with brush/scrub cover, open scrub, floodplains and dry riverbeds. Sandy soils are an essential habitat requirement. Avoid areas such as mopane woodland where the soil is hard, hard clayey soil and areas of tall grassland. In the Kruger, they are found in the sandveld portions of the mopane/bushwillow woodlands, mixed bushwillow woodlands, tree mopane savanna, mopane shrubveld, thorn thickets, Lebombo Mountain bushveld, thorn veld, rugged veld, alluvial plains and sandveld communities habitats.

Tree Squirrel

Paraxerus cepapi

Ger: Ockerfuß Buschhörnchen; **Fre:** Écureuil des bois de Smith; **Afr:** Boomeekhoring; **Nde:** ubusinti, ubuhlula, isikhale; **Xho:** unomatse; **Zul:** ingwejeje yasezihlahleni, intshidane yasezihlahleni; **Set:** samane, setlhora, sepêpê, kôtôkwê, ntuke; **Swa:** ingwejeje; **Xit:** xindzi, maxindlani, maxidyani, sindyane; **Tsh:** tshisindi, tshithura.

Status: not endangered

Mass: ♂ 100–250 g; ♀ 130–265 g. **Head-and-body length:** ♂ 13–19 cm; ♀ 13–19 cm. **Tail length:** ♂ 11–21 cm; ♀ 11–21 cm. **Distinguishing features:** Bushy tail is the same length as the body, or longer. 5 cm-long black whiskers are prominent. **Life-span:** ± 10 yrs. **Predators:** Main predators include virtually all carnivores their size or larger, birds of prey and snakes.

Front: 2 cm
Hind: 3 cm

DESCRIPTION

The coat is coarse and grizzled. The colour varies geographically: greyish in the west and buff or reddish brown in the east. The flanks and upper legs are less grizzled than the upperparts, and the lower limbs are grizzled but even in colour. The underparts are yellowish white. The tail is grizzled and has indistinct blackish bars.
Scent glands: Anal.
Senses: Good sight, very good hearing and good sense of smell.

DISTRIBUTION

Occur commonly and widely in all the ecozones of the Kruger.

BEHAVIOUR

Diurnal, being least active in the hotter hours of the day. Generally a solitary animal, but groups have been reported in the Mpumalanga and Northern provinces of South Africa. Groups are comprised of a dominant male, and one or more females and their offspring. The territory range of 4,3 km² is defended by the male and is marked with urine, anal gland secretions and secretions deposited during mouth wiping. Members of the same group also mark each other with anal gland secretions. Social relations between group members are maintained through mutual grooming.

Tree squirrels are terrestrial and arboreal, and spend considerable time foraging on the ground. They shelter in nests lined with grass and leaves, in natural holes in trees or in holes made by other species, for example, woodpeckers. They are fond of basking in the morning sun before setting off to forage.
Calls: Contact calls include a long 'chuck-chuck-chuck', rattles and croaks. Alarm calls include loud clicks for ground predators, and rattles and high-pitched whistles for avian predators.
Alarm signals: Tail flicking. Flee to holes or trees, making leaps of up to 2 m, or lie flat and motionless on branches or in dense foliage until the threat has passed.
Aggression: Chasing and biting. Groups may mob-attack, chasing and biting with their tails flicking, whilst clicking and rattling.

REPRODUCTION

Breed all year, with a peak in the summer rainy season. 1-3 cubs, weighing 10 g each, are born after a gestation period of 53–57 days, in leaf and grass-lined nests.

Indistinct blackish bars mark the tail

They are blind and sparsely haired at birth; their eyes open at 8 days. They leave the nest at 3 weeks, remaining on nearby branches and close to the nest-hole entrance until 5 weeks. They are weaned at 5–6 weeks.

DIET
Omnivorous, feeding on grasses, flowers, leaves, seeds, nuts, bark, lichen, fruit, berries, gum, termites and ants. They cache food, such as nuts and seeds, by burying them in soil. Water independent, obtaining enough moisture from their food, but will drink when water is available.

HABITAT
Commonly occur in savanna woodlands, especially mopane, *Acacia*, mixed *Acacia/Terminalia* and mixed *Acacia/Combretum* woodlands. Avoid forest and open grassland. Occur in all the habitats of the Kruger.

Greater Canerat

Thryonomys swinderianus

Ger: Großer Rohrratte; **Fre:** Aulacode; **Afr:** Grootrietrot; **Nde:** ivondo; **Zul:** ivondwe; **Set:** bodi; **Swa:** livondo; **Xit:** nhleti; **Tsh:** tshedzi.

Status: not endangered 〗B

Mass: ♂ 3,2–5,2 kg; ♀ 3,4–3,8 kg. **Head-and-body length:** ♂ 48–61 cm; ♀ 46–49 cm. **Tail length:** ♂ 18–19 cm; ♀ 18–19 cm. **Distinguishing features:** Second largest rodent in southern Africa, the largest being the porcupine. The muzzle overhangs the nostrils, jutting out in front. **Life-span:** 2,5 yrs has been reported in captivity, but this seems too short for a mammal of this size and the life-span may indeed be longer. **Predators:** Main predator is man: the meat is popular with indigenous populations. Other predators include leopard, baboon and pythons.

Front: 3 cm
Hind: 5 cm

H

DESCRIPTION

The body is short and stocky. The fur is stiff and bristly. The upperparts are speckled dark brown, the underparts greyish white. The lips, chin and throat are also white. The tail is brown above and paler underneath, and is covered with short, bristly hairs. The ears are broad and short, and are almost completely hidden by the fur. The incisors are grooved. Canerats are excellent swimmers. The first and fifth digit on the feet are reduced to stumps.

Scent glands: None present.

Senses: Poor sight, very good hearing and sense of smell.

DISTRIBUTION

Occur commonly in ecozone H of the Kruger.

BEHAVIOUR

Predominantly nocturnal, with some early morning and late afternoon activity. Generally solitary, but mixed male-female colonies of 8–10 individuals have been reported in restricted habitat areas. They follow distinct runs within the home range, which is marked with dung and piles of cut grass stems. Often, portions of the runs are covered by shallow water; resting spots in these cases are found on drier ground on grass tussocks or elevated patches of ground.

Canerats shelter on piles of debris and reed stems, in dense cover, and in holes in streambanks. They also shelter in holes under tree roots if grass and reed cover are available.

Calls: Contact calls include booming grunts and whistles. Alarm calls include growls and loud whistles. They also thump the ground with their hindfeet.

Alarm signals: Flee, then freeze until closely approached, then flee again. May also thump the ground with their hindfeet.

Aggression: Butting with the muzzle; the overhang of the muzzle protects the nostrils from blows. When pursued, they often take refuge in water.

REPRODUCTION

Breed in the summer rainy season. 1–8 (average 4) pups, weighing 80–190 g each, are born after a gestation period of 152 days, in holes lined with grass and leaves. They are fully furred at birth, with their eyes open, and can follow their mother within an hour. They are weaned at 1 month.

The overhanging muzzle is characteristic

DIET

Herbivorous, feeding on vegetation such as roots, shoots, reeds, grass stems in damp areas, sedges, the bark of certain trees and fruit. Also take cultivated crops, such as maize, wheat, sugar cane and potatoes. Water dependent, drinking regularly.

HABITAT

Reed beds and areas of dense tall grasses with thick reed and cane-like stems, within 50 m of rivers, lakes, streams and swamps. Also found in marshy areas. Not found in desert or semi-desert. Occur in the riverine communities habitats of the Kruger.

Common Molerat

Cryptomys hottentotus

Ger: Hottentotten Graumull; **Fre:** Rat-taupe hottentot; **Afr:** Vaalmol.

Status: not endangered ☽ B

Mass: ♂ 110–145 g; ♀ 100–155 g. **Head-and-body length:** ♂ 10–18 cm; ♀ 10–16 cm. Specimens from the Cape region are about half the above weight and size. **Distinguishing features:** Body is distinctly cylindrical in shape. The mouth closes behind the prominent white, ungrooved incisors. Eyes are very small. Ears are not visible externally. **Life-span:** Unknown. **Predators:** Main predators include mole snakes and barn owls.

DESCRIPTION

The fur is short, soft and silky. The colour of the upperparts varies according to distribution, and ranges from buffy-brown to the colour of the local soil. The under-parts are paler. Northern populations have a white patch on the forehead. The short tail is fringed with hair. The incisors grow continually throughout its life and are used for digging. Soil is pushed out with the feet. The molerat's closest relative is the porcupine. The soles of the feet are naked.

Scent glands: None present.

Senses: Poor sight, very good hearing, good sense of smell.

DISTRIBUTION

Occur in all ecozones of the Kruger, except D, and occur only in the transition regions of ecozone P. Two subspecies are found in the Park. *C.h. natalensis* is restricted to the area south of the Olifants River, and occurs at higher densities in the sandier soils towards the south and west. *C.h. hottentotus* is found in the basalt and sandy soils in the northern and eastern parts of the Park, and occurs at higher densities to the areas north of the Olifants River.

BEHAVIOUR

Nocturnal, but may come to the surface during the daytime after heavy rains. Colonies of up to 14 individuals may be formed, and comprise a dominant breeding pair and subordinates (offspring of the breeding pair and some non-related individuals). The subordinates dig and defend the burrow systems and care for the young.

Molerats are subterranean dwellers. They move in subsurface runs, which are visible on the surface, particularly after rain, as lines of mounds of fresh soil. On average, burrows are 15–30 cm deep, and up to 1 km long. They contain many side tunnels, a nesting chamber and a storage chamber for food, which is located near the nesting chamber.

The minimal home range covers 1,5 km². The burrow systems are defended as territories.

Calls: Contact calls include squeaks and hissing snorts. Alarm calls include grunts and squeaks.

Alarm signals: The body is pumped up and down and the hindfeet are drummed on the ground. They flee by darting down burrow systems, sealing the entrance behind them with soil that is pushed back with the feet.

Aggression: The head is thrown back with the mouth open, ready to bite and attack with the incisors.

The large incisors are used for digging burrows and defence

REPRODUCTION

Breed in the summer rainy season. 1–3 pups, weighing 8 g each, are born after a gestation period of 35–110 days, in nesting chambers lined with corms, roots, root bark and some surface plant material. The pups are blind at birth; their eyes open after 14 days. They take solid food at 10 days, and are weaned at 2–3 months.

DIET

Omnivorous, feeding on fleshy roots, bulbs, tubers, rhizomes, grass, grass stolons, leaves (including aloe), and many corms that may be toxic to other mammals. May occasionally take small vertebrates. Also take cultivated root crops such as carrots and potatoes. Roots are cached in storage chambers in the burrows.

Common molerats appear to be water independent, obtaining enough moisture from their burrow systems, which are usually saturated with condensation.

HABITAT

Wide range of soil habitats, from sandy soils to heavier, stonier soils. Common in sandy alluvium, but not found in red clay soil or hard soil associated with mopane woodlands. Occur in all the habitats of the Kruger Park, except the thorn thickets, and are only found in the transition regions of the mopane/bushwillow woodlands.

Woodland Dormouse

Graphiurus murinus

Ger: Waldlandschläfer; **Afr:** Boswaaierstertmuis.

Mass: ♂ 24–34 g; ♀ 24–34 g. **Head-and-body length:** ♂ 80–115 mm; ♀ 80–115 mm. **Tail length:** ♂ 60–95 mm; ♀ 60–95 mm. **Distinguishing features:** Very bushy tail with a white tip. The face has a dark mask. **Life-span:** ± 5 yrs. **Predators:** Main predators include birds of prey, snakes and small carnivores.

DESCRIPTION

The fur is soft and woolly. The upperparts are grey or buffy grey, the underparts buffy white. A darker facial mask is present. The tail is bushy, with 18 mm-long hair. Its upper surface is slightly darker than the body, the underside is paler. The tail ends in a white tip, and the feet are white. The head is rounded, the ears are small and the muzzle is blunt. Woodland dormice are very good climbers; well-developed pads on the feet allow for tremendous agility and balance. A unique feature of dormice is that their tails detach easily and portions of the tail tissue are regenerated. The hair may then grow as a distinct 'brush'.

Scent glands: None present.

Senses: Good sight, very good hearing and sense of smell.

DISTRIBUTION

The distribution of woodland dormice is patchy within the Kruger, and they are nowhere common. They occur in savanna woodland in ecozones A, B, D, G, I, L, N and P.

BEHAVIOUR

Nocturnal and solitary. Predominantly arboreal, although they may spend short periods on the ground. In captivity, they display territorial behaviour and they are most probably also territorial in the wild.

Woodland dormice shelter in nests, in holes and in crevices lined with debris. They also shelter in houses where they are found in nests in roofs, under floors, and in switchboards, for example.

They may undergo periods of torpidity, lasting a few days, or may enter full hibernation, if the food supply is insufficient or when temperatures drop.

Calls: Contact calls include clicks, growls, twitters and whistles. Alarm calls include a two-part 'spit-urr'.

Alarm signals: Alarm signals consist of the warning call repeated rapidly, finally ending in a piercing shriek.

Aggression: Raise the bushy tail and claws, threatening with an open-mouthed gape. Other signs of aggression include chasing, attacking and biting. The opponent, once killed, is often eaten.

REPRODUCTION

Breed in the summer rainy season. 2–6 pups, weighing 3,5 g each, are born after a gestation period of 24 days. The pups are born in nests lined with debris. Woodland dormice pups are blind, deaf and naked at birth, and are weaned at 1 month.

The dark facial mask is distinctive

DIET

Omnivorous, feeding on vegetable matter, seeds, fruit, insects, invertebrates, lizards, small vertebrates, eggs and carrion. In the Kruger, they have shown a strong preference for the large millipede, *Doratogonus flavifilis*. Water independent, obtaining enough moisture from their food and from dew, but will drink when water is available.

HABITAT

Nearly all habitats, favouring woodland, particularly *Acacia* woodland, thickets, forests and rocky areas. In the Kruger, found in woodland areas in the mixed bushwillow woodlands, mopane/bushwillow woodlands, thorn thickets, delagoa thorn thickets, Lebombo Mountain bushveld, mopane shrubveld, sourveld and sandveld communities habitats.

Rat-like Rodents

The family Muridae comprises 17 subfamilies, about 280 genera and over 1 300 species. Of this, 5 sub-families, 15 genera and 19 species are found in the Kruger National Park, and are listed under the sub-family headings below. Overall ranges for physical characteristics and distribution maps are given for each subfamily.

Grooved-toothed Rats (Subfamily Otomyinae)

Ger: Lamellenzahnratten; **Fre:** Rats des marais à queue courte; **Afr:** Groeftandrot

Species: Angoni Vlei Rat, *Otomys angoniensis*

Status: not endangered	

Mass: ♂ 100–260 g; ♀ 100–260 g. **Head-and-body length:** ♂ 120–220 mm; ♀ 120–220 mm. **Tail length:** ♂ 60–120 mm; ♀ 60–120 mm. **Distinguishing features:** Long, shaggy coats. *Otomys* spp have grooved upper incisors and a blunt muzzle. *O. angoniensis* has buffy brown patches at the base of the ears and on the throat. **Life-span:** Unknown. **Predators:** Main predators include birds of prey, snakes and small carnivores. Indigenous populations consider some species a delicacy.

DESCRIPTION
The shaggy fur is buff-brown to darker brown. The underparts are much paler, tending to be greyish. The short tail is dark and paler underneath. The ears are large and rounded.
Scent glands: Anal.
Senses: Good sight, very good hearing and sense of smell.

DISTRIBUTION
Found in suitable habitat in ecozones B and D, and in the northern parts of ecozones H and N of the Kruger.

BEHAVIOUR
Predominantly diurnal, with some nocturnal activity. Solitary, or occur in pairs or family colonies. Most species of grooved-toothed rats live in dome-shaped nests made of grass and other vegetable material. Nests are constructed in clumps of grass, on ground that is raised above water level. Well-defined runs lead from the nests to the feeding grounds. The home range and runs are marked with piles of short lengths of grass.
Calls: Contact calls include squeaks. Alarm calls include squeaks and squeals.
Alarm signals: Flee for cover.
Aggression: Slow approach with body held low and the tail shivering. An attack may be preceded by a broad side stance. Submissive animals rear up on their hind haunches to show their vulnerable bellies and may fall over while doing so. This is done to prevent attack, as flight would result in them being pursued and their rumps being bitten severely. Other signs of aggression include vocal 'chits' while sitting on the hind haunches.

REPRODUCTION
Breed in the summer rainy season. 1–5 pups, weighing 10–15 g each, are born after a gestation period of about 40 days. They are fully furred at birth, with their eyes closed;

The Angoni vlei rat (above) has brown patches on the throat and ears

their eyes open after a few days. Pups of most species nipple-cling for 7–14 days.

DIET

Herbivorous, feeding on grasses, herb and reed stems, reed rhizomes as well as bark, roots and seeds. They are water independent, obtaining enough moisture from their food, but will drink when water is available.

HABITAT

Grasslands, open savanna, dense secondary growth, marshes and swamps. *O. angoniensis* occurs in grassland and woodland savanna, and is particularly found in drier regions, preferring marshy and swamp areas in these regions. *O. angoniensis* occurs marginally in swampy areas and reed beds in the sourveld, thorn thickets, and northern sandveld and riverine communities habitats of the Kruger.

Gerbils (Subfamily Gerbillinae)

(Data for *Tatera* spp).

Ger: Rennmaus; **Fre:** Gerbille; **Afr:** Nagmuis.

Species: Bushveld Gerbil, *Tatera leucogaster.*

Status: not endangered

Mass: ♂ 60–125 g; ♀ 60–125 g. **Head-and-body length:** ♂ 120–160 mm; ♀ 120–160 mm. **Tail length:** ♂ 140–170 mm; ♀ 140–170 mm. **Distinguishing features:** *T. leucogaster* has a distinct dark line down the upper surface of the tail, white markings above and behind the eyes, and the sides of the muzzle are white. The soles of the feet are dark in colour in this particular species. **Life-span:** ± 4 yrs. **Predators:** Main predators are birds of prey, snakes and small carnivores.

DESCRIPTION

The fur on the upperparts is tawny to reddish brown, and the underparts are white. The eyes and ears are large, the hindlegs are long. The prominent muzzle is hairy. The soles of the feet are naked.

Tatera spp are reservoirs for the *Yersinia pestis bacillus*, which causes plague.
Scent glands: None present.
Senses: Poor sight, very good hearing and sense of smell.

DISTRIBUTION

Occur commonly and widespread in suitable soil in all the ecozones of the Kruger.

BEHAVIOUR

Gerbils are nocturnal. They may be solitary or may occur in pairs, but they are generally found in small family colonies. *T. leucogaster*, however, occurs in pairs.

In sandy soils, gerbils excavate their own burrows. Burrows are distinguished by a mound of fresh sand at the entrance, especially in the mornings. The burrow entrances are situated at the base of bushes and grass clumps. The burrows are usually complex, with many entrances and tunnels that interconnect underground. Chambers are lined with vegetable debris. The burrows of *T. leucogaster* lead to o chamber, 20–45 cm below the surface, and are about 40–45 mm in diameter. In mopane woodland areas, gerbils may shelter in old termite mounds or in holes under tree roots.

Gerbils are fond of sand bathing.
Calls: Contact and alarm calls include squeaks.
Alarm signals: When disturbed outside their burrows, gerbils rush back to the shelter of their burrows, sealing the entrance behind them. When disturbed in their burrows, they move away from the source of disturbance, closing the burrows behind them.
Aggression: Crouching, chasing, attacking, and biting.

REPRODUCTION

Breed all year, with a peak in the summer rainy season. 2–9 (average 4) pups, weighing 4,5 g each, are born after a gestation period of 21–24 days, in grass lined nesting chambers in the burrow system. Pups are blind and naked at birth their eyes open at 10 days and they are furred by 14 days. They take solid food a 18 days and are weaned at 3 weeks.

Bushveld gerbil (above) – note the characteristic white markings above and behind the eyes

DIET

Omnivorous, feeding on stems, grass roots, bulbs, seeds, termites and small insects. Most species cache food within the burrow, however, *T. leucogaster* buries seeds. Water independent, obtaining enough moisture from their food and from dew, but will drink when water is available.

HABITAT

Variety of habitats with well-drained sandy soil. Not found in rain-forest or margins of the Sahara Desert. *T. leucogaster* prefers light, sandy soil and sandy alluvium, and may also be found on hard ground, although it is not found on red clay. Occur in suitable soil in all the habitats of the Kruger.

Dendromurines (Subfamily Dendromurinae)

Ger: Klettermäuse und Fettmäuse; **Fre:** Dendromurinés; **Afr:** Klimmuise en Vetmuise.

Species: Grey Climbing Mouse, *Dendromus melanotis;* Chestnut Climbing Mouse, *Dendromus mystacalis;* Fat Mouse, *Steatomys pratensis.*

Status: not endangered	☽

Mass: ♂ 7–70 g; ♀ 7–70 g. **Head-and-body length:** ♂ 50–145 mm; ♀ 50–145 mm. **Tail length:** ♂ 30–215 mm; ♀ 30–215 mm. **Distinguishing features:** *Dendromus* spp have a distinct dark band running down the length of the back to the base of the tail. Grooved upper incisors. *D. melanotis* has white patches at the anterior base of the ears. *Steatomys* spp have large ears with a white patch at the base, the limbs and tail are short. They have a white patch at the base of the ears. **Life-span:** ± 3 yrs. **Predators:** Main predators include birds of prey, particularly owls; snakes and small carnivores. *Steatomys* spp are considered a delicacy by some indigenous populations.

DESCRIPTION

The upperparts of *Dendromus* spp vary from fawn to grey or rich brown; the underparts are greyish. Tails are long and semi-prehensile. *Dendromus* spp are good climbers, although they tend to restrict activity to tall grass and low bushes (under 2 m). They steady themselves while climbing by curling their tail around grass stems and twigs.

    Steatomys spp have shiny, brownish-grey fur with white underparts. Their tails are darker than their bodies, and are paler underneath. They are often fat and lethargic. In winter, they accumulate fat under the skin and become torpid. *Steatomys* spp can be distinguished from *Dendromus* spp by their feet: they have 4 toes on the forefeet, and 5 on the hindfeet (all with sharp claws).

Scent glands: None present.

Senses: Poor sight, very good hearing and sense of smell.

DISTRIBUTION

D. melanotis is found in ecozones B, H and N of the Kruger, occurring at Willem Picket near Pretoriuskop, at Crocodile Bridge, and in the Punda Maria and Pafuri regions. *D. mystacalis* is rare within the Kruger, having been reported in tall grasslands in ecozones B, D, E, H and L, but particularly in the Pretoriuskop area. *S. pratensis* is found in suitable habitat in ecozones A, B, D, E, H, L and N, occurring particularly around the Pretoriuskop, Punda Maria and Pafuri areas.

BEHAVIOUR

Dendromurines are nocturnal. They are solitary or occur in pairs, and are predominantly terrestrial, although *Dendromus* spp spend considerable amounts of time climbing among grasses and low bushes.

    Dendromus spp construct ball-shaped nests of shredded grass leaves, in abandoned burrows, or more commonly between grass stems or bush twigs, 1 m above ground level. Unlike other *Dendromus* spp, *D. melanotis* shelter in subterranean dwellings. Their burrows are up to 50 cm deep and 4–6 cm in diameter. They contain simple, open-ended tunnels that lead to a nesting chamber with a bolt exit.

    Steatomys spp make deep burrows with several entrance holes that are plugged with loosely compacted soil. The burrows are 30 mm in diameter, 0,02–1 m deep, and slope down from the surface to a chamber lined with shredded vege-

Grey climbing mouse

tation. In winter, *Steatomys* spp become torpid for up to 2–3 weeks at a time.

Calls: Contact and alarm calls include squeaks.

Alarm signals: Generally they freeze when disturbed, then flee for cover. *Dendromus* spp are good jumpers, making leaps of up to 45 cm when surprised or frightened. *Steatomys* spp respond to being dug out by digging away from the source of disturbance, blocking the passage behind them. If pursuit continues, they dig upwards until they break the surface, then flee. If caught, *Steatomys* spp are known to feign death.

Aggression: *Dendromus* spp fight ferociously with one another, and these disputes often result in the death of one of the opponents. They also fight predators, and have been reported to kill snakes.

REPRODUCTION

Breed in the summer rainy season. 1–5 pups, weighing 1 g each, are born after a gestation period of 23–28 days. They are blind, deaf and naked at birth. Their eyes open between 10 and 14 days while their ears open at 15 days. They are independent at 1 month.

DIET

Omnivorous, feeding on grass seeds, termites, grasshoppers, crickets, moths and small beetles. *Steatomys* spp eat roots and bulbs. Dendromurines are water independent, obtaining moisture from food and from dew, but will drink when water is available.

HABITAT

Dendromus spp are found in a variety of habitats: from the Drakensberg Mountains to the scrub of the Kalahari Desert. They are associated with stands of tall, coarse grass, 1–2 m high, particularly where the grass is thickened with other vegetation, for example, the rank vegetation of riverine habitats. In the Kruger, they are particularly associated with *Hyparrhenia* spp grasses.

Steatomys spp are found in savanna, woodland and semi-arid areas, preferring areas with sandy soils, in particular sandy alluvium.

All species occur in the sourveld, sandveld and riverine communities habitats of the Kruger. *D. mystacalis* and *S. pratensis* occur in thorn thickets, thorn veld, and mopane shrubveld habitats; *S. pratensis* also occurs in the mixed bushwillow woodlands.

Pouched Rats (Subfamily Cricetomyinae)

Ger: Hamsterratten; **Fre:** Rats blague; **Afr:** Wangsakrot.

Species: Giant Rat, *Cricetomys gambianus;* Pouched Mouse, *Saccostomus campestris.*

Status: not endangered

)

Mass: ♂ ♀ *Cricetomys* spp 1,0–2,8 kg; *Saccostomus* spp 40–85 g. **Head-and-body length:** ♂ ♀ *Cricetomys* spp 280–450 mm; *Saccostomus* spp 120–190 mm. **Tail length:** ♂ ♀ *Cricetomys* spp 360–460 mm; *Saccostomus* spp 30–80 mm. **Distinguishing features:** *Cricetomys* spp have large, naked ears. *C. gambianus* has a distinctive black facial mask. **Life-span:** *Cricetomys* spp: 4 yrs (in captivity); *Saccostomus* spp: 3 yrs (in captivity). **Predators:** Main predators include birds of prey, snakes and small carnivores.

Giant Rat

H

Hind: 5 cm

DESCRIPTION

Cricetomys spp are grey, greyish brown or brown, with paler underparts. The terminal half of the tail is white. *Cricetomys* spp are very good climbers.

Saccostomus spp are grey or greyish brown with whitish underparts.

All species have large cheek pouches (with those in *Saccostomus* spp being particularly large), in which food is temporarily stored and transported.

Scent glands: None present.

Senses: Poor sight, very good hearing and sense of smell.

DISTRIBUTION

C. gambianus occurs in the northwestern parts of econzone N of the Kruger, at the Soutpansberg foothills, west of Punda Maria.

S. campestris occurs in woodland and woodland savannas in ecozones A, B, C, D, H, I, L and N of the Kruger, but is nowhere common.

BEHAVIOUR

Pouched rats are solitary and nocturnal, but some early morning and late afternoon activity has been reported for *C. gambianus*. They shelter in self-dug burrows, or in modified abandoned burrows or termite mounds, and under rocks, tree trunks and tree roots. Burrows have a nesting chamber in which food is stored; unused food is discarded in mounds within the nesting chamber.

C. gambianus burrows have 1–3 entrances, with characteristic pellet-sized piles of soil at the entrances. Burrows average 100–160 mm in diameter, and have up to 5 chambers, one being a latrine, another the nesting chamber. The latter is used for storing food, and is lined with leaves and sticks; its entrances are sealed with sand and rocks. On average, chambers are 260–660 mm in diameter, 160–360 mm high, and 660–820 mm below the surface. The home range covers 0,02–0,1 km². In captivity, these rats display territorial behaviour: dribbling urine, assuming ritualistic handstand positions whilst depositing dung, and rubbing cheeks.

S. campestris burrow systems may be simple or complex and are usually 380 mm below the surface. In cold weather, they may enter short periods of torpor.

Calls: *C. gambianus:* chirrups (likened to those of a canary).

Alarm signals: Relatively docile and easily caught.

Aggression: All species are tame, but bite when bullied. Aggression is also shown by sitting on the hind haunches, while snapping with the teeth. *C. gambianus* sit on

Pouched mouse

their haunches and push opponents away with the forequarters. They blow up the cheek pouches and release a noisy blast of air.

REPRODUCTION

C. gambianus breeds all year, with a peak in the summer rainy season. 2–4 pups, weighing 19–33 g each, are born after a gestation period of 6 weeks in nesting chambers lined with leaves and sticks. They are blind and naked at birth; skin pigmentation starts developing at 4 days, they are furred at 10 days, and their eyes open at 3–4 weeks. They leave the nest at 3 months.

S. campestris breeds all year, with a peak in the summer rainy season. 5–10 pups, weighing 2,8 g each, are born in nesting chambers after a gestation period of 3 weeks. They are blind but fully furred at birth; their eyes open at 3 weeks. They are weaned at 25 days.

DIET

Omnivorous, feeding on fruit, nuts, seeds, grains, bulbs, tubers, roots and leaves. *Saccostomus* spp also occasionally take insects. Food is collected in the cheek pouches and transported back to the burrows to be eaten.

S. campestris is water independent. *C. gambianus* is water dependent, drinking regularly, but also obtains moisture from fruit.

HABITAT

Cricetomys spp are found in a variety of habitats. *C. gambianus* is common in forest and woodland with high rainfall (over 800 mm annually), and is also common in urban areas where shrubs and hedges are used for cover. *C. gambianus* is found in the sandveld communities habitats of the Kruger.

Saccostomus spp are found in savannas, open woodlands and semi-arid areas with scrub cover, preferring areas with sandy soil. In the Kruger, *S. campestris* occurs in woodland and woodland savannas in the mixed bushwillow woodlands, thorn thickets, Lebombo Mountain and Malelane Mountain bushveld, mopane shrubveld, sourveld and riverine and sandveld communities habitats.

Murid Rats and Mice (Subfamily Murinae)

Ger: Murid Ratten und Mäuse; **Afr:** Murid Rotte en Muise.

Species: Spiny Mouse, *Acomys spinosissimus;* Single-striped Mouse, *Lemniscomys rosalia;* Water Rat, *Dasymys incomtus;* Woodland Mouse, *Grammomys dolichurus;* House Mouse, *Mus musculus;* Pygmy Mouse, *Mus minutoides;* Natal Multimammate Mouse, *Mastomys natalensis;* Multimammate Mouse, *Mastomys coucha;* Tree Rat, *Thallomys paedulcus;* Red Veld Rat, *Aethomys chrysophilus;* Namaqua Rock Mouse, *Aethomys namaquensis;* House Rat, *Rattus rattus.*

Status: not endangered

Mass: ♂ 2,5–180g; ♀ 2,5–180g. **Head-and-body length:** ♂ 45–210 mm; ♀ 45–210 mm. **Tail length:** ♂ 35–320 mm; ♀ 35–320 mm. **Distinguishing features:** *Lemniscomys* spp have a variable number of dark, solid or broken dorsal lines down the mid-back, with a blackish dorsal mid-line. *Mus* spp have a blackish facial mask, *Thallomys* spp a blackish eye mask. *Grammomys* spp have very long, finely haired tails. **Life-span:** ± 3–4 yrs (in captivity). **Predators:** Main predators include birds of prey, particularly the barn owl and spotted eagle owl; snakes and small carnivores.

DESCRIPTION

Acomys, Lemniscomys, Grammomys and *Aethomys* spp have buff, tawny, grey, rust, red or brown upperparts, with white or paler underparts. *Acomys* spp have a coarse, spiny fur. *Dasymys* and *Rattus* spp have dark grey to brown-black upperparts, with greyish-white underparts. *Dasymys* spp have a shaggy coat. *Mus* spp are buffy brown, *Thallomys* spp are tawny, grey or brown, and both have paler underparts. *Mastomys* spp are grey or brown with white underparts. *Dasymys* spp are good swimmers and are semi-aquatic. *R. rattus'* tail touches the ground when walking. *Rattus* and *Mastomys* spp are hosts for *Yersinia pestis*, which causes plague, and for *Salmonella typhimurium*, which causes typhus. *Mastomys* spp are also hosts for the Lassa Fever, Banzi and Witswatersrand Viruses, and for *Eschericia coli* and *Pasteurella pneumotropica*. The diseases are transmitted to humans through infected fleas.

Scent glands: Salivary and perianal. Males also have preputial glands.

Senses: Poor sight, very good hearing and sense of smell.

DISTRIBUTION

A. spinosissimus occurs in ecozones N and M of the Kruger, in the Punda Maria area and in the sandstone ridges north and south of the Luvuvhu River. *L. rosalia* occurs in woodlands and grassy plains in all the ecozones.

D. incomtus is found in the damp habitats near watercourses in ecozones B and N, in the Pretoriuskop and Punda Maria areas.

G. dolichurus occurs in the extreme northeastern parts of ecozone H, in the riverine forests along the Limpopo and Luvuvhu rivers.

M. musculus has been reported in a building in Shangoni on the western border. *M. minutoides* occurs commonly throughout ecozones B, C, D, I, L and N. *M. coucha* has been reported in ecozones F and L, occurring at Satara and the Xitangeni Dam but its distribution probably corresponds with that of *M. natalensis*, which occurs commonly throughout all the ecozones, as do *A. chrysophilus* and *A. namaquensis.*

T. paedulcus occurs in savannas and woodlands in ecozones D, I, L and N. *R. rattus* has been reported in ecozones B and D, at the Pretoriuskop and Skukuza rest camps.

Note the brown-black coat of the house rat (above)

BEHAVIOUR

All the murid rat and mice species are nocturnal, with the exception of *L. rosalia*, which is diurnal, and *D. incomtus*, which is diurnal with activity peaks at dawn and dusk. Social structures vary greatly, even within species, with limited data available.

Acomys spp and *L. rosalia* are solitary, or occur in pairs or family colonies. *Aethomys* spp occur in pairs or family colonies. All shelter in nests lined with vegetable debris: *Acomys* spp beneath rocks, in gerbil and other rodent warrens, and in termite mounds and houses; *L. rosalia* under tall or matted grasses; *Aethomys* spp in rocky crevices, holes in trees and termite mounds, and under piles of debris.

Huge piles of debris cover the entrances to *A. namaquensis'* shelters. *Lemniscomys* spp follow well-defined runs within their home range; these are lined with small piles of cut grass stems.

The nests of *D. incomtus* are dome-shaped and are constructed of finely shredded grass. They are 20 cm in diameter and are buried deep in grass tussocks. Well-defined runs, which are lined with piles of grass stems, are followed within the home range. Runs may be shared with *Otomys* and *Dendromys* spp.

Nests of *Mus* and *Rattus* spp are constructed of any soft, shredded debris. *M. minutoides* is solitary and shelters under logs, in hollows under trees, under piles of debris and in termite mounds. *M. musculus* occurs in pairs or family colonies, and shelters in buildings. *M. musculus* males hold harem colonies, comprised of up to 10 females with their young. They defend a territory range of a few square metres, which is marked with urine. *Rattus* spp shelter in walls, under the floors of buildings, and under piles of debris. They use well-defined runs, which are marked with greasy smears from the fur and feet.

Grammomys and Thallomys spp are arboreal. Grammomys spp are solitary. Their nests are 0,5–2 m above ground, or they shelter in holes in trees and in old weavers' nests. The entrances to their burrows are screened with thin grass. The nests of Thallomys spp are constructed with leaves, grass and twigs. They are situated in hollows in or under trees, in forks in trees, under piles of debris and under loose bark, and are so large that the nest material can fill a wheelbarrow. These constructions are used more as night-time playgrounds or shelters for roaming. Thallomys spp follow well-defined runs, which are lined with twigs. Tree branches within the home range are marked with perianal gland secretions.

Mastomys spp occur in family colonies. They shelter in self-dug or abandoned rodent burrows, or under tree roots, under piles of debris, under rocks, and in cracks in the soil.

Calls: Contact calls include squeaks and twitters. Alarm calls include squeaks, chirps and screeches. Some species may produce sounds that are not audible to the human ear.

Alarm signals: Generally flee for cover. *Grammomys* spp generally climb upwards, seeking a shelter in which to hide.

Aggression: Some species are very aggressive, biting their opponents to death.

REPRODUCTION

Breed in the summer rainy season, with the exception of *Mastomys* spp, *Rattus* spp and *A. chrysophilus*, which breed all year with a peak in the summer. *M. minutoides* gives birth to 2–7 young; *M. musculus*, 1–12; *D. incomtus*, 2–9; *Mastomys* spp, up to 22, (average 7–9); *Rattus* spp, 5–12; the remainder 2–5. Pups weigh between 0,9 and 4,2 g at birth, depending on the species. The gestation period is 19–24 days, except for *Rattus* spp, which is 21–30 days. Pups are blind and naked at birth, with their ears closed and toes fused. Their ears unfold and

open at 1–2 days, their toes separate at 4–5 days, their eyes open at 10–14 days, and they are furred at 18 days. Pups are weaned at about 3 weeks, except for *Rattus* spp pups, which are weaned at 1 month. *Thallomys*, *Grammomys* and *Aethomys* spp pups nipple-cling.

DIET

Omnivorous. *Acomys*, *Lemniscomys*, *Mus*, *Rattus*, *Aethomys*, *Grammomys* and *Thallomys* spp take grass, seeds, leaves and insects. *Acomys*, *Mastomys*, *Mus* and *Rattus* spp also take invertebrates, and *Mus* and *Rattus* spp also feed on carrion. *Mastomys* spp are cannibals. *Acomys*, *Grammomys* and *Mastomys* spp also take wild fruit, stems, and wood fibres. *Thallomys* spp also take roots and gum.

Dasymys spp feed on succulent stems, semi-aquatic grasses and flowers, reeds and insects.

Most species appear to be water dependent, drinking regularly, except *Thallomys*, *Mastomys* and *Dasymys* spp, which are independent of water, obtaining enough moisture from succulents and from their food. If the humidity in the nest is high, *M. musculus* is also independent of surface water.

HABITAT

Acomys spp occur in deserts and drier areas and are not found in moist forest. *A. spinosissimus* prefers rocky areas with sandy alluvium along rivers, dry woodland and thickets. In the Kruger, it is found in the sandveld communities and alluvium plains habitats.

Lemniscomys spp occur in grasslands, and *L. rosalia* is found in grasslands in all the habitats of the Kruger.

Thallomys spp occur in dry, *Acacia*-dominated woodlands and savannas. In the Kruger, *T. paedulcus* is found in the thorn thickets, Lebombo Mountain bushveld, mopane shrubveld and sandveld communities habitats.

Aethomys and Rattus spp occur in grassland, savanna woodland and scrub, with *Aethomys* spp preferring rocky habitats. *R. rattus* also occurs in buildings or near human habitation, and in thick underbrush in thickets, forests or under rocks. *A. chrysophilus* and *A. namaquensis* occur in all the habitats of the Kruger: *A. chrysophilus* in woodland; *A. namaquensis* in rocky areas. *R. rattus* occurs in the sourveld and thorn thickets habitats of the Kruger.

Single striped mouse (above); House mouse (top); Red veld rat (bottom)

Mastomys spp occur in buildings, forest clearings, savannas and woodlands. They are found in most habitats, except in the driest regions of sub-Saharan Africa. Likewise, *M. natalensis* and *M. coucha* are found in all the habitats of the Kruger Park.

Dasymys and *Grammomys* occur in damp areas. *Dasymys* spp occur in grassy areas along rivers, marshes, swamps and reed beds. *Grammomys* spp are found in riverine forest, thickets in woodland, and reed beds.

In the Kruger Park, *D. incomtus* is found in the sourveld and sandveld communities habitats; *G. dolichurus* is found in the extreme northeastern riverine communities habitats.

Mus spp occur in nearly all habitats, with *M. musculus* occurring in buildings and *M. minutoides* occurring in grassland savanna and woodland. In the Kruger, *M. minutoides* occurs in the Malelane and Lebombo Mountain bushveld, mopane shrubveld, thorn thickets, sourveld and sandveld communities habitats.

Bats

The order Chiroptera comprises 18 families, about 200 genera and hundreds of species worldwide. Of these, 7 families, 18 genera and 42 species are found in the Kruger National Park, and are listed under the family headings below. Overall ranges for each family are given for physical characteristics and distribution.

Fruit Bats

Ger: Frucht Fledermäuse; **Fre:** Mégachiroptères; **Afr:** Vrugtevlermuise.

Species: Peter's Epauletted Fruit Bat, *Epomophorus crypturus;* Wahlberg's Epauletted Fruit Bat, *Epomophorus wahlbergi;* Egyptian Fruit Bat, *Rousettus aegyptiacus.*

Status: not endangered

Mass: ♂ 0,011–1,500 kg; ♀ 0,011–1,500 kg. **Head-and-body length:** ♂ 50–400 mm; ♀ 50–400 mm. **Forearm length:** ♂ 24–170 cm; ♀ 24–170 cm. **Distinguishing features:** Also known as flying foxes because of the 'dog-like' head. Tail is very short or absent. The brown eyes are noticeably large. The tubular ears lack tragi. **Life-span:** ± 20–30 yrs. **Predators:** Main predators include birds of prey.

DESCRIPTION

R. aegyptiacus is grey-brown with black wings. *Epomophorus* spp are varying shades of brown, and have white tufts of fur at the base of the ears and white circular patches (epaulettes) on the shoulders.

Fruit bats have two claws on the wing structure: one on the flexible thumb, and one on the second finger. The wings are broad and crepe textured. The teeth are blunt and simple.

Scent glands: *Epomophorus* spp have scent glands under the epaulettes on their shoulders.
Senses: Good sight, very good hearing, and good sense of smell.

DISTRIBUTION

R. aegyptiacus is found in ecozone N, occurring along the Limpopo and Luvuvhu rivers. *E. wahlbergi* is found in ecozones B, C and N, occurring in the Pretoriuskop, Malelane and Punda Maria areas, particularly in riparian forests. *E. crypturus* occurs throughout the Kruger, in all ecozones except K; it is particularly common in riparian forests.

BEHAVIOUR

Fruit bats are nocturnal, and form colonies. *E. crypturus* congregates in hundreds, *E. wahlbergi* in dozens. Both roost under the canopy of thick foliage in evergreen trees.

R. aegyptiacus congregates in thousands and roosts in caves. Females gather in nursery groups, and males form bachelor groups.

In winter, fruit bats may undergo periods of torpor.

Calls: Contact calls include chattering. Muffled snuffling noises are associated with feeding. The calls of *Epomophorus* spp are often mistaken for those of frogs. Only *R. aegyptiacus* have echo-ranging capabilities. Echo-ranging signals sound like 'clicks' to the human ear.

Aggression: Many species spar aggressively, and may bite and strike out with the clawed thumbs. Sparring may be accompanied by loud shrieks and cackles.

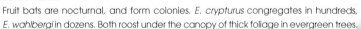

Peter's epauletted fruit bat

REPRODUCTION

Breed in the summer rainy season. 1 (rarely 2) pup, weighing one fifth of the mother's body weight, is born after a gestation period of 105 days. Pups are blind at birth and the ears are folded closed. The pups' eyes open at about 10 days. They nipple-cling for about 6 weeks, and are weaned at 4–5 months.

DIET

Fruit bats, as their name implies, are fructivorous, feeding on fruit, flowers, nectar and pollen. *R. aegyptiacus* also takes leaves and buds. In the Kruger Park, *E. wahlbergi* mainly eats the fruits of *Ficus sycomorus, Diospyros mespiliformis* and *Mimusops zeyheri*. *E. crypturus* favours the fruits of the *Ficus* spp, *Diospyros mespiliformis* and of *Xanthoceris zambesiaca*.

Fruit bats are water independent, obtaining enough moisture from fruit and condensation (on their fur and on cave walls, etc.), but will drink when water is available.

HABITAT

Fruit bats require the presence of fruiting trees all year, and are found in savannas, woodlands and forest mosaics. All species are found in the sandveld communities habitats of the Kruger Park. *E. crypturus* and *E. wahlbergi* are found in the sourveld and Malelane Mountain bushveld habitats, and *E. wahlbergi* is found in almost all the other habitats of the Kruger, except the rugged veld.

Sheath-tailed Bats

Ger: Scheidenschwanz Fledermäuse; **Fre:** Emballonuridés; **Afr:** Skedestertvlermuise.

Species: Tomb Bat, *Taphozous mauritianus.*

Status: not endangered	☽ B

Mass: ♂ 3–30 g; ♀ 3–30 g. **Head-and-body length:** ♂ 37–100 mm; ♀ 37–100 mm. **Tail length:** ♂ 6–30 mm; ♀ 6–30 mm. **Forearm length:** ♂ 32–80 mm; ♀ 32–80 mm. **Distinguishing features:** Tail is half sheathed. The eyes are noticeably large. Ears are often joined together on the forehead. **Life-span:** Several years. **Predators:** Man has the biggest negative impact on bat populations due to habitat modification. Main predators are birds of prey.

DESCRIPTION

The fur is soft and short. *T. mauritianus* is grizzled grey with white underparts. When in flight, air enters the skin pockets below the wrists, producing a whirring sound. The wings are long and narrow.

Scent glands: Most species have a gland on the wing, and a throat gland. *T. mauritianus* has a throat gland.

Senses: Good sight, very good hearing, good sense of smell.

DISTRIBUTION

Although *T. mauritianus* is rare within the Kruger, it is widespread, occurring in suitable habitat in ecozones A, B, C, E, G, I, L, N, M, and P.

BEHAVIOUR

Sheath-tailed bats are predominantly nocturnal, but some daytime activity has been reported. Most species are found in pairs, but *T. mauritianus* occurs in pairs or groups of pairs.

Sheath-tailed bats roost on tree trunks, in hollow trees, rock faces and rock crevices, on the walls of buildings, particularly in ruins or under thatched roofs with overhangs. Roosting sites on painted walls characteristically have brown urine stains, covering 150 x 100 mm. Other roosting sites are marked with greasy smear from the throat gland.

T. mauritianus has been observed to return to the same roosting site every year.

Calls: Contact calls include chirrups and screeches. The short echo-ranging signals 75–20 kHz and 1–6 pulses/msec, are emitted through the mouth.

Alarm and aggression: Generally gentle creatures that do not fight among one another, nor bite, even when captured. They are reluctant to fly when disturbed and will move away from the source of disturbance by scurrying sideways along vertical surfaces.

REPRODUCTION

Breed in the summer rainy season. A single pup, weighing one fifth of its mother's body weight, is born after a gestation period of 3–4 months. It is weaned at 1–4 months.

DIET

Insectivorous, feeding on insects, particularly butterflies and moths. Occasionally also take fruit. Water dependent, drinking regularly.

Tomb bat (above and below) – note the large eyes

HABITAT

Sheath-tailed bats occur in open savanna woodland and forest fringes. In the Kruger Park, they are found in the mixed bushwillow woodlands, mopane/bushwillow woodlands, Malelane and Lebombo Mountain bushvelds as well as in the mopane shrubveld, sourveld, thorn veld, delagoa thorn thickets, sandveld communities and alluvial plains habitats.

Slit-faced Bats

Ger: Schlitznasen Fledermäuse; **Fre:** Nyctères; **Afr:** Spleetneusvlermuise.

Species: Common/Egyptian Slit-faced Bat, *Nycteris thebaica;* Wood's Slit-faced Bat, *Nycteris woodi.*

Status: Wood's Slit-faced Bat – IUCN: NT

Mass: ♂ 10–30 g; ♀ 10–30 g. **Head-and-body length:** ♂ 45–75 mm; ♀ 45–75 mm. **Tail length:** ♂ 43–75 mm; ♀ 43–75 mm. **Forearm length:** ♂ 36–60 mm; ♀ 36–60 mm. **Distinguishing features:** Prominent slit extending from nostrils over the eyes. Nostrils are bound at the sides by a series of lobes (or nose leaves). Ears are longer than the head, and are fused in the middle of the forehead. The long tail is enclosed in a membrane with a T- or Y-shaped tip. **Life-span:** Unknown. **Predators:** Man has the biggest negative impact on bat populations, due to habitat modification. Main predators are birds of prey.

DESCRIPTION

Instantly recognizable by the very long ears, which are longer than the head and by the prominent slit running from the upper lip to the forehead. The fur is long and silky. The upperparts are reddish brown or brown with a greyish tinge while the underparts are whitish grey to buff-grey. The delicate wings are broad and short.

Scent glands: None known.

Senses: Good sight, very good hearing, good sense of smell.

DISTRIBUTION

N. woodi occurs in ecozone N of the Kruger, in the Pafuri area. *N. thebaica* occurs commonly throughout ecozones A, B, D, E, I, M, N and O, and in the northern parts of ecozone L.

BEHAVIOUR

Nocturnal, and form colonies. *N. thebaica* colonies comprise hundreds of bats while *N. woodi* is found in smaller groups. Prefer cool, dark and moist roosting sites. Roosting sites include caves, rock ledges, rock cavities, hollow trees, tree branches, mine adits, roofs, as well as aardvark and porcupine burrows. In winter, slit-faced bats may undergo periods of torpor.

Calls: Contact calls include quiet 'whispers'. The short echo-ranging signals 100–80 kHz and 0,25–1 pulses/msec, are emitted through the nose.

REPRODUCTION

Breed in the summer rainy season. A single pup, weighing one fifth of its mother's body weight, is born after a gestation period of 150 days. The new born pup is transported by nipple-clinging to its mother. It is weaned after 45–60 days.

DIET

Insectivorous, feeding on insects, including butterflies, moths, flies, crickets, cicadas and grasshoppers. Spiders and scorpions are also taken. Water dependent, drinking regularly. Apart from drinking at a specific water supply, moisture can also be obtained by licking condensed water from their fur and from the cave's walls.

Common slit-faced bat

HABITAT

Slit-faced bats are found in a variety of habitats, but are not found in desert areas. Although they have a wide habitat tolerance, they forage at lower levels in thickets, reeds and areas of dense undergrowth. *N. thebaica* and *N. woodi* occur in woodland savanna. In the Kruger Park, *N. woodi* is found in woodland savanna in the sandveld communities habitats. *N. thebaica* is found in the mixed bushwillow woodlands, tree mopane savanna, sourveld, thorn thickets, as well as the Lebombo Mountain bushveld, thorn veld, alluvial plains, sandveld communities, and the northern parts of the mopane shrubveld habitats.

Horseshoe Bats

Ger: Hufeisennasen Fledermäuse; **Fre:** Rhinolophidés; **Afr:** Saalneusvlermuise.

Species: Peak-saddle Horseshoe Bat, *Rhinolophus blasii;* Geoffroy's Horseshoe Bat, *Rhinolophus clivosus;* Darling's Horseshoe Bat, *Rhinolophus darlingi;* Rüppell's Horseshoe Bat, *Rhinolophus fumigatus;* Hildebrandt's Horseshoe Bat, *Rhinolophus hildebrandtii;* Lander's Horseshoe Bat, *Rhinolophus landeri;* Bushveld Horseshoe Bat, *Rhinolophus simulator;* Swinny's Horseshoe Bat, *Rhinolophus swinnyi.*

Status: Peak-saddle Horseshoe Bat – IUCN: NT))

Mass: ♂ 4–40 g. ♀ 4–40 g. **Head-and-body length:** ♂ 35–110 mm; ♀ 35–110 mm. **Tail length:** ♂ 25–45 mm; ♀ 25–45 mm. **Forearm length:** ♂ 35–70 mm; ♀ 35–70 mm. **Distinguishing features:** A prominent nose leaf – its lower portion shaped like a horseshoe – covering the upper lip and surrounding the nostrils. Triangular, upright leaf with complex folds over small eyes. The ears are large and pointed. **Life-span:** ± 20 yrs. **Predators:** Man has the biggest negative impact on bat populations, due to habitat modification. Main predators are birds of prey.

DESCRIPTION

The fur is long and soft. The upperparts are greyish brown to brown, with paler underparts. The wings are short and rounded.

Scent glands: None known.

Senses: Good sight, very good hearing, good sense of smell.

DISTRIBUTION

R. clivosus is found in ecozones D and N of the Kruger, occurring in the Punda Maria, Pafuri and Skukuza areas. *R. darlingi* occurs widely throughout ecozones A, B, C, H, I, N and P. *R. fumigatus* and *R. hildebrandtii* occur in ecozones I and N: *R. fumigatus* in the Pafuri area, the Matshitshindzudzi area south of Pafuri, and in the Olifants River Gorge; *R. hildebrandtii* in the Punda Maria and Pafuri regions, and marginally in the Lebombo Mountains. *R. landeri* is found in eco-zones E and N, occurring in a cave near Girivana, west of Satara, and in the Pafuri and Xirhombe Picket areas. *R. simulator* is found in ecozones F and G, occurring in the central districts and in the Pafuri area. *R. swinnyi* occurs in eco-zone N, in the Pafuri area.

BEHAVIOUR

Horseshoe bats are nocturnal. The social structure varies according to species: *R. swinnyi* is solitary or occurs in pairs; *R. blasii* forms small colonies of 3–4 individuals; *R. fumigatus* and *R. landeri* form colonies of up to 12 individuals; *R. simulator* and *R. darlingi* colonies of several dozen; *R. hildebrandtii* colonies of hundreds; and *R. clivosus* colonies of up to 10 000. All species roost in caves and mines. *R. fumigatus, R. clivosus, R. landeri,* and *R. hildebrandtii* also roost in rock crevices, rock ledges, hollow trees and roofs.

All species hang by their hindfeet from the ceilings of their roosts.

In winter, horseshoe bats may undergo periods of torpor or enter full hiber-nation. During torpor/hibernation, the heart rate may be reduced to as little as 2 beats/min.

Calls: Contact calls are not audible to the human ear. The long, echo-ranging sig-nals, 120–40 kHz and 10–60 pulses/msec, are emitted through the nose.

Hildebrandt's horseshoe bat

REPRODUCTION

Breed in the summer rainy season. 1–2 pups, weighing 2–3 g each, are born after a gestation period of 60–75 days. Some species delay ova fertilization by storing sperm in a vaginal pocket. Pups are weaned at 2 months.

DIET

Insectivorous, feeding on insects only. Water dependent, drinking regularly. Apart from drinking at a water supply, moisture can be obtained by licking condensed water from their fur and from cave walls.

HABITAT

Horseshoe bats occur in savanna woodland. All species are found in the sandveld communities habitats of the Kruger. Additionally, *R. clivosus* is found in the thorn thickets habitats; *R. fumigatus* and *R. hildebrandtii* in the Lebombo Mountain bushveld habitats; *R. landeri* occurs in the thorn veld habitats; *R. simulator* in the knobthorn/marula savanna habitats; and *R. darlingi* inhabits the mixed bushwillow woodlands, mopane/bushwillow woodlands, Malelane and Lebombo Mountain bushvelds, riverine communities and sourveld habitats.

Leaf-nosed Bats

Ger: Rundblattnasen Fledermäuse; **Fre:** Hipposideridés; **Afr:** Bladneusvlermuise.

Species: Sundevall's Leaf-nosed Bat, *Hipposideros caffer;* Commerson's Leaf-nosed Bat, *Hipposideros commersoni.*

Mass: ♂ 4–130 g; ♀ 4–130 g. **Head-and-body length:** ♂ 25–150 mm; ♀ 25–150 mm. **Tail length:** ♂ 0–60 mm; ♀ 0–60 mm. **Forearm length:** ♂ 30–110 mm; ♀ 30–110 mm. **Distinguishing features:** A prominent horseshoe-shaped nose leaf, an erect leaf with complex folds (not triangular as in *Rhinolophidae* spp). The eyes are small and inconspicuous. Pointed ears are very large, and are almost as wide as they are long. **Life-span:** ± 12 yrs. **Predators:** Man has the biggest negative impact due to habitat modification. Main predators are birds of prey.

DESCRIPTION

H. commersoni is the largest insectivorous bat in southern Africa. It is fawn in colour; the head and neck are paler. The overall colour of *H. caffer* varies greatly: whitish in semi-desert areas; golden to grey-brown in temperate and tropical regions and other areas. The fur on the upper parts is long and woolly. Leaf-nosed bats have well-developed canine teeth.

Scent glands: *H. caffer* has a gland behind the nose leaf.

Senses: Good sight, very good hearing, good sense of smell.

DISTRIBUTION

H. commersoni occurs seasonally in ecozone N of the Kruger, in the Pafuri area. *H. caffer* is found in dry open savannas throughout the Kruger in ecozones B, C, D, E, F, G, I, L, M, N and O.

BEHAVIOUR

Leaf-nosed bats are nocturnal, forming colonies. *H. caffer* and *H. commersoni* form colonies of up to hundreds of individuals, but *H. caffer* is also solitary at times. In colony formations, *H. caffer* individuals roost close to each other, without touching. Prefer cool, dark and moist roosting sites. Both species roost in caves, mines, rock crevices and in buildings. *H. commersoni* also roosts in hollow trees. *H. commersoni* appears to be migratory as it only occurs in the Kruger in the summer.

In winter, leaf-nosed bats may undergo periods of torpor.

Calls: Contact calls include piercing, high-pitched whistles. The long echo-ranging signals, 160–50 kHz and 0–60 pulses/msec, are emitted through the nose.

Alarm and aggression: When disturbed, individuals clamber further back into recesses, pushing their backs against the wall. *H. commersoni* may bite.

REPRODUCTION

Breed in the summer rainy season. 1–2 pups, weighing one fifth of their mother's body weight, are born after a gestation period of 120 days. Delayed foetal development occurs in some species. Pups nipple-cling for the first few weeks. They are weaned at about 2 months.

Sundevall's leaf-nosed bat

DIET

Insectivorous, feeding on a variety of insects and small vertebrates. They are water dependent, drinking regularly. Apart from drinking at a water supply, moisture can also be obtained by licking condensed water from their fur and from cave walls.

HABITAT

Leaf-nosed bats occur throughout a range of forest types (these include high forests and riparian forests), forest mosaics, woodlands and savanna woodlands.

In the Kruger Park, *H. commersoni* occurs in savanna woodland and riverine forest in the sandveld communities habitats.

H. caffer occurs in the knobthorn/marula savanna, tree mopane savanna, the sourveld as well as in the Malelane Mountain and the Lebombo Mountain bushvelds, thorn thickets, thorn veld, mopane shrubveld, sandveld communities and alluvial plains habitats of the Kruger.

Free-tailed Bats

Ger: Freischwanz Fledermäuse; **Fre:** Molossidés; **Afr:** Losstertvlermuise.

Species: Ansorge's Free-tailed Bat, *Tadarida (Chaerephon) ansorgei;* Little Free-tailed Bat, *Tadarida (Chaerephon) pumila;* Angola Free-tailed Bat, *Tadarida (Mops) condylura;* Midas Free-tailed Bat, *Tadarida (Mops) midas;* Madagascar Large Free-tailed Bat, *Tadarida (Tadarida) fulminans;* Egyptian Free-tailed Bat, *Tadarida (Tadarida) aegyptiaca.*

Status: Madagascar Large Free-tailed Bat – IUCN: NT ☽

Mass: ♂ 8–170 g; ♀ 8–170 g. **Head-and-body length:** ♂ 40–130 mm; ♀ 40–130 mm. **Tail length:** ♂ 14–80 mm; ♀ 4–80 mm. **Forearm length:** ♂ 27–85 mm; ♀ 27–85 mm. **Distinguishing features:** The large head has a 'bull-dog' appearance. Many stiff hairs on the face. Wrinkly lips and creased ears. Although only one third to one half of the tail is free (not attached to a membrane on either side), it is noticeably freer than the tails of bats belonging to other families. The ear creases and antitragi are characteristic of the family, and aid in distinguishing the different genera: *Mops* – join over the forehead; *Tadarida* – meet across the nose but do not join; *Chaerephon* – join above the bridge of the nose. **Life-span:** ± 8–20 yrs (species dependent). **Predators:** Man has the biggest negative impact on bat populations, through habitat modification and the use of pesticides. Main predators include birds of prey and weasels. Free-tailed bats are also susceptible to parasites.

DESCRIPTION

The short fur is adpressed to the body. The upperparts are generally brown or dark reddish brown, and the underparts paler. The leathery wings are long, narrow and pointed.

Scent glands: Many species have throat, face, muzzle and perineal glands. Some *Chaerephon* spp have glands on top of the head. *Tadarida* spp have facial glands.

Senses: Good sight, very good hearing, good sense of smell.

DISTRIBUTION

T. ansorgei is rare within the Kruger, and has been recorded in ecozones I and N, occurring in the Lebombo Mountains and Pafuri areas. *T. fulminans* occurs in ecozone N, in the Pafuri region. *T. condylura* and *T. pumila* occur commonly in suitable roosts in most ecozones: *T. pumila* does not occur in ecozone J, and *T. condylura* does not occur in ecozones B, C and J. *T. midas* is found in ecozones D, N and P, occurring in the Skukuza, Phalaborwa and Pafuri areas, at Malitube near Punda Maria, and on the Limpopo River at Scrutton, about 30 km west of the Park border. *T. aegyptiaca* is found in ecozones A and D, occurring in the Skukuza and Malelane areas.

BEHAVIOUR

Free-tailed bats are nocturnal, forming colonies. All species form large colonies of hundreds, with the exception of *T. fulminans*, which generally forms colonies of under 20 individuals, and *T. condylura*, which forms colonies of dozens. All species roost in caves, in rock crevices, under rock ledges and in mines. *T. midas* also roosts under bridges and roofs, and *T. aegyptiaca* and *T. pumila* also in tree hollows. In the Kruger, however, *T. condylura* is the only *Tadarida* and *Chaerephon* species that also roosts in caves.

In winter, free-tailed bats may undergo periods of torpor.

Calls: Contact calls include squeaks, squeals, chirps and screeches. The short

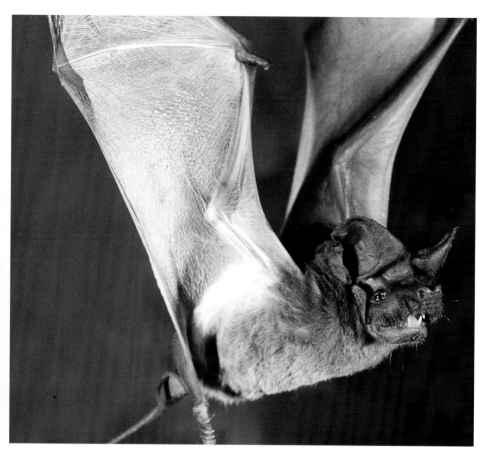

Angola free-tailed bat

echo-ranging signals, 60–20 kHz and 8–10 pulses/msec, are emitted through the mouth.

REPRODUCTION

Breed in the summer rainy season. 1–2 pups are born after a gestation period of 60–90 days. Pups weigh between 3 and 10 g, depending on the species. They are weaned at 2 months.

DIET

Free-tailed bats are insectivorous, feeding solely on insects. They are water dependent, having to drink water regularly. Apart from drinking at a water supply, moisture can also be obtained by licking condensed water from their fur and from cave walls.

HABITAT

All species are found in savanna woodland. *T. condylura* and *T. pumila* are also found in forests; and *T. aegyptiaca* is found in all habitats except forest.

All species, except *T. aegyptiaca*, occur in the sandveld communities habitats of the Kruger. *T. midas* is found in the thorn thickets and mopane/bushwillow woodlands habitats, *T. ansorgei* in the Lebombo Mountain bushveld habitats, *T. condylura* in nearly all the habitats, except the sourveld, Malelane Mountain bushveld, and rugged veld; and *T. pumila* occurs in all habitats except the rugged veld, and can be found roosting in the roofs of staff and other dwellings throughout the Park.

T. aegyptiaca is found in the mixed bushwillow woodlands and thorn thickets habitats of the Kruger.

Common, Evening and Vesper Bats

Ger: Gewöhnliche und Glattnasen Fledermäuse; **Fre:** Vespertilionidés; **Afr:** Gewone vlermuise.

Species: Schreibers' Long-fingered Bat, *Miniopterus schreibersii;* Rufous Hairy Bat, *Myotis bocagei;* Temminck's Hairy Bat, *Myotis tricolor;* Welwitsch's Hairy Bat, *Myotis welwitschii;* Anchieta's Bat, *Pipistrellus anchietai;* Kuhl's Bat, *Pipistrellus kuhlii;* Banana Bat, *Pipistrellus nanus;* Rüppell's Bat, *Pipistrellus rueppellii;* Rusty Bat, *Pipistrellus rusticus;* Butterfly Bat, *Chalinolobus variegatus;* Botswana Long-eared Bat, *Laephotis botswanae;* Cape Serotine Bat, *Eptesicus capensis;* Long-tailed Serotine Bat, *Eptesicus hottentotus;* Melck's Serotine Bat, *Eptesicus melckorum;* Somali Serotine Bat, *Eptesicus somalicus zuluensis;* Lesser Yellow House Bat, *Scotophilus borbonicus;* Yellow House Bat, *Scotophilus dinganii;* Schlieffen's Bat, *Nycticeius schlieffenii;* Damara Woolly Bat, *Kerivoula argentata;* Lesser Woolly Bat, *Kerivoula lanosa.*

Status: Lesser Yellow House Bat – IUCN: CR; Schreiber's Long–fingered Bat, Anchieta's Bat – IUCN: VU; ☽ Somali Serotine Bat – IUCN: NT

Mass: ♂ 4–50 g; ♀ 4–50 g. **Head-and-body length:** ♂ 32–105 mm; ♀ 32–105 mm. **Tail length:** ♂ 25–75 mm; ♀ 25–75 mm. **Forearm length:** ♂ 22–55 mm; ♀ 22–55 mm. **Distinguishing features:** Massive head with a short muzzle, no nose leaves. Ears are widely separated with noticeable ear tragi. Long tails are enclosed in a membrane. **Lifespan:** ± 4–20 yrs (species dependent). **Predators:** Man has the biggest negative impact on bat populations due to habitat modification. Main predators are birds of prey and weasels. These bats are susceptible to parasites.

DESCRIPTION

Kerivoula spp have thick, woolly fur and grizzled grey upperparts. All other species have short fur, which is adpressed to the body. The overall body colour is generally varying shades of brown, except in *Myotis* spp (copper coloured) and in *C. variegatus* (dark reticulations on a yellowish background). All species have paler underparts, except *Scotophilus* spp whose underparts are distinctly yellow.

Scent glands: Muzzle gland in most species. *Scotophilus* spp have swollen glands situated in the corner of the mouth.

Senses: Good sight, very good hearing, good sense of smell.

DISTRIBUTION

K. lanosa, K. argentata, E. hottentotus, C. variegatus, P. rueppellii, P. rusticus, M. bocagei, E.s. zuluensis and *L. botswanae* occur in ecozone N of the Kruger. *K. lanosa, K. argentata, E. hottentotus, C. variegatus, P. rueppellii* and *M. bocagei* occur in the Pafuri area; *P. rusticus* in the Pafuri and Punda Maria areas; *L. botswanae* in the Punda Maria area and *E. s. zuluensis* in the Xitangeni Windmill, Tshashanga and Pafuri areas.

M. tricolor is found in ecozones F and N, occurring in the Pafuri and Satara areas. *M. schreibersii* occurs commonly throughout the Park in ecozones A, B, C, D, E, I, L and N. *M. welwitschii* is found in ecozones B, D, F and N, occurring near the Sabie River, and in the Matukwale Dam, Punda Maria and Pafuri areas.

E. melckorum is found in ecozones D and N, occurring in the Skukuza and Pafuri areas. *E. capensis* is rare within the Kruger, but is widely distributed throughout ecozones A, B, D, I, and the northern parts of ecozones L and N.

P. anchietai and P. kuhlii occur in ecozone D in the Skukuza area. *P. nanus* is found in ecozones B, C, D, F and N, occurring in the Pretoriuskop, Skukuza, Malelane, Satara and Pafuri areas.

Temminck's hairy bat

N. schlieffenii occurs commonly throughout eco-zones A, D, G, L, N and P, near permanent water.

S. borbonicus is found in ecozones A, D, E, N and P, occurring near Satara at Nsemani Windmill, in the Skukuza and Phalaborwa Gate areas, and in the extreme northern regions of the Park. *S. dinganii* occurs in ecozones A, B, C, D, E, N, O and P, but is nowhere common.

BEHAVIOUR

Common bats are nocturnal. Social structure varies according to species, and little data is available regarding their natural history. *Miniopterus* spp are found in colonies, from a few individuals up to thousands, roosting in caves, mines, rock crevices and trees.

M. welwitschii and *M. bocagei* are solitary, roost-ing in trees, with *M. bocagei* also being found in palm leaves and in between bunches of bananas. *M. tricolor* occurs in colonies of dozens of individuals and roosts in caves and mines.

Pipistrellus and *Scotophilus* spp occur in small colonies of up to 12 individuals, and roost in trees, tree hollows, and occasionally in roofs, but *P. kuhlii* is generally found in the leaves of banana growths.

Eptesicus spp occur in colonies of 2–4 individu-als, roosting in foliage, the loose bark of trees, or in roofs. Unlike the other bats in this genera, *E. hotten-totus* roosts in caves and mines.

Nycticeius spp are solitary, and usually roost in buildings.

Kerivoula spp are solitary or occur in small colonies of up to 5 individuals. They roost in dead foliage and bark or in disused birds' nests.

In winter, some species may undergo periods of torpor, or enter full hibernation.

Calls: Contact calls include clicks, squeaks and screeches. Alarm calls include shrieks. *Eptesicus* spp may produce audible clicks as they fly. The short echo-ranging signals, 120–20 mHz and 0,25–4 puls-es/msec, are emitted through the mouth.

REPRODUCTION

Breed in the summer rainy season. 1–2 pups are born after a gestation period of 40–70 days. Pups weigh between 0,5 and 6 g at birth, depending on the species. Some *Miniopertus* and *Scotophilus* spp delay implantation of fertilized ova. Some *Nycticeius* and *Myotis* spp delay fertilization of ova. Pups are weaned at 1–2 months.

Lesser yellow house bat

DIET

Insectivorous, feeding on insects only. Water dependent, drinking regularly. Apart from drinking at a water supply, moisture can also be obtained by licking condensed water from their fur and from cave walls.

HABITAT

All species occur in savanna woodland, with *Pipistrellus*, *Scotophilus*, *Kerivoula* and *Chalinolobus* spp usually occurring in areas associated with riverine habitats. In the Kruger, *P. anchietai* and *P. kuhlii* are found in the thorn thickets habitats. All species except *P. anchietai* and *P. kuhlii* are found in the sandveld communities habitat of the Kruger. Additionally, *M. tricolor* is found in the knobthorn/marula savanna; *M. welwitschii* in the mixed bushwillow woodlands, thorn thickets and knobthorn/marula savanna habitats; *P. nanus* in the sourveld, Malelane Mountain bushveld, thorn thickets and knobthorn/marula savanna habitats; *E. capensis* in the mixed bushwillow woodlands, sourveld, thorn thickets, Lebombo Mountain bushveld and northern mopane shrubveld habitats; *E. melckorum* in the thorn thickets habitats; *S. borbonicus* in the mixed bushwillow woodlands, mopane/bushwillow woodlands, thorn thickets and thorn veld habitats; *S. dinganii* in the mixed bushwillow woodlands, mopane/bushwillow woodlands, tree mopane savanna, sourveld, Malelane Mountain bushveld, thorn veld and thorn thickets habitats; *M. schreibersii* in the mixed bushwillow woodlands, sourveld, Malelane and Lebombo Mountain bushvelds, thorn veld, thorn thickets and mopane shrubveld habitats; and *N. schlieffenii* in the mixed bushwillow woodlands, mopane/bushwillow woodlands, thorn thickets, knobthorn/marula savanna and mopane shrubveld habitats.

Appendix 1: Field signs and tracking tips

ELEPHANT
ELEPHANT ◆ *Loxodonta africana*
Faeces are roughly spherical, very coarse and fibrous with undigested fragments of wood and bark (rhino faeces are comparable in size but are more cylindrical). Elephants demolish trees and bushes and often leave ragged ends on branches. Mud smears can be found on trees and rocks. Anything above 1,8 m can only be made by elephants. They often dig holes in riverbeds.

RHINOCEROS
WHITE RHINOCEROS ◆ *Ceratotherium simum*
Faeces are dark and contain undigested grass fragments (twigs in black rhino faeces). Use middens when defecating. Mud smears mark trees, termite mounds and rocks. Their presence can also be determined by the presence of polished rubbing spots. Take special care of wind direction, their sense of smell is acute. Rhinos are creatures of habit and use the same waterholes and resting spots.

BLACK RHINOCEROS ◆ *Diceros bicornis*
Dung contains undigested twigs with ends cut at 45°. Use middens when defecating. Mud smears mark trees, termite mounds and rocks; also have typical polished rubbing spots. Feeding spots are recognized by neatly pruned bushes with twigs trimmed off at 45°. Take special care of wind direction, their sense of smell is acute. Rhinos are creatures of habit and use the same waterholes and resting spots.

ZEBRA
BURCHELL'S ZEBRA ◆ *Equus burchelli*
The dung looks like a kidney-shaped lump, and is 5 cm or more across, characteristically with a crack across the middle and often loosely stuck together.

HIPPOPOTAMUS
HIPPOPOTAMUS ◆ *Hippopotamus amphibius*
Dung heaps near paths. Hippo leave the water during the night to graze, travelling on well-worn paths. Hippo trails wear into two parallel ruts.

GIRAFFE
GIRAFFE ◆ *Giraffa camelopardalis*
Giraffe droppings are dark pellets, 2 cm x 3 cm, tapered at one end and blunt at the other. The faeces are more scattered than those of antelope due to the long drop. Their browsing prunes trees into an hourglass shape.

ANTELOPE
BUFFALO ◆ *Syncerus caffer*
Droppings are flattened cowpats. One of the most formidable of the big 5. Take care of wind direction. Buffalo have good eyesight. When the herd moves, bulls lag behind to investigate.

ELAND ◆ *Taurotragus oryx*
Droppings are 2–3 cm long, tapered or rounded at one end, blunt at the other; sometimes in cylindrical clumps. Broken down branches, horned mud patches. The front hooves of eland make a clicking noise when walking.

NYALA ◆ *Tragelaphus angasii*
Droppings are 1,5 cm long with a small bump at one end and a hollow at the other. Most active during early evening. Horned up soil and thrashed bushes.

KUDU ◆ *Tragelaphus strepsiceros*
Droppings are 2 cm long, slightly longer than wide, with a short point at one end and a hollow at the other. Thrashed bushes, horned up soil, broken down branches. Kudu rest in thick bush during the heat of the day and often move cautiously toward water early in the morning or at the end of the day.

BUSHBUCK ◆ *Tragelaphus scriptus*
Droppings are distinctive tubular clusters of pellets, sometimes looking like miniature black maize cobs. Clusters are 2–3 cm across.

SABLE ANTELOPE ◆ *Hippotragus niger*
Faeces 2 cm long, tapered at one end, hollow at the other, with scratch marks in the soil produced by solitary bulls. Thrashed bushes.

ROAN ANTELOPE ◆ *Hippotragus equinus*
Dung pellets are 2 cm long, tapered at one end, hollow at the other; similar in size to sable's, but roan do not leave scrape marks. Thrashed bushes. Roan remain at the same area for a few days, may be found at the same spot the following day.

BLUE WILDEBEEST ◆ *Connochaetes taurinus*
Blue wildebeest droppings are dark pellets, sometimes in clusters. Middens and bare, trampled patches on territories. Often have a favourite sleeping spot and may be found there early in the morning. They also visit the waterhole regularly.

TSESSEBE ◆ *Damaliscus lunatus*
Middens containing dung pellets 0,5 cm long, tapered at one end, hollow at the other. Worn trails. Scars on tree bark on territory borders.

WATERBUCK ◆ *Kobus ellipsiprymnus*
Droppings are rounded clumps of flattened pellets, or separate pellets 2 cm long, tapered at one end and blunt at the other. Highly territorial, may be found at the same spot the next day.

SOUTHERN REEDBUCK ◆ *Redunca arundinum*
1,5 cm long droppings, tapered at one end, blunt at the other. Flattened grassbeds in patches of tall grass.

MOUNTAIN REEDBUCK ◆ *Redunca fulvorufula*
Droppings are clusters of squashed, round pellets.

GREY RHEBOK ◆ *Pelea capreolus*
Droppings are 1 cm long, tapered at one end, blunt at the other.

IMPALA ◆ *Aepyceros melampus*
The dung pellets are 1,5 cm long, tapered at one end, blunt or hollow at the other. During the rut, horned bushes, middens are a common sight.

KLIPSPRINGER ◆ *Oreotragus oreotragus*
Dung middens up to 1 m across and 10 cm deep. Pellets are 0,5–1 cm long, 0,5 cm across, tapered at both ends (more elongated than droppings from rock rabbits, dassies and mountain reedbuck, which share the habitat). Blobs of black preorbital gland secretion on the tips of twigs. Nearly always found in pairs on a rocky hill, which is occupied for life.

STEENBOK ◆ *Raphicerus campestris*
Steenbok faeces are mixed with soil (not necessarily buried); the pellets are shiny, long and thin, 1 cm x 0,5 cm, with a narrow point at one end. These antelope are highly territorial and animals spotted at a particular place will probably be there the following day.

SHARPE'S GRYSBOK ◆ *Raphicerus sharpei*
Large middens up to 1 m across and 10 cm deep; the pellets are 1 cm long, tapered at one end, blunt at the other.

ORIBI ◆ *Ourebia ourebi*
Droppings are 1 cm long with a short narrow point at one end, sometimes in middens. Oribis lie down in open meadows. Bitten-off grass stems with black secretion on top.

SUNI ◆ *Neotragus moschatus*
Droppings are 0,5 cm long, tapered at one end, blunt at the other, in middens. Trails through undergrowth. Black blobs of preorbital gland secretion on short stems and twigs.

COMMON DUIKER ◆ *Sylvicapra grimmia*
Droppings are 1 cm long, 1 cm across, with a short point at one end, blunt or slightly hollow at the other, sometimes in middens.

RED DUIKER ◆ *Cephalophus natalensis*
Dung pellets are 0,5 cm long, tapered at one end, hollow at the other, deposited in middens.

WARTHOG, BUSHPIG
WARTHOG ◆ *Phacochoerus aethiopicus*
Dung is soft, flattened segments, stuck together in rough, often misshapen cylinders, with a distinctive unpleasant smell when fresh. Mud smears low down on trees and rocks. Rooting in both hard and soft ground (bushpig only in soft ground). Trees scraped with tusks. Mud wallows.

BUSHPIG ◆ *Potamochoerus larvatus/porcus*
Droppings are segmented cylinders looking rather like dried figs, up to 8 cm in diameter, sometimes in middens containing up to 40 (average 10) droppings. Patches of soil churned up by rooting. Tusk marks on bark.

GENET

GENET ♦ *Genetta genetta, Genetta tigrina*
Droppings are cylindrical, up to 5 cm long and 1 cm thick, nearly always contain insect fragments. Musky odour of scent marks, faeces and urine.

HYAENA

SPOTTED HYAENA ♦ *Crocuta crocuta*
Middens contain large numbers of white faeces (dark when very fresh), lumpy cylinders with tapered ends. Spotted hyaena dens are less likely than brown hyaena dens to have large accumulations of bones. Scent marks are brown smears (white when very fresh) on bunches of grass stems.

CATS

LION ♦ *Panthera leo*
Droppings are segmented sausages with tapered ends, 4 cm thick, usually with hair and bone fragments. Very dark faeces point to a diet of meat with little bone, light-coloured faeces indicate more bone in the diet.

LEOPARD ♦ *Panthera pardus*
Faeces are segmented sausages with tapered ends 2 cm–3,5 cm thick, nearly always with hair and bone fragments; they are left exposed sometimes in prominent places. Carcasses in trees, feathers and fur plucked from kills. Scrapes on the ground. Claw marks on bark.

CHEETAH ♦ *Acinonyx jubatus*
Droppings are short, segmented sausages with tapered ends, about 3 cm thick. Urine marks on trees and rocks. Carcasses with most of the bones and skin intact.

CARACAL ♦ *Felis caracal*
Faeces are segmented sausages with tapered ends, up to 2 cm thick; may be buried or left

exposed. Kills can be identified by tooth marks and bruising on the throat or nape of the neck, sometimes claw marks on the shoulders, marks of canine teeth 24 mm–30 mm apart (same for black-backed jackal; dogs from fox terrier size upwards make marks which are 35 mm–60 mm apart). Hair or wool sometimes plucked. Feeding starts inside hindleg. Guts not removed (leopard removes guts).

JACKAL

BLACK-BACKED JACKAL ♦ *Canis mesomelas*
Droppings are cylindrical with tapered ends, 1 cm–2 cm thick, usually containing hair, insect fragments and bone chips, often deposited in a prominent position such as on top of a rock or a clump of grass. On sheep and lamb kills: teeth marks either side of the windpipe, with spacing between punctures 23 mm–30 mm (35 mm–60 mm for domestic dogs terrier size and upwards). Carcass opened on the flank, kidneys, liver, heart and tips of ribs eaten, no large bones broken (domestic dogs often bite at the back, flanks and hindlegs, and eat large bones).

BABOON

CHACMA BABOON ♦ *Papio ursinus*
Droppings are irregular and roughly rounded; they are often deposited on top of rocks. When fresh, have a strong, distinctive odour. Stones and rocks turned over in search of food.

PORCUPINE

PORCUPINE ♦ *Hystrix africaeaustralis*
Droppings are rounded, 2 cm–3 cm across, or cylindrical, 4 cm–7 cm long, stuck together in clumps, black and often containing fibres from roots and bark. Detached quills are often found. Diggings, debarked trees and roots, tooth marks 1 cm–5 cm apart on food remnants and bones (no other rodent leaves such wide marks).

(reproduced (modified) with the permission of www.AfricanHunting.com).

Appendix 2: Predator/prey relationships in the Kruger National Park

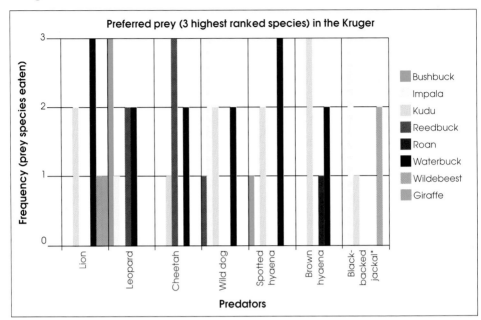

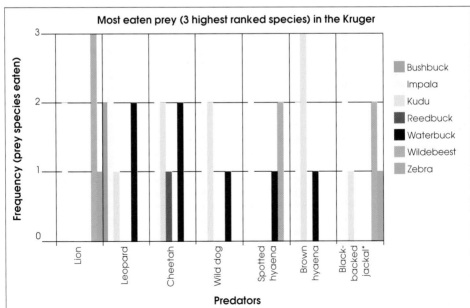

Note: 4 prey species per predator – 2 prey species are taken at equal frequencies. * Includes juveniles.

Predation pressure in the Kruger Park

PREY (incl. juveniles)	Lion	Leopard	Cheetah	Caracal	Serval	Br. Hyaena	Sp. Hyaena	Wild dog	Jackal	Baboon	Crocodile	Pythons	Martial Eagle	%
Giraffe	99.4		0.3								0.3			100
Zebra	97.0	1.6	0.6			0.4		0.2			0.2			100
Buffalo	99.0	0.4	0.1			0.1	0.1				0.3			100
Eland	90.0	5.1	2.0			0.6		2.3						100
Nyala	26.1	48.0	3.4					17.0		1.0	4.5			100
Kudu	77.3	5.5	4.6			2.0	0.5	9.3			0.8			100
Bushbuck	11.9	69.0	4.4			0.1	0.7	9.9		0.4	3.3		0.3	100
Sable	93.3	2.1	1.7			0.7		2.2						100
Roan	88.7	1.6	1.6			0.8		7.3						100
Wildebeest	97.7	0.9	0.6			0.1	0.2	0.4			0.1			100
Tsessebe	71.1	7.2	6.7			1.6		13.4						100
Waterbuck	82.4	5.7	3.4			0.8	0.5	5.8			1.4			100
Sth Reedbuck	16.9	46.0	21.8			0.4	0.2	13.3		0.2	1.0	0.2		100
Mnt Reedbuck	30.0	50.0						20.0						100
Impala	29.8	34.4	11.9			0.2	0.7	20.5	0.8	0.1	1.5	0.1		100
Klipspringer	5.0	85.0						2.5			2.5		5.0	100
Sharpe's Grysbok	3.8	58.5	3.8	1.9			1.9	20.7	1.9				7.5	100
Steenbok	2.5	55.5	12.6	4.2	0.8		0.2	11.8	5.9		1.7	2.5	2.5	100
Oribi		50.0		0.6	0.3				50.0					100
Duiker	5.0	49.5	19.0			0.3		20.8		2.4	0.6	1.5	·	100
Warthog	72.7	20.2	4.0			0.2	0.2	1.9			0.6	0.2	0.1	100
Baboon	9.5	77.0				9.4					2.7	1.4		100

Glossary

Alpha The first letter of the Greek alphabet used to describe the top-ranking member of a group, for example, the alpha male.

Adpressed Pressed close to or lying flat against something.

Agglutinate To unite or adhere; to stick or clump together.

Antelope Common name applied to a large group of ruminants in the family Bovidae that possess hollow, unbranched horns, which are never shed. Comprised of approximately 150 species that occur mainly in Africa.

Antitragus Projection on ear, opposite the tragus.

Aquatic Living in fresh water (but also move readily on land).

Arboreal Living mainly in trees.

Boss Heavy horn mass at the base of horns, as found in wildebeest and buffalo.

Browser An animal that feeds mainly on the shoots, stems and leaves of trees, shrubs and bushes.

Callosity Patch of thickened skin.

Carnivore An animal that feeds mainly on animal meat; a member of the order Carnivora.

Cheek pouch Pockets that extend from the cheeks to the neck, which are used for the temporary storage of food.

CITES Convention of Trade in Endangered Species of Wild Fauna and Flora.

Clan A social grouping of at least two individuals, usually pertaining to carnivores.

Cowlicks A projecting tuft of turned-up hair (usually over the forehead) that grows in a different direction from the rest of the hair and will not lie flat.

Crepuscular Active at dawn and dusk.

Dermis The inner layer of the 2 layers of skin of vertebrates, the outermost layer being the epidermis. The dermal layer is the sensitive connective tissue layer of skin, containing nerve endings, sweat and sebaceous glands, and blood and lymph vessels.

Dew claw A digit that fails to touch the ground; the innermost digit in carnivores.

Digitigrade Walking on the toes rather than on the whole underside of the foot.

Diurnal Active mainly during daylight hours.

Dung midden A site where faeces is deposited regularly, accumulating into piles.

Ecology A study of organisms (plants and animals) in relation to their environment.

Ecozone An area of particular ecology.

Endemic Restricted to a particular region.

Forbs Herbs and other grasses found in abundance in grasslands.

Gallery forest Trees and other vegetation lining watercourses, and extending the forest habitat into savanna and arid zone habitats.

Gestation period The time between conception and birth, when young are carried in the womb.

Grazer Animal that feeds on grasses and herbs.

Ground horning Using the horns to toss or dig into soil. A dominance and/or aggression display, advertising the level of aggression or dominance status of an antelope by the degree to which soil is tossed or dug into.

Harem The females ('wives' and 'concubines') belonging to a dominant male.

Herbivorous Feeding on plants.

Herd A social grouping of at least two individuals. The term is usually applied to ungulates.

Holt A lair or den (particularly otters).

Home range The area that an animal covers while performing its day-to-day activities (for example, searching for food, shelter and mates).

Indigenous Originating in and native to a particular region or country.

Inguinal Pertaining to the groin.

Insectivorous Feeding mainly on insects.

Interdigital Between the digits (toes, hooves).

Invertebrates Animals without a backbone, for example spiders and insects.

IUCN International Union for the Conservation of Nature & Natural Resources; World Conservation Union.

Klipspringer Afrikaans for rock jumper.

Kopje Cape Dutch for a small hill.

Leveret A young hare.

Maternal imprinting The process whereby offspring is isolated from all other group members until the maternal bond between mother and offspring has been established.

Mine adit A near-horizontal passage leading into a mine – the passage is used as an entrance, for ventilation or drainage.

Miombo Woodland Zone Vegetation zone within the southern savanna (see map: Major Ecozones of Africa, p 14), dominated by broad-leaved, deciduous, and leguminous trees.

Mob attack/Mobbing response Cooperative attack by members of a group.

Monogamous Having only one sexual partner, with permanent pair bonds being formed.

Montane Pertaining to African mountain habitats, including grassland, forest, bamboo, moorland.

Native Person, animal or plant indigenous to a certain region or country.

Nocturnal Active during the night.

Nomad A wanderer, having no defined place of residence but moving from place to place.

Nose-leaf Characteristic flaps of skin surrounding the nasal passages of nose-leafed bats.

Oestrus Behaviour associated with ovulation, occurring in most female mammals (excluding humans), being the only time when the female is sexually receptive; 'in heat'.

Olfactory Pertaining to the sense of smell.

Omnivorous Feeding on both animal and plant matter.

Pan A hollow or basin in the ground in which water collects in the rainy season; a natural waterhole.

Perianal Pertaining to the area around the anus.

Perineal Pertaining to the area between the anus and the genitals.

Plantigrade Flatfooted, walking on the whole underside of the foot.

Predator An animal that preys on other animals.

Preorbital In front of the eyes.

Preputial Pertaining to the loose skin (foreskin) over the penis.

Reticulation Resembling or forming a network.

Rhinarium The naked fleshy area at the tip of the muzzle, which encloses the nostrils.

Rut Period of concentrated sexual activity; the mating season.

Savanna Extensive areas of natural grasslands with scattered trees; characteristic of regions with extended and defined wet and dry seasons.

Scats Animal excretions/ droppings.

Scent gland A specialized area of skin, packed with complex chemical compounds that are secreted to communicate information regarding identity and reproductive status, for example.

Sebaceous gland The most common type of cutaneous (skin) scent gland. It secretes sebum, an oily substance composed of fat and epithelial (outer tissue) debris.

Skink Any one of numerous species of lizards of the family Scincidae; have a shiny scale-covered body and rudimentary legs; found in tropical regions worldwide.

Solitary Unsociable; living alone.

Sounder Collective name for a group of pigs.

Sourveld Afrikaans for tall grassland that is not nutritious, and unpalatable to livestock during the dry season.

Species A group of interbreeding individuals, derived from a common ancestor, with common characteristics and qualities.

Spoor Footprint.

Steenbok Afrikaans for brick buck; 'steen' referring to the brick red colour of their coats.

Stolon A shoot from the base of a plant that bends to the ground or grows horizontally above the ground, and produces new plants from buds at its tips.

Stotting action Action of jumping into the air with all four legs held stiff and straight, performed by several antelope species when alarmed.

Style trotting Exaggerated trotting, emphasized by raising the legs higher than usual. The action is associated with alarm and/or aggression in antelope; equivalent to the stotting action of smaller antelope.

Subdesert An area that receives more rainfall than true, sandy deserts, but less rainfall than arid regions.

Substrate 1. An underlying layer; a substratum. 2. Subsoil. 3. The substance acted on by an enzyme. 4. The base on which an enzyme resides.

Symbiotic A mutually beneficial partnership between two unrelated organisms that depend on each other for survival.

Termitary Termite mound or hill (*pl.* termitaria).

Terrestrial Living mainly on the ground.

Territory An area occupied by an individual or group, and effectively defended against other members of the same species.

Tragus (*pl.* tragi) A small cartilaginous process situated in front of the external opening of the ear.

Ungulate an animal that has hooves, belonging to the former order Ungulata, which is now divided into the orders Persissodactyla and Artiodactyla.

Vegetation horning Using the horns to thrash vegetation. A dominance and/or aggression display, advertising the level of aggression or dominance status of an antelope by the degree to which vegetation is thrashed.

Veld Afrikaans for open area dominated by grasslands (veld = savanna).

Vertebrate An animal with a backbone.

Vlei Afrikaans for an area of marshy ground.

Suggested further reading

ALTRINGHAM, J. D. 1996. *Bats – Biology and Behaviour.* Oxford University Press, Oxford.

BERE, R. 1970. *The World of Animals: Antelopes.* Arco Publishing Co., New York.

DE GRAAFF, G. 1981. *The Rodents of Southern Africa.* Butterworths & Co (SA), Durban.

DE V. PIENAAR, U. 1980. *Small Mammals of the Kruger National Park.* National Parks Board of South Africa, Pretoria.

DE V. PIENAAR, U. 1987. *Field Guide to the Mammals of the Kruger National Park.* Struik Publishers, Cape Town.

ESTES, R.D. 1991. *The Behaviour Guide to African Animals.* University of California Press, Los Angeles.

ESTES, R.D. 1993. *The Safari Companion: A Guide to Watching African Mammals.* Chelsea Green Publishing Co., Vermont.

GRYZIMEK, B. (Ed) 1990. *Gryzimek's Encyclopaedia of Mammals.* Vols. 1-5. McGraw-Hill Publishing Co., New York.

JACANA EDUCATION. 2000. *Kruger National Park Ecozone Map.* Jacana Education, Houghton (www.jacana.co.za, marketing@jacana.co.za)

KINGDON, J. 1984. *East African Mammals*, Vol. I-V. University of Chicago Press, Chicago.

KINGDON, J. 1997. *The Kingdon Field Guide to African Mammals.* Academic Press, San Diego.

MACDONALD, D.W. (Ed). 1984. *The Encyclopaedia of Mammals.* Vol. 1. George Allen & Unwin, London.

SKINNER, J.D. & SMITHERS, R.H.N. 1990. *The Mammals of the Southern African Subregion.* University of Pretoria, Pretoria.

SMITHERS, R.H.N. 1992. *Land Mammals of Southern Africa: A Field Guide.* Southern Book Publishers, Johannesburg.

ZAMBATIS, G. 1997. *Checklist of the Mammals of the Kruger National Park*, Archive Skukuza.

STUART, C & T. 1997. *Field Guide to the Larger Mammals of Africa*, Struik, Cape Town.

STUART, C & T. 1988. *Field Guide to Mammals of Southern Africa*, Struik, Cape Town.

MILLS, G & HES, L (Eds) 1997. *The Complete Book of Southern African Mammals*, Struik, Cape Town.

Index to scientific names

Sigmoceros lichtensteinii 46
Steatomys pratensis 184
Suncus lixus 160
Sylvicapra grimmia 70
Syncerus caffer 30

T
Tadarida aegyptiaca 202
Tadarida fulminans 202

Tadarida ansorgei 202
Tadarida condylura 202
Tadarida midas 202
Tadarida pumila 202
Taphozous mauritianus 194
Tatera leucogaster 182
Taurotragus oryx 32
Thallomys paedulcus 188
Thryonomys swinderianus 174

Tragelaphus angasii 34
Tragelaphus scriptus 38
Tragelaphus strepsiceros 36

Index to Afrikaans common names

A
Aap
 Blou 140
 Samango 142
Aardwolf 88

B
Bobbejaan
 Kaapse 138
Bok
 Riet 52
 Rooi 58
 Steen 62
 Water 50
Boomeekhoring 172
Bosbok 38
Bosrot
 Afrikaanse 188
Buffel 30

D
Das
 Klip 78
 Geelkol 80
Duiker
 Gewone 70
 Rooi 72

E
Eekhoring 172
Eland 32
Erdvark 82

G
Gemsbok
 Baster 42
Grysbok
 Sharpese 64

H
Hartebees
 Lichtensteinse 46
Haas
 Kol 150
 Vlak 152

Hiëna
 Bruin 86
 Geflekte 84

I
Ietermagog 148

J
Jagluiperd 94
Jakkals
 Rooi 104
 Witkwas 106

K
Kameelperd 28
Kat
 Boskat
  Tier 98
  Vaal 100
 Rooi 96
Klaasneus
 Bos 162
 Klip 164
 Kortneus 166
Klipdas 78
Klipspringer 60
Koedoe 36
Konyn
 Natalse rooiklip 154
Krimpvarkie
 Suid-Afrikaanse 156
Kwagga
 Bont 24

L
Leeu 90
Luiperd 92

M
Mol
 Gouemol
  Geel 158
  Julianase 158
 Vaal 176

Muis
 Dwerg 188
 Eenstreep 188
 Huis 188
 Klim
  Grys 184
  Roeskleur 184
 Klip
  Namakwalandse 188
 Nag
  Bosveldse 182
 Stekel 188
 Stert
  Boswaaier 178
 Veld
  Natalse Vaal 188
  Vaal 188
 Vet 184
 Wangsak 186
 Woud 188
Muishond
 Dwerg 118
 Gebande 116
 Grootgrys 124
 Kleinwitstert 120
 Kommetjiegat 128
 Mellerse 122
 Stink 136
 Swartkwas 126
 Witstert 130
Muskejaatkat
 Kleinkol 114
 Rooikol 112

N
Nagaap
 Nagaapie 146
 Bos 144
Njala 34

O
Olifant 16
Oorbietjie 66
Otter
 Groot 132

Index to English common names

Photographic credits

Heike Schütze with exception of the following:
A Kemp (AK), Clem Haagner (CH), Daryl & Sharna Balfour (D&S), DDP Photography (DDP), Gallo Images (GI), J & B Photographers (J&B), John Visser (JV), Lanz von Hörsten (LVH), Leonard Hoffman (LH), KZNPB - KwaZulu-Natal National Parks Board, Lorna Stanton (LS), Martin Harvey (MH), National Parks Board (NPB), Naas Rautenbach (NR), N Greaves (NG), Nigel Dennis (ND), Photo Access (PA), Peter Pickford (PP), Roger de la Harpe (RLH), Shaen Adey (SA), Struik Image Library (SIL).

Front cover: (clockwise) Elephant LvH/SIL, White rhino ND/SIL, Blue Wildebeest ND/SIL, Lion ND/SIL, Giraffe ND/SIL, Chacma baboon ND/SIL. Back cover: Elephant Shrew LH/SIL. Spine: ND/SIL.

AK: page: 81; GI: page: 125 CH; D&S: page: 89, 121; JV: page: 171, 177; MH: page: 169; DDP: page: 89 ND, 111, 109; NR: page: 195 (bottom); KZNPB: page 133 (RLH), 143 (RLH), 145. NPB: page: 47 LS, 69 (top), LS (bottom), 83, 97, 107, 113, 131, 137, 153, 155, 159, 161, 163, 165, 167, 175, 183, 185, 187, 191 (bottom), 197, 199, 201, 203, 205, 206; PA: page: 10 J&B, 101 J&B, 195 NG (top); SIL: page: 1 (ND), 8 ND (both), 9 ND (top & center), LVH (bottom), 11 ND, 13 ND (both), 17 ND, 18 ND, 19 ND (top),LVH (bottom), 21 SA, 23 ND, 25 ND, 27 ND, 29 ND (both), 31 ND (top), LVH (bottom), 33 ND (top), 35 ND (both), 37 ND (both), 39 ND (both), 41 ND, 43 ND, 45 ND, 49 ND, 51 ND (both), 55 D&S, 57 ND, 59 ND (both), 61 PP (top), ND (bottom), 63 PP (top), ND (bottom), 65 ND, 71 PP (both), 73 RLH, 75 ND, 85 PP, 87 ND, 91 ND, 93 RLH, 95 ND, 99 ND, 103 ND, 105 ND, 109 ND (both), 117 PP, 119 ND (both), 127 PP, 139 ND (both), 141 ND, 147 ND, 149 PP, 151 PP (top), LH (bottom), 157 RLH, 173 ND (both), 179 LH, 181 PP, 191 PP (top), 214 ND.

ILLUSTRATION CREDITS
SIL/Penny Meakin: Page 123